Problems in SLA

SECOND LANGUAGE ACQUISITION RESEARCH
Theoretical and Methodological Issues
Susan M. Gass, Jacquelyn Schachter, and Alison Mackey, Editors

Monographs on Research Methodology

Of Related Interest

For a complete list of other titles in LEA's Second Language Acquisition Series, please contact Lawrence Erlbaum Associates, Publishers

Problems in SLA

Michael H. Long
University of Maryland

LEA
LAWRENCE ERLBAUM ASSOCIATES, PUBLISHERS
2007   Mahwah, New Jersey   London

Lawrence Erlbaum Associates, Inc., Publishers
10 Industrial Avenue
Mahwah, New Jersey 07430
www.erlbaum.com

Cover design by Tomai Maridou

Library of Congress Cataloging-in-Publication Data

Long, Michael H.
Problems in SLA / by Michael H. Long.
         p.   cm.—(Second language acquisition research)
         Includes bibliographical references and index.
ISBN 0-8058-3580-6 (cloth : alk. paper)—ISBN 0-8058-6084-3
   (pbk. : alk. paper)—ISBN 1-4106-1433-6 (e book)
1. Second language acquisition.   I. Title.   II. Series.

P118.2.L667 2006
418—dc22   2005037986
                                                          CIP

Books published by Lawrence Erlbaum Associates are printed on acid-free
paper, and their bindings are chosen for strength and durability.

Printed in the United States of America
10   9   8   7   6   5   4   3   2   1

Contents

Preface

Mike Long
University of Maryland

Second language acquisition (SLA) is a young science, to the extent that it deserves the name at all, struggling to emerge and differentiate itself from such fields as education and applied linguistics. It shows many signs of scientific youth, including disagreements as to the proper scope of inquiry and, not unrelated, an intemperate rush to theory. *Problems in SLA* is essentially a proposal concerning how the field might develop greater coherence and a clearer focus than it has now, and do so systematically, in part through guidance from work in the philosophy of science.

As it is used in the title, "problems" has three intended meanings. First, it is a technical term in the theory of scientific progress first articulated by L. Laudan (1977), which has been refined in numerous writings since that time. Although not without problems (in the lay sense) of its own, I believe strongly that Laudan's work on theory construction, comparative theory evaluation, research traditions, and change and progress in science offers valuable insights for SLA researchers.

Writers continue to disagree on the issue, but my own view is that one of several current obstacles to progress in SLA is theory proliferation. The extent of the problem is documented in chapter 1, "Second Language Acquisition Theories," in which I also discuss some of the often-overlooked differences between a theory of SLA and a theory of language teaching. In chapter 2, "Problem-Solving and Theory Change in SLA," I try to show how Laudan's ideas can help in this area. Among other things, Laudan's concept of "research tradition" offers a way of seeing the wood from the trees with respect to multiple theories in any field, and his problem-solving notion is a useful yardstick when it comes to comparative evaluation of theories.

The second sense of "problems" refers to substantive issues in SLA, both conceptual and (especially) empirical, in need of resolution. According to Laudan, the number and importance, or weight, of each that theories in a field can account for constitute the principle criteria by which those theories are to be evaluated. There are many such problems of both kinds in SLA, of course, but some are more important than others, for several reasons. First, they may concern anomalous findings (in the traditional sense of the term in the philosophy of science) for various SLA theories (i.e., problematic results that suggest flaws in, or limitations on, one or more current understandings of how second languages are learned, of when and why they are not, or of individual variation in the processes involved). Second, they may represent anomalies in Laudan's special sense of the term (i.e., findings explained by one or more theories, but not by others, which therefore represent anomalies for those other theories and an especially important metric for theory evaluation). Third, they may be matters of fundamental interest to any SLA theorist, and/or to practitioners in such allied fields as language teaching, literacy, and education through the medium of a second language, language policy, or language and the law.

Empirical findings in two lines of SLA research important in all three senses are the focus of part II. In chapters 3 and 4, respectively, I review recent literature on two controversial issues, sensitive periods for language learning, and the role of implicit negative feedback—in particular, recasts—in SLA. The intention is to contribute to our understanding of the substantive issues, and simultaneously to illustrate the varying status of each as, in Laudan's terms, unsolved problems, solved problems, or anomalies for different SLA theories.

In keeping with the orientation—theory, research, and practice—of the series in which this book appears, whereas part I concentrates on theory, and part II on research, part III concerns practice, in this case, the practice of language teaching. In chapter 5, "Texts, Tasks, and the Advanced Learner," I focus on parts of an embryonic theory of language instruction I call Task-Based Language Teaching (TBLT). Motivated in part, although by no means wholly, by work in SLA, TBLT was first sketched in methodology courses at the University of Pennsylvania from 1980 to 1982, and elaborated over the years in graduate seminars at the University of Hawai'i and, since 2003, in SLA courses in the School of Languages, Literatures, and Cultures at the University of Maryland.

TBLT eschews all kinds of linguistic syllabus, overt or covert, along with the *synthetic* teaching methodologies that traditionally accompany them. Instead, it employs an *analytic* methodology (the terms are Wilkins') and a genuine task syllabus, the content of which (selection) is determined by the results of a task-based learner needs analysis, the sequencing of elements in which (grading) remains problematic. The syllabus is delivered following 10, putatively universal *methodological principles*, themselves realized through an array of *pedagogic procedures*, selection among which reflects their appropriateness for local needs, and is made by the classroom teacher as the expert on those needs. Some methodological principles (e.g., MP 2: "Use task, not text, as the unit of analysis," MP 3: "Elaborate, not simplify, input," and MP 6: "Focus on form, not forms") are original to TBLT; others (e.g., as MP 1: "Support integral education," MP 7: "Provide negative feedback," and MP 10: "Individualize instruction") derive from long-standing traditions in language teaching and/or general education. Chapter 5 summarizes TBLT's psycholinguistic underpinnings and provides a rationale for the choice of *task* as the appropriate (but not unproblematic) unit of analysis in course design and delivery—especially, but not only, for the advanced learner—in place of *text*, which persists as the starting point in traditional synthetic approaches, including most so-called content-based instruction.

The third meaning of "problems" refers to the many problems in the lay sense of the word that confront SLA as a field and need to be resolved. Some (e.g., confusions over the field's scope) are partly, again, reflections of the fact that SLA is a young science, many of whose practitioners hail from a variety of disciplines outside SLA itself. Others (e.g., attacks on mainstream SLA research by postmodernists in applied linguistics) are the product of differences in epistemological beliefs between SLA researchers and outside commentators, leading to disagreements as to what count as legitimate research methods and valued findings. Still others concern various features of SLA's social structure (e.g., the wide range of content and standards in the formal training available and in the field's professional publications and associations). Such problems are by no means unique to SLA; in fact, the history of science shows them to be quite common in emerging disciplines. The issues and means of resolving them are typically treated within the philosophy and sociology of science and the sociology of knowledge. I address several of them in chapter 6, "SLA: Breaking the Siege."

Like most books, the ideas in this one have benefited—quite possibly, more than I am aware of—from the insights of many individuals over the years, including several who hold radically different positions on the matters at hand, and from one another, and some of whom might wish to dissociate themselves from directions taken and conclusions drawn in what follows. At the risk, therefore, of causing unintended distress in a few cases, I would like to acknowledge the debt I believe I owe for discussion over the years of the issues treated in the chapters that follow, and/or for their own work on one or more of them: Evelyn Hatch, Diane Larsen-Freeman, John Schumann, the late Russ Campbell, Steve Krashen, Herb Seliger, Fred Eckman, Tere Pica, Sue Gass, Manfred Pienemann, Malcolm Johnston, Dick Schmidt, Craig Chaudron, Robert Bley-Vroman, Graham Crookes, Kenneth Hyltenstam, David Birdsong, Eric Kellerman, Larry

Laudan, Catherine Doughty, Peter Robinson, William O'Grady, Nick Ellis, Lydia White, Alan Beretta, Kevin Gregg, Robert DeKeyser, Geoff Jordan, and last, but by no means least, the late, and dearly missed, Charlene ("Charlie") Sato.

Charlie was born to a blue-collar family on a sugar plantation in Lahaina, Maui. Her father was a fourth generation Japanese-American, her mother a Japanese war bride from Osaka. When Charlie was just one year old, the family moved to Wahiawa, a working-class town set among the pineapple fields of central O'ahu. A native speaker of Hawai'i Creole English (so-called 'Pidgin'), she was educated at the local high school, Leilehua (a proud "Mule" to the day she died), then at U.C. Berkeley (B.A. in linguistics), the University of Hawai'i at Manoa (M.A. in linguistics, M.A. in ESL), and UCLA (Ph.D. in applied linguistics). We met as Ph.D. students at UCLA and later married.

For 14 years, Charlie taught sociolinguistics, SLA, and pidgin and creole studies, and served as chair of the Ph.D. Program in Second Language Acquisition in UH-Manoa's Department of ESL (now Second Language Studies). Her spirit and energy, like her chuckle, were infectious. Before her untimely death from ovarian cancer in 1996, age just 44, Charlie had already made valuable contributions to the fields of SLA, sociolinguistics, pidgin and creole studies, and educational linguistics. One can only guess what might have followed. A tireless fighter for social justice and the rights of working people, the focus of much of her scholarship grew out of the social conditions she knew firsthand, and often resulted in concrete suggestions for their improvement. She remains an inspiration to me and to all who knew her. This book, wholly inadequate for the purpose though it is, is humbly dedicated to her memory.

ACKNOWLEDGMENTS

I thank Susan Gass, Jacquelyn Schachter, and Alison Mackey (series editors), and Cathleen Petree, Tanya Policht, and all at Lawrence Erlbaum Associates, for their help in making this book a reality.

The author and publisher are grateful to Michael Byram and Routledge for permission to reproduce extracts from M. H. Long, Second language acquisition theories. In M. Byram (Ed.). *Encyclopedia of language teaching.* London: Routledge, 2000.

I
Theory

CHAPTER ONE

Second Language Acquisition Theories

Second language acquisition (SLA), like applied linguistics, is an interdisciplinary field with widely varying interpretations placed on it, and varying demands made of it. For these reasons, and because it continues to be developed by individuals from diverse disciplinary backgrounds and with varied epistemological allegiances, it has become increasingly fragmented during the past 15 years, and is characterized by a multiplicity of theories (broadly construed). The theories differ substantively, and in at least five other ways: source, scope (or domain), content, type, and form.

Until recently, with only a few exceptions, research of very different kinds by numerous individuals, groups, and even whole "schools" working under the rubric of one of these theories, or with no theory, has tended to continue in relatively untroubled isolation, without this being seen as problematic. Of late, however, circumstances have changed, portending a period of change in SLA theory, and in the way research is conducted: There is growing public pressure for accountability from SLA researchers. Increasingly robust empirical findings on several issues have lent support to some theories, but cast doubt on others. And, because all theories are at some level interim understandings of what theorists ultimately seek to explain—in this case, how people learn second languages—identifying faulty understandings, and amending or culling the theories concerned, constitutes progress, whereas persistence of a plethora of theories, especially oppositional ones, obstructs progress.

Acceptance of the need for absolute or comparative theory evaluation involves coming to terms with what are sometimes controversial and conflicting evaluation criteria used for theory assessment in other fields and/or developing (sometimes equally controversial and conflicting) new ones. Of particular, and long-running, concern in this regard is the unwarranted assumption in some quarters that SLA theories should be judged by their relevance for language teaching.

HOW SLA THEORIES DIFFER

SLA is a broad, expanding, and diverse field. It encompasses, at the very least, the simultaneous and sequential learning and loss of second (third, fourth, etc.) languages (L2) and dialects, by children and adults, with differing motivations, abilities, and purposes, as individuals or whole communities, with varying access to the L2, in formal, informal, mixed, foreign, second, and lingua franca settings. Researchers come to SLA with varied training in a variety of disciplines, including—but not limited to—linguistics, applied linguistics, psychology, anthropology, education, and SLA. SLA theory and research findings are utilized in many fields, including first language acquisition, theoretical linguistics, neurolinguistics, language learning in abnormal populations, language teaching, education, and psychology.

Not surprisingly, given all this heterogeneity, the past three decades have witnessed the production of numerous theories of "the" SLA process. As discussed here, there is a tendency for researchers whose original graduate training was in a discipline outside SLA to bring with them into the field expertise and interests in issues and research methods that reflect this different training. Naturally enough, they then work on those issues, and as the pioneers doing the early research on the same topics in SLA, they import theories from other fields or develop new ones. The results are often little more (or less) than retrospective explanations of their own initial L2 findings. Whatever their merits, the theories developed apply only to a particular behavioral domain in many cases, and sometimes in a domain that others in the field would view as falling outside second language *acquisition* altogether (e.g., as treating one or another aspect of second language *use*).

As a result of these and other factors—by some accounts, and depending on what one counts—the literature offers as many as 60 theories, models, hypotheses, and theoretical frameworks, many of which are sketched here. These terms are often used nontechnically in the SLA literature (for review, see Crookes, 1992) and in much of what follows. Some view this situation as one of healthy, even inevitable, theoretical pluralism. Certainly, the proliferation is made more likely by the absence of one or more widely (cf. universally) accepted theories governing work in the field, a situation that in itself is indicative of the field's immaturity, and by some accounts, signals prescientific chaos likely to obstruct progress as long as it lasts.

SOURCE

The first way in which SLA theories differ is by *source*, that is, in their (primary) origins inside and/or outside the field. A number of theories have emerged, at least in part, from empirical research findings on second language learning. Examples include the ZIZA Group's Multidimensional Model (Meisel, Clahsen, & Pienemann, 1981), Krashen's Monitor Theory (Krashen, 1985), Schumann's Acculturation Model (Schumann, 1986), Cummins' Linguistic Interdependence Hypothesis for bilingual proficiency (Cummins, 1991), and Ellis' Integrated Theory of Instructed Second Language Acquisition (R. Ellis, 1990). Other theories have been imported ready-made from related areas of cognitive science, notably from linguistics and psychology. Linguistic models tested as theories of SLA, or as parts of same, include Chomsky's and others' theories of Universal Grammar (UG; e.g., White, 1996, 2003a, 2003b), Prince and Smolensky's Optimality Theory (e.g., Eckman, 2004), Bickerton's Bioprogram Hypothesis (e.g., Huebner, 1983), Givon's Functional-Typological Model (e.g., Sato, 1990), O'Grady's general nativist theory (e.g., Wolfe-Quintero, 1992), and Bresnan's Lexical-Functional Grammar (e.g., Picnemann, 1998). Work introduced from psychology includes Giles' Accommodation Theory (e.g., Beebe & Giles, 1984), Bates' and MacWhinney's Competition Model (e.g., Kilborn & Ito, 1989), various connectionist models (e.g., Gasser, 1990), and several models based on Anderson's and others' distinction between declarative and procedural knowledge (e.g., K. Johnson, 1996).

DOMAIN, OR SCOPE

Theories also differ with respect to *domain*, or *scope* (i.e., as to what they purport to explain, or their "coverage"). Most nativist theories, for example, focus primarily, or thus far even exclusively, on phonology, syntax, and morphology, and at the level of form only, whereas some functionalist theories (e.g., Bates & MacWhinney, 1989; Givon, 1979) attempt to account for the acquisition of all levels of language, consider data from all levels when seeking explanations, and attribute a major role to communicative function in driving language acquisition (indeed, language change of all kinds). The acquisition type and context of interest (naturalistic or instructed, foreign or second, individual or community, etc.) also varies. The primary focus of Schumann's Acculturation Model, for example, is naturalistic acquisition by learners as members of groups. The central claim is that the degree to which members of such identifiable communities as Koreans in Los Angeles, Turks in Germany, Arabs in Israel, or Americans in the Middle East acquire the surrounding L2(s) will be a function of the extent to which they adapt to the new culture. This will depend on the social distance between their group and that new culture; social distance, in turn, is determined by eight factors: social dominance (the relative status and power of the groups in question), integration pattern (assimilation, acculturation, or preservation), enclosure (self-sufficiency in terms of such things as first language (L1)-medium clubs, newspapers, employment opportunities, shops, and churches), cohesiveness, community size, cultural congruence (e.g., shared or conflicting values and religious beliefs), attitude (positive to hostile), and intended length of residence (projected stay in the target language environment). Whereas the Acculturation Model speaks to naturalistic learning only, the domain of Ellis' theory, as its name implies, is the classroom. Krashen's Monitor Theory sets out to handle both naturalistic and instructed acquisition, but other things being equal (e.g., *if* each of the three theories were successful in their respective domains, and *if* they were comparable in other ways), the broader scope of Krashen's theory would make it the preferred choice.

CONTENT

Theories differ, thirdly, with respect to *content* (i.e., in the variables, and kinds of variables, that make up their explanatory core) and at a broader level, the relative importance accorded internal or environmental factors. Theories such as Schumann's Acculturation Model and Gardner's Socio-Educational Model (Gardner, 1988) draw primarily on social and social-psychological variables for their accounts, attempting to predict *that* SLA will or will not occur, and the degree of likely success, mostly as a function of group membership and intra- and inter-group relations. White's UG-based theory and Eckman's functional-typological approach (Eckman, 1996), on the other hand, invoke linguistic theory and related findings from studies of child first language acquisition (L1A), attempting to predict *how* acquisition will occur at the level of the individual, not the group, and as an internal cognitive process, not a social one, mostly as a function of prior linguistic knowledge and L1–L2 relationships. Whereas social-psychological models tend to make claims about general learning outcomes, assessed via global measures of L2 proficiency, researchers working within the UG and functional-typological frameworks test detailed claims about learning sequences, and about the ease, difficulty, and learnability of particular phonological and grammatical structures for speakers of certain types of L1 learning certain types of L2.

In White's UG-motivated work, for example, speakers of languages like French, which allows adverbs to be placed between verb and direct object (*Je bois toujours du café*), are expected to have difficulty with languages like English, which disallows this (**I drink every day coffee*), but not vice versa (see White, 1991a, and elsewhere, and for an alternative analysis; Schwartz & Gubla-Ryzak, 1992). (The facts about adverb placement are manifestations of a broader underlying structural difference between these and other languages.) English speakers should be able to learn the new option that French permits by encountering instances of verb–adverb–direct object strings in the input (positive evidence), whereas French speakers face the very different task of noticing the absence of such strings in the language they are learning, and so may need, or at least benefit from, various kinds of "correction" or explicit grammar instruction (negative evidence). Such an asymmetrical prediction is different from, and more accurate than, one that would have been derived from the old Contrastive Analysis Hypothesis (CAH; i.e., difficulty predicted for adverb-placement for both French *and* English speakers), with *any* L1–L2 difference being seen as a potential difficulty for the learner.

Also illustrating the level of detail and focus on process, but operating within a very different linguistic framework, Eckman's functional-typological approach, with its related Markedness Differential Hypothesis (MDH) and Structural Conformity Hypothesis, draws upon work on typological linguistic universals, combined with knowledge of L1–L2 contrasts, to make precise predictions about SLA in or out of classrooms. For example, where the presence of one structure (e.g., voiced stops: /b/, /d/, /g/) in the world's languages always implies the presence of another (e.g., voiceless stops: /p/, /t/, /k/), in various positions (word-initial, medial, or final), but not the reverse, the first structure is said to be "unmarked" relative to the second, and the second "marked" relative to the first. Unlike the discredited CAH, which predicted, wrongly, that (all) such differences between L1 and L2 would be difficult to learn (and all L2 features similar to those in the L1 simple), the MDH predicts, generally correctly, that learners will have problems with those areas of the L2 that differ from, and are more marked than, the L1. Again unlike the CAH, which could not predict difficulty if L1 and L2 both allowed the "same" structure, the MDH predicts varying degrees of difficulty, generally correctly, in such grammatical domains as relative clauses. Thus, where L1 and L2 both allow relativization, but from different levels in a six-tier noun phrase accessibility hierarchy, previously demonstrated to constitute an implicational markedness scale in the world's languages (Keenan & Comrie, 1976), ease or difficulty with L2 relative clause formation can be accounted for in part by whether the more marked structures occur in the L1 or L2 (see, e.g., Hamilton, 1994, and for review, Eckman, 1996).

TYPE

Schumann, Gardner, and other theorists focus on SLA as a social process, and draw primarily on situational and social-psychological variables to explain success and failure at the level of whole communities. White, Eckman, and others, conversely, emphasize SLA as a mental process, with the individual as the unit of analysis, and rely primarily on different kinds of linguistic theory to account for interlanguage development. Most of these and many other models fall into one or other of two broad camps: nativist (special, general, or hybrid) and empiricist.

Special nativist SLA theories (e.g., those of White, Krashen, and others) assume continued access by L2 acquirers, including adults, to genetically transmitted abilities specific to language learning—used for that, and nothing else—including innate knowledge of highly abstract syntactic principles and of the parameters along which languages can vary (UG), or of a set of universal semantic distinctions (Bickerton, 1984), which are held to govern child L1A and adult SLA alike, the latter sometimes with modifications brought about by prior learning of the L1.

General nativist proposals, such as those of O'Grady and Wolfe-Quintero, hold that SLA proceeds without UG or any such language-specific innate knowledge and abilities, and is instead accomplished through use of modularized general cognitive mechanisms. In O'Grady's (1996) formulation, there are five (perceptual, propositional, conceptual, computational, and learning) innate mechanisms, which suffice *both* for language and other kinds of learning, although possibly supplemented by a few (nonsyntactic) concepts used only for language. In O'Grady's account, the relative failure of most adult SLA (following the relatively uniform success of child L1A) is posited to be due to degradation of, or reduced access to, three of the five modules.

Hybrid nativist models, such as those of Clahsen and Muysken (1986), and Bley-Vroman (1990—his Fundamental Difference Hypothesis), are special nativist for L1A, usually holding it to be governed by UG, but general nativist for SLA, proceeding via general problem-solving procedures of various kinds. Bley-Vroman (1997), for example, proposed that adult SLA is accomplished by a general human cognitive categorization ability, manifested in SLA as the learning of variously weighted, category-based, and linked "constructions," or "patterns," roughly equivalent to phrase-structure rules, the learning process mediated by such phenomena as "noticing" (Schmidt, 1995), input frequency, saliency, and prototype effects.

From a theory construction point of view, although the success of particular exponents of these three general positions in predicting the facts about child and adult first and second language acquisition will ultimately determine their fate (see, e.g., Schwartz, 1992), general nativist theories have the initial advantage of being less powerful than special nativist theories, because they set out to handle the same data without recourse to innate linguistic knowledge. Special nativist and general nativist theories, in turn, are less powerful than hybrid nativist theories, because they attempt to explain the data on both first and second language acquisition using only one set of innate abilities, whether or not language specific, whereas hybrid theories assume both language-specific knowledge and general learning mechanisms, *and* are discontinuous (i.e., in this case, posit very different processes for child and adult and/or L1 and L2 acquisition). The discontinuity is usually motivated by the need to account for putative "sensitive period(s)" effects (i.e., maturational constraints). Young children typically become native-like in a first or second language if allowed continued access to the language concerned, and do so in about the same time period, despite wide variations in intelligence, linguistic exposure, or the kind of language(s) involved; adults, conversely, typically exhibit partial, often gross, failure under the same conditions, this despite what on the surface, at least, would seem to be the distinct advantage of cognitive maturity, improved memory, and prior success with their native language (for reviews of findings, see, e.g., DeKeyser, 2000; Hyltenstam & Abrahamsson, 2003; Long, 1990b, and chap. 3 in this volume). General nativist theories need to account for the seeming lack of decline in the ability to perform other general learning tasks at the same age(s) as the closure(s) of the one or more putative sensitive periods. Discontinuous (hybrid nativist) models would require an alternative motivation altogether should the alleged biological scheduling turn out to be illusory, or alternatively, should not one, but several sensitive periods be discovered for different linguistic systems.

In contrast to nativist theories, *empiricist* models are "data-driven," with linguistic input acting on universal cognitive, not linguistic, architecture. As conceived here, they include a greater variety of theories than those in the nativist camp, ranging from functionalist linguistic accounts, through social-psychological models, to connectionism. Some empiricist positions are referred to as "social-interactionist" (e.g., Gass, 1997) or "cognitive-interactionist" (e.g., Andersen, 1989). Most theorists stress that the environmental factors they consider important interact with internal mental abilities—hence, "interactionist" theories—and their views by no means signal a return to behaviorism. In all cases, however, in combination with internal factors, the learners' or learner groups' linguistic *experience* is said to play a stronger determining role in acquisition than anything countenanced by nativists of whatever stripe.

Experience can refer to the amount and quality of contact with the target language and its speakers, as in the case of the Acculturation and Socio-Educational Models, and as in several "skill-building" models of acquisition. The latter are usually based on variants of the idea from general cognitive psychology that learning (here, language learning) is chiefly a matter of converting declarative knowledge (knowledge that) into procedural knowledge (knowledge how) through a process of automatization (for review, see K. Johnson, 1996, pp. 77–151). Experience can also refer to emerging judgments of the relative importance of attending to particular linguistic features of the L2 in the input, as in Bates' and MacWhinney's Competition Model (MacWhinney, 1997). The Competition Model recognizes that such phenomena as word order, subject–verb agreement, case marking, lexical meaning, animacy, and pragmatic knowledge can all function—and sometimes compete with each other—as differentially available, reliable, and valid cues to meaning within and across languages (e.g., to such matters as which NPs in an utterance are subject and object). SLA, on this view, is in part a matter of learning new cues and cue strengths. In connectionist models (see, e.g., Elman et al., 1996; Plunkett, 1995), numerous encounters with forms and meanings in the input result not in the acquisition of rules of grammar, but in the formation of new connections, and modifications to the strengths of existing connections, between nodes in vastly complex neural networks. And, finally, experience can refer to both global L2 contact and detailed linguistic features of the input, or conversational experience, as in the so-called Interaction Hypothesis (Long, 1996) and the Experience Model (Hatch, Flashner, & Hunt, 1986).

To illustrate, Hatch et al. (1986) claim that all linguistic knowledge (phonological, morphological, syntactic, semantic, pragmatic, etc.) can be accounted for in terms of the interaction of cognitive, social, and linguistic systems, that "language clarifies and organizes experience and, conversely, that language grows out of experience" (p. 5). Elsewhere, following several child language acquisition researchers, Hatch (1978) claimed that "language learning evolves *out of* learning how to carry on conversations" (p. 404), although she suspected that the process might not work as well for certain aspects of a new language. These hypotheses were borne out by the results of a longitudinal study (Sato, 1986, 1988, 1990) of two Vietnamese brothers, age 8 and 10, acquiring English through submersion (cf. immersion) in state school classrooms in the United States. Sato found, for example, that the boys' earliest attempts at relativization and other complex syntax were supported by use of conversational scaffolding across utterances and speakers, whereas their development of inflectional marking of past time reference could be hindered by the same conversational scaffolding and/or interlocutors' situational knowledge, which often made overt morphological marking expendable. Sato concluded that conversation was *selectively facilitative* of development, a view since adopted by many social and cognitive interactionists in SLA (for review, see Gass, 1997; Long, 1996).

Although attributing far greater importance to the linguistic environment and to the social context for language acquisition, as already noted, empiricist models also assume considerable cognitive resources on the learner's part, including prior (but not innate) linguistic knowledge. The cognitive component of Andersen's cognitive-interactionist theory of SLA (Andersen, 1989), for example, includes two causal processes, "nativization" and "denativization," which are mental mechanisms that function in combination with (to date) 12 operating principles as part of the learner's mental acquisition apparatus. Some of those principles (e.g., "Keep track of the frequency of occurrence of every unit and pattern that you store") are drawn directly from Slobin's 40+ operating principles for child first language acquisition. Others are variants of principles that researchers claim govern many kinds of language development, including historical change, pidginization, creolization, and first language acquisition, and are also attested in SLA. Examples include the Multifunctionality Principle and the One-to-One Principle. In SLA, the latter states that "An interlanguage system should be constructed in such a way that an intended underlying meaning is expressed with one clear invariant surface form (or construction)" (Anderson, 1989, p. 51). Still others were originally derived primarily from cross-linguistic studies of interlanguage development, although they may also operate in such processes as pidginization and creolization. Examples are the Transfer to Somewhere and Reflexification principles. Andersen (1989) claims these 12 principles interact with each other and with one of, or (sequentially) both, the internal nativization and denativization mechanisms, so as to shape systematic variation and diachronic change in SLA. Nativization, according to Andersen, denotes "a composite of (presumably universal) processes" by which, especially when access to the L2 is restricted, as in early stages of SLA or in pidginization and creolization, a learner "creates an internal representation of the [target] language" (p. 48), often resulting in a system very different from that of the input. Conversely, Andersen claims that where access to linguistic input is unrestricted, as in most advanced SLA, denativization operates, and learners gradually restructure their initially idiosyncratic internal systems toward the target as a result of processing linguistic input (i.e., toward external, not internal, norms; p. 49). Like hybrid nativist models, in cases where nativization precedes denativization, Andersen's theory is discontinuous.

As each of these illustrations shows, empiricist theories tend to be data-driven in a second sense (i.e., in often, not always, having originally been derived inductively from empirical findings on interlanguage development). This is in contrast to most (not all) nativist models, which have usually been imported wholesale from outside the field (e.g., from linguistics), and then applied deductively in the design and interpretation of studies. An advantage most empiricist models share, as a result, is that they are often better supported empirically than many nativist models, especially during early stages in their development (which shows the danger inherent in evaluating rival theories, especially early on, simply in terms of their empirical adequacy). Empiricist models tend to be pitched at a level closer to the data they set out to explain. Although increasing the likelihood of their being "correct," in a superficial sense, at any one time, the lower level of abstraction can also reduce their potential scope and, hence, their interest. This differing ontogeny of nativist and empiricist models is usually also reflected in differences in form.

FORM

SLA theories, like theories in general, also differ in *form*. In some cases, the theorist's interim explanation consists of little more or less than a collection of statements, based on repeated empirical observations of the phenomena of interest that were consistent with *hypotheses* about those phenomena. Although recognizing that refutations may lie around the next corner, the statements attempt to capture patterns in the findings, general truths about the beast, and take the form of *generalizations*. When the findings are repeated often enough, without exceptions, and with a consensus among researchers in the field as to what has been discovered, these generalizations may attain the status of *laws*. This form of theory is known as *set-of-laws* (cf. the law of gravity or the laws of thermodynamics). There are very few, if any, laws in SLA as yet, but at least one theorist (Spolsky, 1989) has adopted this general approach to SLA theory construction, producing a listing with brief surveys of supporting empirical findings of over 100 statements of this kind, which are generalizations of greater or lesser certainty. Examples include: "Like first language knowledge, second language knowledge is marked by variability" (Spolsky, 1989, p. 40), "The younger one starts to learn a second language, the better chance one has to develop a native-like pronunciation" (p. 96), and "The closer two languages are to each other genetically and typologically, the quicker a speaker of one will learn the other" (p. 117).

Theories cast in set-of-laws form are useful in that they provide a sort of stock-taking, or a handy inventory of what we know (or think we know) about something. They are limited in at least two ways, however. First, the statements they contain are often unrelated, as with the previous three examples, usually having arisen from independent lines of inquiry. Testing any of them must generally be conducted separately, therefore, which is expensive in research costs, time, and energy. Second, because generalizations and laws started life as hypotheses, and the hypotheses had to be operationalizable to be empirically testable, they, and the generalizations and laws to which some of them eventually gave rise, could not and cannot contain *constructs*. Constructs abound in SLA, and include parameter, module, Monitor, nativization, cue validity, markedness, affective filter, "*i* + 1," social distance, noticing, learnability, teachability, sensitive period, generative entrenchment, fossilization, and so on. Theories in set-of-laws form stop at description, therefore, rarely providing anything more than implicit *explanations* for the phenomena they concern. If true, then *why* is it, for example, that "The younger one starts to learn a second language, the better chance one has to develop a native-like pronunciation?" In some sense, then, rather than constituting a theory of a *process* like SLA, theories in set-of-laws form are better seen as storehouses of information, repositories of the widely accepted facts (if facts they be) about the *product* that an SLA theory needs to explain (Long, 1990a). To be satisfactory, a SLA theory should be able to explain *why* younger starters do better, *why* developmental sequences are unaffected by instruction, and so on, and not merely capture the observations themselves. To do this, they need to avail themselves of constructs, in the short term at least, and to posit explanatory *mechanisms* of some kind. And it is here that a second form of theory is more successful.

Causal-process theories (in some other fields, but not always in SLA, regrettably) contain definitions of their constructs and concepts, with operational definitions of at least some of the latter, existence statements, and deterministic and/or probabilistic causal statements, which are interrelated. Together, they specify how or why SLA will occur, not just that it will or when it will occur. Chomsky's so-called Principles and Parameters theory of the 1980s, as exemplified in the work of White, Schwartz, and others, O'Grady's and Wolfe-Quintero's general nativist models, and Pienemann's Processability Theory, are examples of causal-process theories in SLA. The interrelatedness of statements in such theories means that some unoperationalized (unobservable) constructs, mechanisms, and processes are permitted and unproblematic, for whereas the statement containing the unoperationalized item is not itself testable, a related statement is, and if the second survives the test, then the related statement containing the explanatory construct receives indirect support. Problems only arise when each of a pair of statements contains unoperationalized constructs, mechanisms, or metaphors, as with "$i + 1$" and the "affective filter" in what is perhaps the best known causal-process theory in SLA, Krashen's so-called Input Hypothesis. According to Krashen (1985):

> In order to acquire, two conditions are necessary. The first is comprehensible (or even better, comprehend*ed*) input containing "$i + 1$," structures a bit beyond the acquirer's current level, and second, a low or weak affective filter to allow the input "in." This is equivalent to saying that comprehensible input and the strength of the filter are the true causes of second language acquisition. (p. 33)

In a case like this, the whole claim becomes *untestable* (although not necessarily wrong for that, of course).

THE USE AND EVALUATION OF THEORIES

Work of widely different kinds by numerous individuals, groups, and even whole "schools," has tended until recently to continue in untroubled isolation from that of others supposedly working on the same or related issues. However, a number of circumstances have conspired to dispel this mirage of harmonious coexistence. The following paragraphs discuss three scenarios.

First, there is growing public pressure for accountability from researchers in SLA, as in other fields where public money is at stake. An obvious example is the absence, until recently, of research funding theoretical work in the United States, where many SLA researchers live, and the corresponding requirement that the little research funded produce tangible "products" of clear public benefit. Such pressure is made more acute by the importance of advances in SLA theory for so many populations and for addressing so many important social problems—everything from language revitalization to refugee resettlement.

Second, increasingly robust empirical findings on several issues lend support to some theories, and for some whole classes of theories, but they cast doubt on others, and on some whole classes. To illustrate, theories (e.g., Bley-Vroman, 1997; O'Grady, 2003) that posit one or more different mechanisms, and predict differential outcomes, for child and adult language learning are consistent with findings on maturational constraints on language development (see, e.g., De Keyser, 2000). Conversely, so-called full access positions within the UG camp (e.g., Flynn, 1996) cannot explain the widely documented inferior achievement of adults supposedly still equipped with the full innate language learning capacity that served them so well as children.[1] Similarly, the impossibility of learning some (specifiable) L2 items from positive evidence alone (Pavesi, 1986; White, 1991a, 1991b), and the repeatedly documented persistence of errors and error types in learners' interlanguages despite ample opportunity to acquire (e.g., Lardiere, 1998a; Swain, 1991), both mean that a theory predicting native-like mastery simply from exposure to comprehensible language samples (e.g., Krashen, 1985, and elsewhere) is inadequate, at best, or more likely, simply wrong. (For additional examples of problematic empirical findings for various classes of SLA theories, see Long, 1990a.)

Third, because all theories at some level represent researchers' interim understandings of the phenomena they are trying to explain, it follows that identifying faulty understandings, and culling the theories concerned, constitutes progress. Persistence of a plethora of theories, conversely, especially oppositional ones (see Beretta, 1991), obstructs progress, and many theories in and of SLA at present are clearly oppositional (see Long, 1993a, for examples of different kinds of oppositionality among SLA theories).[2] Acceptance of the resulting need for (absolute and comparative) theory evaluation has led more SLA research-

---

[1]Aware of this problem, Flynn and others have repeatedly, but unsuccessfully, sought to explain away findings on maturational constraints on SLA as due to various environmental or motivational factors, not to a loss of capacity for language acquisition. See, for example, Flynn and Manuel (1991).

[2]These claims are elaborated and supported in the final chapter.

ers to begin to familiarize themselves with evaluation criteria used for theory assessment in other fields and/or to propose new ones.

Disciplines with much longer histories and far greater accomplishments than SLA have found it necessary to develop ways of evaluating theories, both in absolute terms, and comparatively (i.e., relative to other theories). Over the past 40 years, various evaluation criteria have been formalized and themselves evaluated by philosophers of science (see, e.g., Cushing, 1989; Darden, 1991; L. Laudan, 1977, 1996a; Riggs, 1992b), and whereas some observers consider it premature, discussions of possible approaches to evaluating SLA theories have begun to appear in the SLA literature (see, e.g., Beretta, 1991; Crookes, 1992; Gregg, 1993, 1996; Jordan, 2004b; Long, 1990a, 1993a; chap. 6 in this volume).

In absolute terms, theories may be judged inadequate because they are too powerful, ad hoc, untestable, say nothing about relevant phenomena, and so on. In relative terms, they may be less adequate than rival theories of the same phenomena because they consistently make less accurate predictions, account for fewer data, require more mechanisms to handle the same data, and so on—and of particular importance, following L. Laudan (1977), in terms of their comparative ability to solve various kinds of differentially weighted empirical problems, an approach described and adopted in chapter 2. Evaluation criteria that have evolved to achieve one or both of these two general goals include, but are not limited to: empirical adequacy, simplicity/parsimony, generality, ability to explain phenomena different from those for which the theory was invented to account, ability to make surprising novel predictions, continuity/rationality, problem-solving ability, explanatory power, consistency, and (the somewhat overlapping) fertility and generative potential (for review, see Long, 1993a).

At a more general level, which of several theories is judged "best" may be a function of two qualities (see Gregg, 1993, p. 285, following Lipton, 1991, p. 61). First, how *likely* is a theory (i.e., how reasonable, or how plausible, is it as an explanation) given what we think we know about the facts? This often simply means, disappointingly, how close it is to those facts (e.g., a claim that structures A, B, C, and D are always learned in a particular order because each is linguistically more complex than the one that preceded it). Second, how *lovely* is it (i.e., how broad and deep an understanding does it provide?)? A "lovelier" theory of the same phenomenon might be less obvious, even somewhat surprising, for example, that A, B, C, and D are always acquired in that order because acquisition sequences always obey markedness relationships, and A, B, C, and D have been shown to be thus ordered, from least to most marked, on an implicational markedness scale.

However acceptable (or accepted) a theory may be when evaluated by these and other standards, it is worth remembering that, by definition, and for two reasons, even the "best" theory can never be shown to be *true*. First, as rationalists (e.g., philosophical realists), the vast majority of researchers in any scientific field believe (unlike postmodernists and relativists) that an objective reality exists independent of any individual's or group's (social) construction of it (i.e., that there are facts of the matter, even though that reality may never be fully comprehended). They also believe that, along with individual differences and particularities of time and place, there are universals (e.g., a universal law of gravity, supported by such repeatedly attested phenomena as apples falling to the ground—not just on Thursdays, around Cambridge, or only when observed by Isaac Newton, but always, everywhere, and regardless of who is doing the observing). In SLA, most researchers believe that, although imperfect, the field's research methods permit theories to be evaluated, among other ways, by assessing the degree to which their predictions are borne out in nature. Are there or are there not people who can attain native-like proficiency in various linguistic subsystems starting SLA after certain ages? Do or do not certain L2 grammatical constructions prove differentially problematic for speakers of certain languages? And so on. They believe it is possible to approximate the truth, in other words, without necessarily ever being able to be sure that a belief *is* the truth. The second reason a theory can never be true is simpler: If all the facts were in and agreed on, and if a process like SLA were fully understood, and agreed to be understood, then there would be no need for a theory about it.

NECESSITY, SUFFICIENCY, AND EFFICIENCY

Another criterion suggested in the applied linguistics literature for evaluating SLA theories is that they be assessed in terms of their pedagogic value and/or their comprehensibility to teachers, a proposal I consider flawed, not to mention demeaning to both researchers and teachers (even when not the same people). In addition to the fact that theories are just that, theories and not "the truth" about SLA, there is a question of focus. As illustrated earlier, the scope of many SLA theories does not extend to the L2 classroom at all. Moreover, even the minority of SLA theories that aspire to classroom relevance address instructed SLA, not language teaching per se, which involves acquisition *plus* a number of situational variables, and so is far more complex. And whereas the goal of most SLA theorists is the least powerful theory that will handle the known facts (i.e., to identify what is *necessary* and *sufficient* for language acquisition), the language teacher and the language teaching theorist alike are interested in the most *efficient* set of procedures, the combination of conditions and practices that will bring about language learning fastest and with least effort, whether or not strictly necessary or sufficient.

To illustrate, Krashen's (1985) Monitor Theory holds that adult learners can and do learn grammatical structures, the meanings and collocations of lexical items, and so on, *incidentally* (i.e., through exposure to those items in communicative use), without conscious awareness while doing something else, just as children (supposedly) learn their first language. One of several applications of Monitor Theory to classroom settings, the Natural Approach (Krashen & Terrell, 1983), essentially advocates recreating in the classroom the conditions that (supposedly) are necessary and sufficient for L1A (which, in contrast to much SL teaching, is widely successful, after all). The two basic tenets of the Monitor Theory have to be instantiated pedagogically in some way. First, the so-called Input Hypothesis, which states that adults, like children, acquire a second language incidentally through exposure to comprehensible target language samples, might be reflected in an emphasis on communicative teacher speech and high interest extensive reading, each containing structures and vocabulary one step ahead of where the learner is now ($i + 1$), and with the learners encouraged to focus on meaning, not the language itself. Second, the so-called Affective Filter Hypothesis, which states that L2 exposure needs to occur in a positive affective climate, might be addressed via pedagogic procedures that cater to student sensitivities and promote a relaxed and supportive classroom atmosphere. The Natural Approach is a case of a theory of SLA masquerading as a theory of language teaching.

Meanwhile, a very different view has been advanced by Schmidt (1995, and elsewhere), who argues, contra Krashen, that incidental learning is *in*sufficient for adult SLA in or out of classrooms. Schmidt claims instead that L2 forms themselves must be "noticed," in the sense of their existence in the input being registered, if learning is to occur, and noticing in this sense is *necessary and sufficient* for acquisition. Schmidt's proposals are based on theory and research findings in cognitive psychology and in first and second language acquisition.

Supporters of a current proposal for language teaching known as *focus on form* (not forms; see, e.g., Doughty, 2001; Doughty & J. Williams, 1998a; Long, 1991; Long & Robinson, 1998) note these conflicting claims. Without necessarily taking sides on the necessity or sufficiency issue, they advocate drawing students' attention to language as object—grammar, vocabulary, collocations, and so on—in context, with the linguistic sequence and timing determined by the students' internal syllabus, not an externally imposed one, during otherwise meaning-based lessons of some kind (e.g., task-based or content-based classes). Although generally favoring Schmidt's view over Krashen's, proponents of focus on form do not all claim such code-focused interventions are necessary for classroom learning, and certainly not in all cases, but that they make learning more *efficient*. Their position is based not only on theoretical grounds (Schmidt's claims, and others), but also on empirical findings (for review, see Doughty & J. Williams, 1998b; Long & Robinson, 1998; Norris & Ortega, 2000; Spada, 1997). A growing number of researchers have reported intentional learning to be more efficient (e.g., to occur faster) than incidental learning, for example. And focus on form has performed nonsignificantly differently from (for other reasons, the less desirable) focus on forms, despite most of the roughly 50 controlled comparisons to date having targeted easy grammar in experiments of brief duration, both factors that favor focus on forms.[3]

The embryonic language teaching theory of which focus on form is but a part is already more *powerful* (a negative when evaluating theories, as noted earlier) than, say, Krashen's theory, because (among others) it has recourse to a mechanism, focus on form, to induce acquisition that Monitor Theory does without. This would be important when evaluating the claims as part of a theory of SLA, but it is immaterial in the classroom context, because the relevant theories against which to judge a theory of language teaching will be other theories of language teaching, not theories of SLA. A relevant comparison, for example, would be between a theory of language teaching that invoked focus on form, on the one hand, and on the other, one which claimed that such interventions were unhelpful, or one holding that an externally imposed linguistic syllabus, explicit grammar rules, translation, structural pattern drills, and so on, were either necessary or more efficient ways of inducing learning of some or all grammatical structures and lexical items.

PUTTING SLA THEORIES IN THEIR PLACE

Almost every theory ever invented in any field has turned out to be wrong, at least in part, and there is no reason to expect current SLA theories will fare much better. That is not a license for so-called eclecticism in language teaching, however. "Eclectic methods" are usually little more than an amalgam of their inventors' prejudices (see, e.g., Sheen, 1998). The same relative ignorance about SLA affects everyone, and makes the eclecticist's claim to be able to select the alleged "best parts" of several theories absurd. Worse, given that different theories by definition reflect different understandings, the resulting methodological mish-mash is guaranteed to be wrong, whereas an approach to language teaching that is based in part on one theory can at least be coherent, and can be subject to the previously discussed caveats, and so has a chance of being right.

That said, theories are what people rely on in the absence of anything else. They are attempts to make sense of experience, and where data are lacking, as is massively the case in SLA and in SL teaching, they go beyond the putative facts of the matter, using logical inference, imaginative speculation, and other ingredients. Therefore, whereas one potential source (not

---

[3]The rationale for focus on form also draws on logical arguments concerning subset relations, to the effect that code-centered interventions are probably necessary, at least for certain classes of target language features and L1–L2 contrasts, if such features are ever to be learned, the need for negative evidence, and more.

the only one, of course) of crucial insights about language learning, the process language teaching is trying to induce, as Hatch (1979) pointed out, SLA theories should always be treated with caution (as no more or less than one or more theorists' current best shot at explaining language learning, never the truth about it) and with downright suspicion whenever advocated as a recipe for the classroom, which will always require consideration of other factors and not "just" SLA—however important a component of a theory of language teaching that may be.

Most SLA theories and SLA theorists are not primarily interested in language teaching, and in some cases they are not at all interested. So although SLA theories may be evaluated in absolute terms and comparatively in a variety of ways—parsimony, empirical adequacy, problem-solving ability, and so on—it makes no sense to judge them solely, or in some cases at all, on the basis of how useful they are for the classroom or how meaningful to classroom teachers. Theories of the role of innate linguistic knowledge in adult SLA, for instance, should be judged on their own terms (e.g., according to how well predictions they make are borne out by empirical findings, not as to whether they say anything about how teaching should proceed). Most do not. By the same token, just as any understanding of how the human body works is likely to be relevant to medical practice at some level, so any theory of SLA is likely to be at least indirectly relevant to language teaching practice, in that SLA is the process language teaching is designed to facilitate. Thus, SLA theories may provide the classroom practitioner with useful new ways of thinking about (e.g., the varied sociolinguistic milieu students inhabit outside the classroom) perceptual saliency, attention, awareness, learnability, and teachability, the role of implicit and explicit learning, learner error, the need for negative feedback, and different kinds of structural differences between the learners' L1(s) and the L2, among many other matters. The theories themselves might not say anything to teachers about how to teach, but perhaps something about who and what it is they are trying to teach (e.g., about whether, depending on L1–L2 relationships, drawing students' attention to some contrasts is essential, facilitative, or not needed at all).

SLA theories may provide insight into putatively universal *methodological principles* for language teaching, in other words, while saying little or nothing about the inevitable and desirable particularity of appropriate classroom *pedagogical procedures*, in which the local practitioner, not the SLA theorist, should always be the expert. A SLA theory might hold provision of negative feedback to be necessary or facilitative, for example (i.e., to be a universal methodological principle), but it will be up to the teacher to decide which pedagogic procedures, ranging from the most implicit corrective recasts to the most explicit spoken and/or written forms of on-record "error correction," are locally appropriate ways of delivering negative feedback for a particular group of learners, depending on such factors as the target linguistic item concerned and learner age and literacy.

Whatever the precise relationship, given that SLA theorists and language teachers share a common interest, L2 development, it would clearly be self-defeating for either group to ignore the other's work.

CHAPTER TWO

Problem Solving and Theory Change in SLA[1]

A look at such journals as *Studies in Second Language Acquisition, Language Learning,* and *Second Language Research* shows that work in SLA has grown more sophisticated over the past three decades, especially where research design and methodology are concerned. It is equally clear, however, that a number of big-picture matters at the "top end" of research methods, principally issues concerning theory construction and evaluation, remain less well developed. In fact, with few exceptions (see, e.g., Beretta, 1991; Crookes, 1992; Gregg, 1993, 2001, 2003; Gregg, Long, Jordan, & Beretta, 1997; Jordan, 2002b, 2004; Long, 1990a, 1993a), they are rarely discussed at all, much less resolved. Yet, most are basic enough to affect overall progress in the field far more fundamentally than appropriate use of this or that data collection device or statistical procedure.

The following are some of the questions in need of consideration with respect to SLA as an emergent scientific discipline. What is the role of theories in guiding and shaping a field of inquiry? What counts as a theory? Is theory proliferation really a problem? When and how can theories be evaluated, either in absolute terms or comparatively, without endangering needed theoretical innovation? What constitutes progress in a field? If 99% of researchers are rationalists, and if they agree on appropriate theory assessment criteria (scope, parsimony, falsifiability, empirical adequacy, etc.), then how is one to explain theory proliferation and theoretical disunity? Con-

[1] I thank Kevin Gregg and Geoff Jordan for helpful comments on an early version of this chapter.

versely, if they are rationalists, but disagree on assessment criteria, then how could one ever expect to achieve or explain theoretical consensus and the emergence of a dominant theory? When, how, and why do theories change?

Valuable help with these and related issues is available from the history, sociology, and philosophy of science, and in particular from the work of the American philosopher of science, Larry Laudan. Laudan's notion of *research tradition* and his *problem-solving* view of science offer a rational explanation of theory evaluation and change, and of progress in SLA.

WHAT IS THE ROLE OF THEORIES IN GUIDING AND SHAPING A FIELD OF INQUIRY?

As described in chapter 1, theories are interim understandings of natural phenomena—what we rely on in the absence of certainty. By positing which the relevant variables may be in some line of inquiry, theories suggest the most fruitful foci for future research. Particular types of theory, notably causal-process theories, not only produce predictions about future findings, but simultaneously offer potential explanations as to why the observations in question will be made. In other words, they provide ready means of interpreting findings.

Theories bring order out of chaos. Instead of numerous lone individuals duplicating effort and consuming time and resources studying anything and everything that moves, theories indicate what is important, offering road maps for research programs. They create communities of scholars working collaboratively on the same important problems (not necessarily advocating the same solutions, of course), and help unify their efforts around agreed-on domains of relevance such that the sum of those efforts is greater than the parts.

For these and other reasons, theories are clearly a good thing. Consequently, it behooves researchers in SLA, as in any discipline, to devote careful attention to the state of theory and theories in the field. To a great extent, progress will be reflected in, and measurable by, theory change.

WHAT COUNTS AS A THEORY?

Where does one theory end and another begin, and how broad does the scope of a "hypothesis,"[2] or claim, have to be before it is accorded theoretical status? Sizable variation in the numbers of theories of SLA reported in the SLA literature—ranging from none (Gregg, 1996) to between 40 and 60 (Long, 1993a)—is probably in large part a function of different verdicts on those issues. Of course, the precise numbers themselves are unimportant,

---

[2]Which term, *theory* or *hypothesis*, authors apply to their own claims is of little help in identifying demarcation lines. Whatever their relative merits, Krashen's Input Hypothesis (Krashen, 1985), for example, purported to offer a theory of SLA of far broader scope than, say, Pienemann's Processability Theory (Pienemann, 1998).

but in general, the larger the number, and if they conflict, the greater the degree of disunity apparent in the field, and the greater the need for comparative theory appraisal.

It is easy to distinguish theories with fundamentally different assumptions, content, or mechanisms. Special nativist theories, like Chomsky's, which assume innate knowledge of basic properties of language and of limits on the ways languages can vary, are obviously different from general nativist theories, like O'Grady's (see, e.g., O'Grady, 1996, 2003; Wolfe-Quintero, 1996), which assume innate cognitive abilities and processing capacities, but not innate knowledge of language per se. Where is the line to be drawn, however, in such cases of rival explanations of (roughly) the same phenomena that *share* similar basic assumptions, content, or mechanisms? Let us consider two of many such cases.

A first example concerns the properties of the innate linguistic inheritance assumed still available to the adult L2 acquirer. Eubank (1996) and Vainikka and Young-Scholten (1996), among others, have claimed that the explanation for nonsuppliance of inflectional morphology is that adult L2 learners retain access only to lexical category projections, and initially lack functional features and/or the feature values (e.g., strong/weak) associated with them, which supposedly do not transfer from the L1—the so-called Weak Continuity and Minimal Trees hypotheses. Putative evidence for this position takes the form of learners in the very early stages who fail to produce overt verbal inflectional morphology associated with such functional categories as AgrP and TP. They have to acquire those elements of syntactic knowledge, or phrase structure, it is maintained, gradually, by projection, through analysis of the L2 input. In contrast, Schwartz and Sprouse (1996) and Lardiere (1998a, 1998b), among others, have indicated that absence of inflectional morphology does not necessarily imply absence of underlying syntactic knowledge. Researchers in this camp purport to have shown that functional categories and their projections are available to the L2 acquirer from the outset—the so-called Full Transfer/Full Access hypothesis. Indeed, Lardiere has argued that they are even to be found in the (putatively fossilized) "final state" of a Chinese acquirer of English, Patty, who controls full clausal phrase structure (e.g., verb-raising) and finiteness despite very low suppliance of related finite verbal inflectional (subject–verb agreement or tense) morphology. The fact that Patty's interlanguage also exhibits perfect distribution of nominative and accusative pronoun case marking also suggests full specification of the functional IP features. Morphological deficiencies, the Full Transfer/Full Access group hold, are due to problems with mapping to PF, not a lack of underlying functional categories, projections, or features.

A second example of rival explanations proposed by researchers sharing the same overall theoretical allegiances concerns Schumann's (1978, 1986) Acculturation Model and Gardner's (1985, 1988) Socio-Educational Model. Schumann's and Gardner's theories share similar underlying assumptions, scope, and content. Schumann and Gardner both invoke a combination of social, psychological, and social-psychological variables to explain success and failure in SLA at the level of the group, mostly as a function of group membership and intra- and intergroup relations. Each attributes greater importance to affective and situational factors than to linguistic or cognitive variables. Empirical tests of both theories have tended to utilize questionnaires and other paper-and-pencil measures of the putative causal variables—attitude, motivation, contact with target-language speakers, and so forth—and (with some exceptions in the case of the Acculturation Model) global L2 proficiency tests as the primary outcome measure.

Should the Weak Continuity/Minimal Trees position, on the one hand, and the Full Access/Full Transfer position, on the other, be considered two variants of the same theory of SLA, subtheories nested within the UG paradigm, or oppositional theories within the same domain? And what of the Acculturation and Socio-Educational Models? Are they, also, two variants of the same basic theory, or are they oppositional theories within the same domain? I suspect most would judge the first case to be one of oppositional theories within the same domain, but both embedded within the same (Chomskyite UG) tradition, and the second a case of two distinct theories. Yet, differences between the two UG camps are in many ways more specific, more explicit, more empirically testable, and potentially more far-reaching in their consequences than those between Schumann's and Gardner's positions. It is noteworthy that advocates of either side in the debate over "access" invariably discuss the significance of their empirical findings for both positions; to the best of my knowledge, such has never been the case in the literature on either the Acculturation or Socio-Educational Model. This might suggest that the two UG "camps" were really rival theories—in the making, at least—whereas the Acculturation and Socio-Educational Models were variants on a common basic theory.

It should also be noted that writing on UG-motivated SLA research makes no reference to work on Schumann's or Gardner's models, and vice versa. At first sight, this is unsurprising, because researchers in each case are so clearly working on theories with such different underlying assumptions, domains, content, mechanisms, and data. The easy explanation for the lack of interchange, in other words, is simply that they are complementary, not oppositional, theories (see Beretta, 1991), and researchers working within one framework therefore have little or no *need* to evaluate work in another. But are they really complementary? Each of these (two, three, or four) theories, after all, purports to be a theory of SLA.[3] Another interpretation of the peaceful coexistence of these and so many other putative theories of SLA is that groups of researchers in these and numerous other areas

---

[3]I leave aside the fact that UG is technically (at most) a property theory (of language), not a full theory of SLA, which would also require a transition theory (see, e.g., Gregg, 1996, 2001, 2003; and for a contrary view, Jordan, 2002a).

have "gone off on their own" (i.e., to their own academic networks, journals, conferences, publishers, and university departments), each finding little or no interest in, and in many cases gradually becoming virtually oblivious to, work in the field outside their own intellectual ghetto—untroubled, as a result, by the often very real, albeit unrecognized, oppositionality. This state of affairs reflects an unhealthy fragmentation of the field of SLA, with concomitant effects on its intellectual coherence, its viability as a science, and its social relevance.

An alternative analysis—one that I favor—is offered by Laudan. On this analysis, the degree of fragmentation may not be quite as severe as it first appears. Researchers, Laudan points out, tend to have enduring, long-standing commitments to clusters of fundamental beliefs broader than those of any particular theory that reflects them, and to a corresponding set of epistemic and methodological norms about how a domain of inquiry should be studied. The two components make up what Laudan calls *research traditions*, a technical term in his theory of theory change—groups of theories with a shared ontology, and agreed-on methodological ground rules. Research traditions are not directly testable (unlike some theories or parts thereof). They can survive the demise of one of their particular subordinate theories.[4]

Viewed in this light, it is easy to see that the Weak Continuity/Minimal Trees and Full Transfer/Full Access positions are properly viewed as theories in the same generative *research tradition*. Vainikka, Young-Scholten, Eubank, Schwartz, Sprouse, Lardiere, Hawkins, White, and others involved in the "access" debate, for example, all clearly share the same assumptions about the existence of an innate language faculty, and about its approximate contents (in the infant, at least), the same focus on underlying linguistic competence as the proper domain of inquiry, and the same research methods (e.g., use—not exclusive use, of course—of grammaticality judgment tests) for probing the dimensions of that competence, and they agree on the standards to be met by their linguistic analyses. They play, that is, by the same rules. Also, if one of the theories in the research tradition (say, Minimal Trees) crashes, it is hard to imagine the adherents to that theory jumping to a completely different tradition (e.g., some variety of functionalism); they are far more likely to switch allegiance to what was hitherto a rival theory within their own research tradition (probably, Full Transfer/Full Access).

Work on the role in language development of Chomsky's and his followers' evolving conceptions of universal grammar is perhaps the easiest, most transparent case of a research tradition in SLA. Other examples might include research on the so-called Input, Interaction, and Output Hypotheses (see, e.g., Gass, 1997, 2003; Hatch, 1978; Long, 1996; Mackey, 1999; Mitchell & Myles, 1998; Pica, 1994) over the years, and on at least some

---

[4]For discussion of Laudan's notion of "research tradition," see Gholson and Barker (1985) and Riggs (1992a, pp. 109–119).

strands of functionalism (see, e.g., Braidi, 1999; Mitchell & Myles, 1998; Sato, 1990). But these are admittedly less clear cases. Thus, Krashen, Long, Swain, and others have periodically reflected a focus on qualitative and quantitative features of linguistic input to learners, their conversational experience, and learner production as a function of both. On the surface, at least, their models share an assumption that interlanguage development is data-driven in an experiential way far removed from the Chomskyan view. The latter has language "unfolding," with the environment important mainly for the "triggers" it contains to stimulate utilization of preexisting innate knowledge about language, as in parameter-(re)setting, with such factors as negative feedback unimportant (see, e.g., Schwartz, 1993). But appearances can be deceptive. Krashen's Input Hypothesis also relied explicitly (see, e.g., Krashen, 1985, pp. 2–3) on the continuing availability to adult second language learners of Chomsky's Language Acquisition Device, and on that count, could be viewed as fundamentally a special nativist theory. Similarly, Swain holds great store by metalinguistic knowledge as an engine driving acquisition (see, e.g., Swain & Lapkin, 1998), a position both Krashen and Long reject.

To take another example of a more ambiguous case, is some version of a Critical Periods Hypothesis (CPH) a theory of (S)LA, or just part of one, and are all the many versions of a CPH each different theories (or hypotheses) within the same research tradition, or just different versions of the same (basic) theory? As described in chapter 3, the formulations differ, among other ways, in whether they posit a one-time loss of overall language learning capacity or different ages for different linguistic abilities, in the linguistic domains they claim to be affected by maturational constraints, and in the neurophysiological processes believed to underlie the constraints. In this case, I would suggest that at least some of the CPHs are oppositional theories in the same domain, but not from the same research tradition at all. For instance, Scovel (1988, and elsewhere) claims that maturation controls only the acquisition of L2 phonology (the window of opportunity for native-like ultimate attainment closing at puberty), whereas many other CPH researchers (see, e.g., DeKeyser, 2000; Hyltenstam, 1992; Hyltenstam & Abrahamsson, 2003; Long, 1990b; Seliger, 1978) believe morphology, syntax, and the lexicon to be affected, too (often well before puberty). Crucially, too, the origin of various versions of the CPH in different research traditions is visible in the explanations offered for loss of ability. Some (e.g., Long, 1990b, 1993b, chap. 3 in this volume; Scovel, 1988; Seliger, 1978) are neurophysiological, others (e.g., Newport, 1990, and elsewhere) general cognitive, and so on.

IS THEORY PROLIFERATION REALLY A PROBLEM?

During the 1980s and 1990s, the field of SLA became increasingly fragmented and characterized by a multiplicity of theories (broadly construed)—as noted in chapter 1, as many as 60 by my count (see Long,

1993a, and, also, chap. 6). As noted, some (e.g., Lantolf, 1996a; Jordan, 2004) consider this a healthy sign; others (e.g., Beretta, 1991; Gregg, 1993, 2000; Long, 1993a) view it as a serious problem.

Shorn of the mix of straw man arguments and misrepresentations, Lantolf's defense of proliferation (Lantolf, 1996a, 2002) boils down to three equally unsupported and unsupportable assertions: (a) Theories are merely metaphors in disguise, spectacles, "grand narratives"; (b) the more theories there are, the more research is generated, so theory proliferation is an indication of the fruitfulness of a field; and (c) proliferation is protection against the tyranny of the paradigm. As described in chapter 6, Gregg (2000, 2002) has provided a trenchant and, in my view, unanswerable critique of Lantolf's position; it is unnecessary to say more.

Jordan's position is more substantive. Unlike Lantolf, he does not endorse proliferation on the spurious postmodernist grounds that one theory is as good as the next, all knowledge is socially constructed, and so on. Quite to the contrary, he acknowledges cases where proliferation is unwarranted, and recognizes that comparative theory evaluation is possible:

> While in my view the proliferation of theories is not, in itself, a problem, there are often good *pragmatic* reasons to support a culling of theories. Where there are contradictions between theories, these must be highlighted and then discussed as fully as possible. In the field of SLA, some theories can be dismissed on conceptual grounds.... Any real contradiction between theories can then, at least in principle, be settled by empirical tests, and after that the decision about the best current theory in a given domain is a question of applying the criteria discussed earlier. (2004, p. 108)

Jordan offers two basic reasons for supporting proliferation. First, he views SLA as too broad a field to be handled by any currently available single theory. To this, I would respond that even if true, that is a justification for two or more complementary (cf. competing) theories of different scope, not proliferation. Also, domains do not sit around waiting for theories to come along to handle them; in a very real sense, it is the theory that identifies the domain.

Second, Jordan accepts Feyerabend's view[5] that scientists should adopt a critical stance and constantly develop theories that challenge the paradigm: "Kuhn's 'normal science' encourages conformity, and suggests that scientists should accept assumptions uncritically. I agree with Feyerabend: scientists should constantly develop theories which challenge the paradigm—and the more theories the merrier" (Jordan, 2004, p. 5). I disagree with Jordan (and Feyerabend). Scientists remain "critical," theories are

---

[5]Whatever one may think of his arguments, Feyerabend's fiery review of Laudan's model, and of *Progress and Its Problems*, in particular (Feyerabend, 1981), still makes delightful reading 25 years after its first publication. See, also, Grobler 1990), and the no-holds-barred exchange between Worrall (1988, 1989) and L. Laudan (1989). Even the toughest reviews in SLA journals are tame by comparison.

tested, and new ones developed as need be, in mature disciplines during periods of normal science, as well as during periods of change. Also, Jordan does not explain *why* constant theory development is a necessary corollary of a critical stance, or why it would necessarily be valuable to develop new theories with which to challenge one or more widely viewed as probably correct. Unless clearly motivated, for example, by some difference of scope or explicitly recognized oppositionality, theory proliferation hinders progress (see chaps. 1 and 6), and ultimately renders both the theorist and the field unaccountable, when the advancement of knowledge about the mind, as well as many important social problems, requires just the opposite.

WHEN AND HOW CAN THEORIES BE EVALUATED, EITHER IN ABSOLUTE TERMS OR COMPARATIVELY, WITHOUT ENDANGERING NEEDED THEORETICAL INNOVATION?

Those agreeing on the need to assess SLA theories would ask several questions: Is the job better done in absolute terms, one theory at a time, or comparatively, with two or more theories pitted against one another? And, in either case, how can theories be evaluated rationally, and the process accomplished without endangering needed theoretical innovation?

The history and philosophy of science literatures yield a wide array of (sometimes overlapping) assessment criteria available for the evaluation of (SLA) theories, in absolute terms or comparatively, including: internal consistency, nontautologousness, systematicity, modularity, clarity, explanatory adequacy, predictive adequacy, scope, generality, lack of ad hocness, extendability, fruitfulness, consistency with accepted theories in other fields, experimental testability, ability to make quantitative predictions, simplicity, falsifiability, fertility as a paradigm for puzzle-solving, explanatory power, problem-solving ability, ability to account for different kinds of data, ability to account for phenomena different from those for which the theory was invented to explain, novel predictive successes, ability to account for data a rival theory cannot handle, simplicity/parsimony, consistency, generality, empirical adequacy, proven fertility, unproven fertility/generative potential, continuity/rationality, pragmatic ("get on with things") relationship with experiment, and ability to resolve fundamental conceptual difficulties. (For explanations of the criteria, sample applications, and evaluation, see Darden, 1991; Jordan, 2004; L. Laudan, 1990; L. Laudan & R. Laudan, 1989; Long, 1993a.)

A particularly promising approach is to be found in Laudan's work (see, e.g., L. Laudan, 1977, 1996a, 1996b, pp. 77–87; 1997). For L. Laudan (1996b, p. 78, and elsewhere), as for Popper, science is fundamentally a *problem-solving activity*. Sciences are not different in kind from other forms of intellectual inquiry, but are generally more "progressive" than nonsciences. There is no set of features that distinguishes all sciences from all nonsciences. More important than attempting to differentiate the two is distinguishing reliable and well-tested claims to knowledge from bogus ones, and theories with broad problem-solving scope from others, regardless of where the theories come from—physics, literary theory, philosophy, or common sense (L. Laudan, 1996b, p. 86).

Scientific progress is measured historically not by various theories' purchase on truth, but by the extent to which new theories solve more problems than their predecessors. It would be futile to try to set up an absolute standard against which to measure each theory independently of any other. It follows that (aside, obviously, from the first theory in a domain) theory evaluation is usually, and should always be, *comparative*. The centrality of comparative evaluation is further suggested by the fact that the coexistence of rival theories is the norm in science, not the exception. For Laudan, the question to ask is whether one theory has more problem-solving effectiveness than another. Is a new theory more progressive (a technical term for Laudan), that is, does it solve more problems or problems of greater significance, or weight?

A potential problem with this approach, of course, Laudan recognizes, is that new theories can only rarely handle the data accounted for by current favorites, much less those data and more. In fact, he points out, the history of science shows that *cumulative retention* is rare; successor theories often entail explanatory losses, as well as gains. Hence, it would be unreasonable and counterproductive to demand that new theories do all the work of older ones, precisely because they are newer and must pass through a period when they have been applied less extensively, to fewer problems, by fewer adherents. Over the past 30 years, for instance, Chomsky's theories have been used to account for a vast array of phonological, morphological, and syntactic phenomena in numerous languages. Recent alternatives, like that of O'Grady (2003), inevitably cannot hope to compete *empirically* for many years, unless the importance of some linguistic problems they solve is considered to outweigh the number of problems Chomskyan generativists have dealt with, or unless the conceptual apparatus involved in the new theory is perceived as having major long-term advantages (e.g., handling some of the same syntactic phenomena without the need to posit innate linguistic knowledge). Laudan points out, therefore, that researchers may consider a theory "acceptable," or "unacceptable," but warranting further investigation, even when it does not preserve cumulativity (i.e., when it initially solves fewer or less significant problems overall than its rivals). That is, scientists are not limited to outright acceptance or rejection, belief or disbelief, in what Laudan calls the "cognitive stances" they adopt toward new theories. Like good wine, theories should not be judged (not finally, at least) before their time.

Thus, it is that rival theories and research traditions may coexist, despite scientists subscribing to the same evaluation criteria. One theory or another is *rationally* evaluated as more or less worthy of being "accepted," "pursued," or "entertained" according to its effectiveness (i.e., its problem-solving ability), its progress (i.e., "the difference between the problem-solving effectiveness of the [theory or] research tradition in its latest form and its effectiveness at an earlier period"; L. Laudan, 1996b, p. 84), and its rate of progress (i.e., "how quickly a [theory or] research tradition has made whatever progress it exhibits"; 1996, p. 84).[6] *Theoretical pluralism* (as opposed to incoherent proliferation) is understandable this way, even among scientists who share common evaluative criteria, and needed theoretical innovation remains protected, both factors that contribute to scientific growth.

WHAT CONSTITUTES PROGRESS IN A FIELD?

For L. Laudan (1996) to reiterate, science is fundamentally a problem-solving activity: "The aim of science is to secure theories with a high problem-solving effectiveness. From this perspective, *science progresses just in case successive theories solve more problems than their predecessors.*" (p. 78, italics in the original) It follows that what constitutes a "problem," and how problems compare with one another in size and importance, are both crucial for the evaluation process and for measuring progress in SLA or any other field.

L. Laudan (1996b, pp. 79–81) distinguishes two general classes of problems: empirical and conceptual. *Empirical problems* are of three kinds: potential, solved, and anomalous (L. Laudan, 1996b, p. 79). *Potential problems* are phenomena accepted as facts about the world for which there is as yet no explanation. *Solved, or actual, problems,* are claimed facts about the world that have been explained by one or more theories. *Anomalous problems* ("anomalous" is a technical term for Laudan with a different meaning from "problematic" or "contrary to prediction," traditional in philosophy of science) are those problems solved by rival theories, but not (yet) by the theory in question. Note that potential or unsolved problems need not be anomalies by this analysis. In Laudan's theory, what makes a problem an anomaly for a particular theory is not whether it currently constitutes a problem for that theory, or looks like doing so for being apparently unsolvable by it, but the fact that a viable rival theory has solved it, while the theory being evaluated has not. Hence, a problem that appears likely to constitute a falsifying instance for a theory may not be an anomalous problem if no other theory can handle it, either, and a fact or a result that does not falsify a theory may yet be an anomalous problem for that theory if it does not account for it and another theory can do so.

The second general class of problems in Laudan's scheme, *conceptual problems,* consists of four kinds, one theory-internal and three external. In-

---

[6]Adequacy and promise were judged the same way in traditional theories of theory change, for example, those of Carnap, Popper, and Lakatos.

ternal conceptual problems arise when a theory is *internally* inconsistent or postulates ambiguous theoretical mechanisms. External conceptual problems exist when assumptions a theory makes about the world are inconsistent with those of other theories, with prevailing metaphysical assumptions, or with widely accepted epistemology and methodology; a theory violates the research tradition of which it is a part; or a theory fails to utilize concepts from more general theories to which it should be logically subordinate (L. Laudan, 1996b, p. 78). Gholson and Barker (1985, pp. 764–765) provide examples of the influence of conceptual problems on theory change in the history of physics and behaviorist psychology. They also suggest that a lack of precision in the definition of such central concepts in Piaget's theory of cognitive development as equilibration, construction, assimilation, and organization made them inadequate both theoretically and experimentally, and may account for Piaget's theory seemingly having entered a period of stagnation. This bodes ill for so-called Sociocultural Theory, founded as it is on even more nebulous core concepts, like "inner speech" and the "Zone of Proximal Development."

Turning for a moment to the history of theory change in SLA, conceptual problems are well illustrated by Krashen's Monitor Theory (MT), and the relatively greater importance Laudan attaches to conceptual as opposed to empirical problems in motivating theory change (see Gholson & Barker, 1985, pp. 764–765; L. Laudan, 1977, pp. 64–66) is supported by the history of MT's demise. Many of the arguments (see, e.g., Gregg, 1984; Ioup, 1984; Larsen-Freeman & Long, 1991; McLaughlin, 1978; White, 1987) leading to the field's abandonment of MT ultimately involved the theory's conceptual problems—in particular, ambiguous, and ambiguously interrelated, theoretical mechanisms—rather than problematic empirical findings, plentiful though those were.

Krashen (see, e.g., 1985, pp. 19–23, and elsewhere) attempted to explain away a number of empirical problems—what would traditionally have been considered anomalous findings—as methodological artifacts, or by recourse to ad hoc modifications and vaguely characterized internal mental states or learner traits. For instance, "natural orders" predicted, but not obtained, in several morpheme accuracy studies (e.g., Fuller, 1978; Krashen, Butler, Birnbaum, & Robertson, 1978; Krashen, Sferlazza, Feldman, & Fathman, 1976) were dismissed (see Krashen, 1979, 1985, pp. 19–24) on such grounds as that researchers had wrongly classified elicitation tasks at the outset of a study as not (big M) Monitorable, that task conditions had been insufficient to invoke Monitor use, or that the results were the product of asserted, not independently measured, individual (trait) differences (e.g., "under-, optimal and over-use" of the Monitor). Persistent errors (e.g., the seeming inability of many school-age Canadian Anglophone students to eliminate basic morphological and syntactic errors from their spoken French after many years of French immersion; see, e.g., Swain, 1991) were attributed to a lack of sufficient comprehensible input, with no indication provided as to how much input *would* be sufficient. Evidence from several studies reviewed in Long (1983a), to the effect that, contrary to the predictions of MT, formal instruction was beneficial for children as well as adults, for advanced learners and not just beginners, in acquisition-rich as well as acquisition-poor environments, and as revealed on integrative and not just discrete-point tests, was in the first and fourth cases simply ignored by Krashen (1985, pp. 28–30) or rejected on rather dubious grounds. The second and third of the four problematic results for MT were due mostly, Krashen maintained, to subjects having been misclassified as "intermediate," when (despite clear descriptions to the contrary by the original researchers) they were really "beginners."

But although empirical problems for MT may have served as early warnings that something was amiss (and even if Krashen had been correct in his various counterarguments), it is conceptual problems that seem ultimately to have led to the theory's rejection (see, e.g., Gregg, 1984; Ioup, 1984; Larsen-Freeman & Long, 1991, pp. 245–249; McLaughlin, 1978; Pienemann, 1985, pp. 45–49; White, 1987). In particular, it became apparent that MT's engine room consisted almost wholly of opaque and ambiguously related metaphors, constructs, and mechanisms. These ranged from (a) Learning and Acquisition (both components of L2 competence, yet according to Krashen & Scarcella, 1978, unable to communicate with one another), through (b) both terms in the "$i + 1$" metaphor (with no explanation as to how L2 rules in an L1–L2 superset–subset relationship could be learned from positive evidence alone), (c) a Natural Order lacking a linguistic rationale for the items included in it, (d) "easy" and "hard" rules, and (e) "rule" and "feel" judgments, to (f) the nebulous Affective Filter. By 1985 (see Krashen, 1985, pp. 49–52, 65–67), the Filter had become crucial for defending MT against seeming counterevidence in such forms as Canadian children, described by Swain (1985), who continued to make basic grammatical errors after 4,000 hours of French immersion, and learners like Wes, reported in Schmidt (1983), doggedly unsuccessful despite massive exposure to supposedly necessary *and* sufficient comprehensible input. Consequently, claims involving those concepts and mechanisms (e.g., the so-called Acquisition-Learning, Input, and Affective Filter Hypotheses) were not testable or falsifiable. In other cases, they were hopelessly circular. For example, to quote Larsen-Freeman and Long (1991, p. 292):

> To which of three "hypotheses" did a morpheme study which produced an "unnatural" order constitute counter-evidence—the Natural Order, Learning/Acquisition, or Monitor Hypotheses? Recall that the "natural order" was held by Krashen to be evidence for the construct *acquisition*, but simultaneously evidence that *learning* either could not be or had not been applied via monitoring. Did a disturbed order mean, therefore, that subjects had used their learned systems to monitor their output or that one or more of the original notions *monitoring*, *natural order* or *acquisition* was faulty?

In addition to internal inconsistency or postulation of ambiguous theoretical mechanisms, MT exhibited conceptual problems of at least two other kinds Laudan warns against. For instance, whatever the makeup of the mysterious Affective Filter, the implausibility of one existing in adults, but not children, who, as Gregg (1984) observed, have emotions, too, was a clear case of the theory making assumptions about the world that were inconsistent with those of theories in social-psychology, and for that matter, with the everyday experience of parents of young children. And for a theory of an acquisition process supposedly driven by comprehensible input containing the magic ingredient, "$i + 1$," sudden invocation of Chomsky's LAD (e.g., Krashen 1985, pp. 2–3) was arguably a case of MT violating the research tradition of which it was otherwise a part, suddenly declaring itself of the nativist persuasion after all.

The degree to which a theory is able to account for empirical problems, L. Laudan continues (1996b, pp. 79–80), is of primary importance to so-called correspondentists, philosophers of science whose accounts of scientific knowledge value the empirical viability of theories over their conceptual coherence. Coherentists, on the other hand, prioritize the degree of fit between a theory's basic conceptual premises and other accepted beliefs. A long-running tension exists between the two camps, L. Laudan notes (1996b, pp. 79–80), but more importance has traditionally been attributed to empirical successes. Laudan's theory of scientific progress (as indicated by theory change) recognizes the importance of both: A theory should solve a maximum number of empirical problems while generating a minimal number of anomalies, and should also eliminate conceptual difficulties. As noted earlier, even a change from an empirically well-supported theory to a less well supported one could be progressive if the new theory resolved significant conceptual difficulties confronting the old one (p. 80).

A theory, L. Laudan maintains (1996b, p. 81), achieves *solutions* to empirical problems, or solves a problem, when it entails a statement of the problem, and to conceptual problems when it avoids a conceptual difficulty of its predecessor. Many different theories may solve the same empirical or conceptual problem, so a theory's worth will depend, among other things, on how many problems it solves. A prerequisite for comparative theory appraisal, therefore, is that at least some theorists agree as to the identity of at least some of the significant problems in SLA. The history of SLA and the current literature reveal long lines of research on many of the same issues, suggesting widespread agreement on many of them, even if most researchers are primarily interested in and/or personally able to work on only a few.

Important empirical problems for SLA theories are salient, robust findings, or significant facts (see Bley-Vroman, 1989; Long, 1990a, Spolsky, 1989, or any SLA textbook, for many potential examples) that are widely accepted as such by reputable scholars. To illustrate, with one or two potential exceptions (see later), a minimally adequate SLA theory needs to be able to explain such phenomena as the following:

Age differences: Why is child SLA generally so successful, but adult achievement so variable, often amounting to failure, despite *prima facie* the advantages adult learners would seem to share, such as superior cognitive development and the valuable experience of already having successfully learned at least one language (i.e., their mother tongue)? Are there critical, or sensitive, periods for SLA? If so, what is their scope and timing, and what underlies them? (This problem is taken up in chap. 3 in this volume.)

Individual variation: Which individual difference variables—age of onset, aptitude, memory, intelligence, attitude, motivation, personality, learning style, and so on—account for (which kinds of) significant variation observed in adult acquirers' rate of acquisition and ultimate L2 attainment?

Cross-linguistic influence: What accounts for the influence of the L1 on some dimensions of process, course, rate, and ultimate attainment in SLA, but not others, and what accounts for similar effects of subsequently acquired languages on earlier acquired ones? What are the roles of, and interactions among, such factors as (various notions of) markedness, subset relationships, perceptual salience, frequency, linguistic complexity, and communicative redundancy?

Autonomous interlanguage syntax: What mechanisms, language-specific or general cognitive systems, and/or characteristics of the linguistic environment underlie well-documented patterns in interlanguage development, especially those not easily explained as a product of L1 transfer or L2 input[7]: common errors and error types, accuracy orders, developmental sequences, gradual approximation (cf. sudden, categorical learning), stabilization, and fossilization?[8]

Interlanguage variation: What linguistic, learner, and environmental sources account for both individual, common, and universal patterns of diachronic and synchronic variation in interlanguage development?

The aforementioned are but five of many potential examples of empirical problems for a theory of SLA. A few comments are in order. First, not all widely attested phenomena will be considered significant problems by all SLA theorists. For example, although no SLA researcher denies that synchronic individual variation is a pervasive feature of interlanguage development—one of its defining features, in fact—Chomskyan generativists may view it as a fact about L2 performance, of little or no consequence

---

[7]One of many examples is the use of pronominal copies in Swedish by speakers of languages that, like Swedish, disallow them, documented by Hyltenstam (1984). Pavesi (1986) observed the same phenomenon in the English of Italian speakers. Resumptive pronouns are disallowed in both English and Italian.

[8]Although neither a conceptually very coherent, nor empirically well-supported, phenomenon, in my judgment (see Long, 2003), fossilization is widely accepted as real within the field.

for a theory of the acquisition of L2 competence (see, e.g., Gregg, 1990). How would two theories be evaluated, one of which explained interlanguage variation, and one of which simply ignored the problem? Probably, each theory would arouse interest (i.e., would be entertained), but pursuit or acceptance of one over the other would depend on its successes in other domains.

Second, each of the previous five sample problems can be unpacked to reveal a number of smaller, more narrowly defined problems. For instance, an explanation may be offered for age differences in SLA in general or, more narrowly, for phonology, and not, say, for morphology and syntax. How would two theories be evaluated, one of which claimed to have explained (all) age differences in SLA as a function of maturational constraints, using an account of differences in L2 phonological attainment as evidence, whereas the second theory claimed to have explained age differences in phonology and collocational abilities, but not morphosyntax, and so by implication, not age differences in general? Is the first theory stronger for solving one major problem, or the second for solving two smaller ones?

Third, how are problems to be weighted? Is providing a satisfactory explanation of age differences more significant than doing the same for crosslinguistic influence or individual differences?

Recognizing that developing a calculus of problem weights is a major undertaking. L. Laudan (1977, pp. 32–40) suggests four conditions or qualities that increase (inflate), and three that decrease (deflate), an empirical problem's significance.

First, *solution* of a problem tends to add weight to it, pressuring rival theories to solve it adequately, too, if they are to be taken seriously—what Laudan refers to as *problem inflation by solution.*[9] Work on so-called poverty-of-the-stimulus cases is one example. Thus, Kanno (1997) showed that English-speaking adult learners of Japanese were able to interpret co-reference relationships in the L2, correctly observing a constraint by which overt pronouns in Japanese are prohibited from taking quantified antecedents. The constraint is considered far too subtle to be learned (i.e., is underdetermined by the input, is not taught, and is absent in English). The same result was obtained for Spanish by Perez-Leroux and & Glass (1997). The Chomskyan solution is that adult L2 learners retain access to/knowledge of, the Overt Pronoun Constraint (i.e., in more general terms, that interlanguage grammars are constrained by UG). The explanation places a burden on rival theories either to dismantle the (for them, now anomalous) findings, or to account for them without recourse to innate knowledge of linguistic universals.

---

[9] L. Laudan (1977, p. 33) notes that solution of a problem is sometimes required for a field to recognize its very existence. An obvious example in SLA consists of the subtle grammatical rules and constraints that are underdetermined by the input, to which researchers within the generative research tradition have drawn attention.

Second, a problem that has proven *anomalous* (in the traditional sense), or intractable, for other theories takes on added significance when one theory manages to solve it—*problem inflation by anomaly solution*. For example, some models of the SLA process posit the availability of universal innate linguistic knowledge to children, but forced adult reliance on only those universal grammatical principles that are instantiated in the L1 (with lack of automatic access to those that are not), plus general problem-solving abilities (see, e.g., Bley-Vroman, 1989—his Fundamental Difference Hypothesis; Clahsen & Muysken, 1986; Schachter, 1988). Those accounts solve the problem of non-native-like attainment by adults, in principle, and simultaneously highlight the inability *in principle* for a "full-access" position like that of Flynn (1996) or Flynn and Manuel (1991) to do so (i.e., to explain failure). (If adults have access to all the linguistic knowledge and acquisition abilities of children, as Flynn and Manuel assert, they should be just as successful as children, but manifestly are not.)

Third, a problem deemed *archetypal* by a particular theory (e.g., "triggered" parameter-resetting and categorical acquisition; e.g., Hilles, 1991), or visible interlanguage restructuring, at least, accrues significance due to its being seen as indicating a process considered fundamental to understanding of a whole domain—so-called *problem inflation by archetype construction*. Fourth, more *general* problems (e.g., age differences in ultimate attainment), that subsume examples of the same phenomena (e.g., accentedness in adult learners' L2 speech) have added importance. Laudan refers to this as *problem weighting by generality*.

Reduction in a problem's significance, or deflation, can be brought about in three ways. First, some problems diminish in importance or even disappear altogether when a field changes its mind about the facts, because they are subsequently found not to be replicable or are recognized to have been idiosyncratic. Laudan calls this *problem deflation by dissolution*. Were sufficiently fine-grained analyses to cast doubt on the reality of fossilization, it would disappear as a problem to be solved, along with the numerous explanations for it currently available.

Second, problems are viewed as less significant when they are appropriated by, or seen as properly belonging to, another field of inquiry—*problem deflation by domain modification*. A worrying example in SLA is the tendency of some researchers, as judged by the cavalier treatment of both issues in their work, to ignore two of the most basic problems confronting the field, the definition and measurement of acquisition itself. Despite occasional attempts to join the dots (e.g., Bachman & Cohen, 1998; Chaudron, 1985; Norris & Ortega, 2003), the feeling seems to be that those are ultimately problems for the field of language testing, not SLA—a perilous stance for the field, given the apparent belief on the part of some language testing specialists that they can indeed do the job with scant regard for SLA research findings.

Third, problems lose weight when a theory that had treated them as archetypal is repudiated—*problem deflation by archetype modification*. Thus, replacement of the *Aspects* model by Extended Standard Theory, and then the Minimalist approach, led to a loss of interest among psycholinguists in such matters as the sequence and depth of transformations. The virtual disappearance of MT from the mainstream SLA literature in the 1990s resulted in a shift in focus from such issues as the role of positive evidence in acquisition, and the use of conscious L2 grammatical knowledge (big-M Monitoring) in production, to work on the role of attention, negative evidence (particularly, negative feedback), and implicit and explicit knowledge in both acquisition and use.

Laudan argues that not all anomalous problems are of equal weight. For Popper and for the logical empiricists, any anomaly, or so-called refuting instance, was comparably important, with even one anomaly being grounds for assigning the theory concerned to the trash heap. Laudan notes, however, following Kuhn, that most theories, including accepted theories, have suffered from anomalies, but not all are abandoned as a result. He rejects Kuhn's claim that the sheer number of anomalies is the deciding factor, pointing out that this view fails to explain why scientists may not be put off by $n - 1$ anomalies, yet suddenly jump ship with the appearance of one more. The latter fact implies a need to view anomalies in terms of their *cognitive importance*, not their number— specifically, the epistemic threat they pose for a theory (L. Laudan, 1977, pp. 36–37).

Although the magnitude of a discrepancy between a prediction and the observed outcome can influence judgments of its seriousness, more important is the existence of rival theories. When a theory is alone in a domain, numerous problematic results are of little consequence. It is the presence of one or more rival theories that makes a difference, underscoring again the importance of *comparative* theory assessment (see L. Laudan, 1997). In particular, a problem for theory X *that theory Y can solve* makes that problem a true anomaly in Laudan's scheme, adds weight to it, and makes it critical. Even then, success for one may not mean rejection for the other. It is when a theory is persistently unable to solve a problem a rival can handle that the problem concerned grows into what L. Laudan terms "an epistemic embarrassment" (p. 40). He notes that this is also why so-called crucial experiments, designed to choose between theories, are rarely decisive immediately. Scientists need time and the evidence of additional unsuccessful attempts to solve the problem before they conclude that, unlike its rival, the theory concerned is inherently unable to do so.

An interesting example in SLA of the importance for theory change of both Laudan's definition of anomaly, as opposed to its traditional meaning in the philosophy of science, and the relevance of comparative theory evaluation, may be found in the debate over the status of "$i + 1$" and related concepts that took place briefly in the mid-1980s. Ioup (1984, pp. 348–350) pointed out the impossibility of testing some of Krashen's most basic claims concerning the role of comprehensible input, so long as there existed no way of determining either a learner's current stage of interlanguage development (*i*), or whether input was one step ahead (+ 1) of that stage. Krashen (1984, p. 351; 1985, pp. 67–68) acknowledged the facts of the matter, but discounted their importance on the grounds that unoperationalizable constructs are (indeed) permitted in causal-process theories. This defense was possible in 1984. A year later, Pienemann (1985, see especially, pp. 45–49) was able to mount a blistering attack on MT, in large part by contrasting Krashen's admitted inability to test the "one step ahead" claim at the core of the input hypothesis with the proven ability of (an early version of) his own Processability Theory (PT) to do so. To the best of my knowledge, Krashen has never attempted to deal with Pienemann's criticisms, and it would in any case be too late now. However, whereas MT was under attack from many directions in the early 1980s, there is little doubt that its inability to solve a problem that a rival theory could, and one with major implications for language instruction—the fact that defining and measuring *learnability* was an anomaly for MT in Laudan's sense—was a significant factor in hastening its decline.

To sum up, empirical problems are generally accepted facts about the domain of inquiry of greater or lesser weight, making the ability of rival theories to solve at least some of them a valid basis for comparative evaluation of those theories. Conceptual problems, conversely, are theory-specific. The two core assumptions of Laudan's problem-solving model of scientific progress are simple: "(1) the solved problem—empirical or conceptual—is the basic unit of scientific progress; and (2) the aim of science is to maximize the scope of solved empirical problems, while minimizing the scope of anomalous and conceptual problems" (L. Laudan, 1977, p. 66). To evaluate theories: "For every theory, assess the number and weight of the empirical problems it is known to solve; similarly, assess the number and weight of its empirical anomalies; finally, assess the number and centrality of its conceptual difficulties or problems" (L. Laudan, 1996b, p. 82).

THEORY PROLIFERATION REVISITED

Were SLA researchers to agree on the need for comparative theory assessment and adopt Laudan's problem-solving approach (or any other set of rational evaluation criteria) for the purpose, there is reason to believe some headway could be made with the problem of theory proliferation currently hindering progress. Conversely, there is no reason to fear that one theory would promptly emerge to dominate the field and that, as a result, new thinking would be stifled.

The history of scientific disciplines—from mathematics and physics, through geology and paleontology, to psychology and linguistics—shows that the *normal* situation is for two or more, and usually from three to six, theories to coexist. Rather than Kuhn's claim that theories change through scientific revolutions, with conceptual, methodological, and philosophy of science issues being agreed on and not debated during times of peace ("normal science") in between, Laudan's problem-solving model sees conceptual debates as constant, and allows for coexisting, competing theories and rival research traditions as the norm, not the exception. The latter view is borne out by histories of science. "Like nature," he writes, "science is red in tooth and claw" (L. Laudan, 1996b, p. 85).

A first reaction to this might be a feeling of reassurance that the huge benefits of normal science need not entail suffocation of creativity or the emergence of alternative paradigms. A second response might be to ask a version of three questions posed by L. Laudan and R. Laudan (1989). If 99% of SLA researchers are rationalists, as is probably a roughly accurate assessment, and if they mostly agree on methodology, accepted findings, and theory assessment criteria, how can we account for the fact that they (ever) disagree (i.e., how can *theoretical disunity* be explained)? Also, how can new theories (ever) be accepted, given that they are almost always less well developed and can handle fewer data than their predecessors (i.e., how can *theoretical innovation* be explained)? And if scientists hold different views on method, accepted findings, or assessment criteria, how can *theoretical consensus* and the emergence of a dominant theory be explained?

Using the history of how, over a 50-year period, Wegener's continental drift theory of 1915 came to supplant the immobilist theory in geology, L. Laudan and R. Laudan showed that scientists do in fact operate with divergent standards and assessment criteria (or perhaps ascribe differential importance to the same criteria), thus explaining both *disunity* and *innovation*. Innovators are the first scientists to have their assessment criteria satisfied. Wegener's theory first satisfied scientists impressed by the range of different kinds of (paleomagnetic, paleoclimatic, and geological) data it could account for (i.e., a *variety of instances criterion*), a range no other single theory could handle. Later, the theory came to appeal to scientists who wanted a theory to explain different phenomena from those it was invented to explain, or who wanted novel predictive successes, the more surprising (unrelated) the better. These later converts were persuaded by two startling novel discoveries around 1965–1967 concerning symmetrical patterns in the magnetism of rocks on either side of recently discovered mid-ocean ridges, and seismological evidence confirming the specific direction of movement predicted for certain underwater fracture zones. These findings satisfied an *independent testability criterion* and a *surprising predictions criterion*, and also meant continental drift theory could account for data the rival immobilist geology theory could not. Continental drift theory was *dominant* by all their divergent criteria, in other words, so allowing *consensus*. A *dominant theory* is one that is superior to all of its rivals by every set of assessment criteria used in a field and is recognized as such by all scientists in that field. Scientists can agree about a theory while disagreeing about what makes a theory good.[10]

---

[10]For critical discussion of Laudan's views on disagreement and consensus in science, see Lugg (1986).

There is currently no dominant theory of SLA, or even one that comes close to satisfying the majority of serious researchers, if only because of the range of interests they have, and consequently, as illustrated in chapter 1 in this volume, the different scope of the theories that interest them. Were one to emerge, however, it is safe to predict that researchers in our field would behave much like those in other scientific disciplines have in the past (i.e., in the way described by the Laudans). First, there would always be a range of cognitive stances toward serious contenders, allowing simultaneous consideration (acceptance, pursuit, entertainment, rejection, etc.) of several. Second, a range of assessment criteria would need to be satisfied. The combination of those two factors means that researchers serious about problem solving in SLA may one day expect to see communities of scholars and end-users harvesting the fruits of theoretically focused, collaborative intellectual endeavor *without* fear of intellectual tyranny.

II
Research

CHAPTER THREE

Age Differences and the Sensitive Periods Controversy in SLA[1]

The striking contrast between children's near uniform success with both first and second language acquisition and adults' near uniform partial failure with either has long attracted considerable research interest. Cases like that of Genie (Curtiss, 1977) suggest that native-like attainment is impossible in late L1A, and even the most successful late L2 starters tend to have detectable and identifiable accents and to make occasional morphological and collocational errors not heard from native speakers. Poor adult second language achievement is especially intriguing given older learners' superior overall cognitive development and prior attainment of native status in their mother tongue. Adults could reasonably be expected to do better, not worse, than children.

For these reasons, among others, many conclude that children must come into the world endowed with an innate capacity for language acquisition, but a capacity, or various parts thereof, that can only function within

[1]For helpful discussion over the years of issues addressed in this chapter, I am grateful to David Birdsong, Robert DeKeyser, and Kenneth Hyltenstam, none of whom, however, is responsible for any remaining errors of fact or interpretation.

one or more "sensitive periods" before either deteriorating or being lost altogether (see, e.g., Long, 1990b; Seliger, 1978).[2] Some (e.g., Bley-Vroman, 1989; Clahsen & Muysken, 1986; Meisel, 1991, 1997) have suggested that child first language acquisition is handled by UG, but adult language learning falls under general problem-solving abilities. Some claim that innate knowledge of universal linguistic principles survives, and what is lost is the ability to reset UG parameters (Eubank & Gregg, 1999). General nativists within the sensitive periods camp (e.g., O'Grady, 1996, 2003) maintain that some modularized general (i.e., non-language-specific) cognitive abilities are fine-tuned for language during the period concerned, and later cannot function that way. Others (e.g., DeKeyser, 2000) believe that what has deteriorated is the capacity for implicit learning. Scholars who agree about the existence of maturational constraints often disagree, in other words, over their scope (pronunciation only, pronunciation and other abilities?), precise timing (age 6, puberty, the midteens, as a one-time catastrophic loss, or a sequence of losses in different domains?), and as to their neurophysiological underpinnings. The literature reveals a variety of oppositional sensitive period claims. This is important when evaluating claims to the effect that "the critical/sensitive period hypothesis" has been refuted. One first needs to ask, "Whose claim? Which version of the hypothesis?"

For SLA theory construction, the issue of age differences is of fundamental importance. If the evidence is clear that adults are inferior learners because qualitatively different from children, then a theory will need to reflect this, whatever the explanation offered; otherwise, the finding will constitute an anomaly (in the traditional sense of that term in the philosophy of science) for that theory. For instance, a theorist might propose that child L1A functions on the basis of innate linguistic knowledge, plus positive evidence alone, and adult L2A on the basis of L1 knowledge, general problem-solving abilities, and positive evidence (perhaps supplemented by negative evidence if it is to be successful in some linguistic domains). Proposing the same theory for child and adult language acquisition, conversely, could not account for the observed differences in outcome, although a theory assuming that the same knowledge and abilities produced inferior results due to different initial states in L1A and L2A might be plausible (see, e.g., Schwartz, 1998). On the other hand, if the data

---

[2]The term *sensitive period* is preferable to *critical period* when discussing the human language learning capacity. Following Oyama (1979), sensitive periods are here defined as times of heightened responsiveness to certain kinds of environmental stimuli, bounded on both sides by states of lesser responsiveness, with abrupt *or gradual* increases or decreases in learning ability (while still reflecting qualitative change) expected and sufficient to support the claim. This conception allows for a degree of variability in such matters as precise ages of onset and offset, in recognition of the fact that even some of the clearest cases of sensitive periods in the animal world (e.g., such as imprinting) are not "developmentally fixed" (i.e., genetically determined and impervious to environmental influence). For alternative definitions and detailed discussion, see Bornstein (1987).

are consistent with the idea of comparable child and adult abilities, despite the difference in outcomes, a theorist might posit the same combination of innate linguistic knowledge and/or general cognitive abilities, plus positive evidence, for all types of first or second language acquisition, regardless of learner age, simply appending various individual difference and/or "situational" factors to handle the age-related variance in results. Separate theories for child and adult L1 and/or L2 acquisition would be redundant and unnecessarily and undesirably powerful.

In short, whatever the conclusion, the existence (or not) of one or more sensitive periods for SLA has major implications for the validity of any SLA theory. Researchers on both sides of the critical period issue agree about the facts to be explained, that marked differences in ultimate attainment constitute one of the most salient features—perhaps the most salient—distinguishing child and adult language acquisition and hence one of the empirical (cf. conceptual) "problems" (L. Laudan, 1977, 1996b, and elsewhere) a viable SLA theory needs to solve.[3] Following Laudan, the failure of any theory to handle the finding means that it constitutes a *potential anomaly* for that theory, and once one theory solves the problem (e.g., through embracing some version of a SPH), an *anomaly* (in Laudan's technical sense) for all theories unable to do so. Where, as is now the case, various theories purport to solve the problem in very different ways, rival explanations for age-related outcome differences become an important reference point for those engaged in comparative theory assessment.

SECOND LANGUAGES IN SOCIETY

Any proven age-related decline in second/foreign language learning ability will be crucial not only for theory and research in language acquisition and other areas of cognitive science, but also for those engaged in a variety of important practical activities. They include language teachers and policymakers (e.g., second and foreign language teachers, politicians, and school district administrators) who decide whether to provide or withhold SL instruction or bilingual education for immigrant children of different ages. They include sign language learners and individuals who work with hearing-impaired populations (e.g., those affected by what can be achieved with and through a late-started sign language). They include people who work with mentally abnormal populations; the language learning capacities of Down syndrome children and some other groups exhibit interesting age-related patterns, for instance. They include social workers and others who deal with children from dysfunctional families; neglected, isolated, and institutionalized children, but not abused children, often suffer language delay (Culp et al., 1991). And on a truly massive scale around the world, they include those who design, teach, or as students receive, initial

---

[3]See Long (1990b), and Spolsky (1989), for some other widely accepted findings in SLA.

literacy experiences or even an entire education program through the medium of a second or third language. This last category involves students in immersion programs, members of linguistic minorities in multilingual societies (e.g., India, Papua New Guinea, Singapore, and the Solomon Islands[4]) that have opted to use a second language (often English) as a medium of instruction at some levels, and speakers of nonstandard varieties of a language (e.g., Hawai'i Creole English and African-American Vernacular English in the United States) in societies where a so-called standard variety serves as the official medium of instruction.[5]

Findings about age and language learning abilities, and explanations for them, are important for all of these groups and many others. Yet, after more than 100 empirical studies (for review, see, e.g., DeKeyser & Larson-Hall, 2005; Harley, 1986; Harley & Wang, 1997; Hyltenstam & Abrahamsson, 2003; Long, 1990b, 1993b, 2005b; Singleton, 1989), and not a little theorizing, scholars continue to differ on the existence, scope, and timing of putative maturational constraints on the human language learning capacity, as well as on implications for practice.

RESEARCH FINDINGS ON CHILD–ADULT DIFFERENCES

The basic facts about age differences in SLA are relatively noncontroversial, accepted by almost all supporters and opponents of the idea of maturational constraints alike.[6] As shown by Krashen, Long, and Scarcella (1979), and confirmed by numerous subsequent studies, young children tend to make slower progress in the early stages of learning the grammar of a second (third, etc.) language, but given sufficient time and exposure, they can (and often do) eventually achieve very high levels of proficiency, even native-like levels, if they start early enough (exactly *how* early is yet to be determined). Older children and adults, conversely, tend to go faster in the early stages, but very few of them, if any, reach such high standards in the long run—however able and motivated they may be, or rich and extensive their learning opportunities. Most end up with a noticeable—sometimes very noticeable—foreign accent, a far smaller vocabulary than in their first language, and a tendency to make all sorts of grammatical and collocation errors, even after long years of trying to improve. As schematized in Figure 3.1, older is initially faster, but younger is better in

---

[4]For the critical role of language choice in education in the Solomon Islands, see Watson-Gegeo (1992).

[5]See Sato (1989) for analysis of a number of such cases.

[6]Thus, an opponent of the idea of biological constraints, Birdsong (1999) writes: "The facts of adult second language acquisition (L2A) contrast sharply with those of first language acquisition (L1A). Whereas the attainment of full linguistic competence is the birthright of all normal children, adults vary widely in their ultimate level of attainment, and linguistic competence comparable to that of natives is seldom attested" (p. 1).

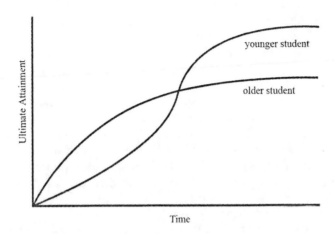

FIG. 3.1. Line graph showing rate/ultimate attainment differences.

the long run. That makes it imperative not to base conclusions about overall capacity on comparisons of progress made too early in the learning process (e.g., after just 10 months), which is to confuse rate and ultimate
attainment.

It is over the *explanation* of these findings, together with the question of
the absolute levels of attainment—native-like or not—of which children
and adults are *capable,* as distinct from what they customarily achieve, that
disagreement persists. Some researchers claim that child–adult differences are not simply quantitative and typical, but qualitative and universal. Specifically, they claim that children who start a SL young enough and
are given sufficient opportunity can (not necessarily will) become native-like in the L2, whereas those starting as adults, or even as older children, cannot do so, however motivated they may be or long they try. They
maintain that the evidence is consistent with the existence of biological
constraints on the human capacity for language acquisition (i.e., one or
more sensitive periods for language learning).

The Exercise and Maturational State Hypotheses

At least two basic versions of a sensitive period hypothesis (SPH) are possible (see Newport, 1990), the second with variants, concerning such matters
as the number and timing of sensitive periods posited, each of which makes
the same prediction for L1A, but different predictions for adult SLA. The
so-called exercise hypothesis (EH) states that once used, or exercised, within
the genetically determined period, the language acquisition capacity is
available, undiminished, for life. It is predicted, therefore, that those starting

L1A as adults will do poorly, and less well than children, but adults who exercised the faculty for L1A within the designated "window of opportunity" will do as well with L2A as children. This position obviously cannot handle the data showing poorer adult than child L2 attainment, and it is has been supplanted by variants of the so-called maturational state hypothesis (MSH). The MSH holds that the genetically inherited, language acquisition capacity operates only within a genetically determined period, and no later, whether or not exercised during that period. It is predicted, therefore, that adult language acquisition, first or second, will be poorer than child first or second language acquisition (see Fig. 3.2). This view has strong, but not universal, empirical support in the literature, mostly from the same studies that rule out the exercise hypothesis. Illustrative findings (by no means the only ones available) in different linguistic domains are shown in Table 3.1.

The demise of the EH does not imply that normal childhood "exercise" of the capacity for L1A or L2A has no effect on subsequent late L2A or L3A. On the contrary, an argument is made later that therein lies the explanation for the benefits of an early start. Mayberry (1993) showed that after an av-

(i) the exercise hypothesis: $C > A$ in L1A; $C = A$ in adult SLA

(ii) the maturational state hypothesis: $C > A$ in L1A; $C > A$ in adult SLA

FIG. 3.2. Predictions of two versions of the SPH.

TABLE 3.1
Child–Adult Differences in Ultimate L2 Attainment

1. Late L1A (ASL) morphology and syntax	Mayberry (1993), Newport (1990)
2. Second dialect phonology	Sibata (1958/1990), Payne (1980), Chambers (1992)
3. SL pronunciation	Oyama (1976), Flege et al. (1995)
4. SL morphology and syntax	Patkowski (1982, 1980), J. Johnson & Newport (1989, 1991), Coppieters (1987), Schachter (1990), D. Lee (1992), DeKeyser (2000)
5. SL lexis and collocation	Hyltenstam (1992), J. Lee (1998), Spadaro (1996)

erage of 50 years of ASL use, subjects who acquired ASL as a second language late (age 9–15), having lost their hearing after acquiring English as L1 at the normal age, outperformed late (age 9–13) acquirers of ASL as a first language, with an average of 54 years of ASL use (matched for chronological age, length of ASL experience, and gender) on an elicited imitation ASL processing task involving immediate recall of long and complex stimulus sentences. Grammatical acceptability judgments were much stronger in the L2A acquirers, whose performance was not significantly different from that of the native (age 0–3) and childhood (age 5–8) signers, suggesting that it is not the capacity for learning syntax that declines or is lost altogether for L2A after a certain age, as distinct from the case of late L1A, where the prognosis for syntax is poorer. Mayberry suggested that improved memory skill from having learned a language early was the likely explanation for the significantly better performance of the late second language ASL acquirers, as compared with the late L1 ASL acquirers, on three other measures: sequencing of constituent structure in the same order as that of stimulus sentences, preservation of the semantic gist of stimulus words and sentences, and short-term memory (STM) span for signed digits. Late L1 acquirers made more errors in their repetitions involving unique lexical substitutions triggered by the surface phonological structure of signs, and unrelated to their meaning. Late second language learners of ASL, in contrast, made few phonologically based, and mostly semantically based, lexical substitutions. Perhaps, Mayberry suggested (1993, p. 36), this was because their prior experience with a first language acquired at the normal age conferred at least two lasting advantages useful in compensating for processing difficulties with L2 (ASL) input: first, general knowledge about how language is structured, together with a large L1 lexicon, which could help them predict sentence meaning and guess appropriately when filling gaps, and second, the option of using the L1 phonological system to recode L2 signs/words in the L1, facilitating the holding of meaning in working memory while producing the repetition.

MULTIPLE SENSITIVE PERIODS

Whereas Lenneberg's and other early formulations of the Critical Period Hypothesis (CPH; see, e.g., Scovel, 1988, 2000) had the loss of ability affecting only L2 pronunciation, with a posited offset at puberty (i.e., around age 13), more recent results suggest that constraints are broader and some set in earlier. Thus, researchers have found raters unable to distinguish L2 speakers from native speakers on a variety of tasks in each of the domains represented in Table 3.1 (i.e., morphology, syntax, lexis, and collocation, not just phonology), but only learners with ages of onset (AOs) of 6 or younger in several cases, regardless of length of residence (LOR). An AO of 0–6 has been implicated for native-like L2 attainment of complex phonological rules in a second dialect to be possible (see, e.g., Chambers, 1992;

Payne, 1980; Sibata, 1958), and even then not guaranteed, although the window for some learners may close as late as age 13 for simple rules and pitch-accent features. Age 6 has also been implicated for native-like attainment of L2 lexis and collocation (Hyltenstam, 1992; J. Lee, 1998; Spadaro, 1996). For morphology and syntax, however, the picture is somewhat different. An AO of age 6 or even younger seems necessary for native-like L1 ASL morphology and syntax to be possible, and even then, is again not guaranteed (Mayberry, 1993; Newport, 1990), whereas for L2 morphosyntax, the window seemingly extends to the midteens (DeKeyser, 2000; Johnson & Newport, 1989; Patkowski, 1982), another possible indication of the influence of exercise on subsequent maturation.

Four studies that illustrate the different patterns for L2 lexis and collocation, on the one hand, and L2 morphology and syntax, on the other, are those by Spadaro (1996) and J. Lee (1998), and DeKeyser (2000) and DeKeyser, Ravid, and Alfi-Shabtay (2004), respectively. Evidence of an earlier AO for lexis and collocation was first reported in the pioneering work of Hyltenstam (1992). Because that work is well known, however, whereas neither Spadaro's nor Lee's studies have been published, the latter are described in some detail here.[7]

Spadaro (1996)

Spadaro compared the performance on nine tasks of a group of 10 NSs of Australian English and 38 comparably (mostly tertiary) educated, extremely proficient NNS immigrants, residents in Australia for substantial periods, during which time they had used English extensively in their work, household, and so forth. The nine tasks were: a speeded written version of the Kent–Rosanoff word association test ($k = 100$), completed in 10 minutes or less; seven unspeeded written tasks developed for the study, typically taking about 30 minutes or less in all; and an oral retelling of a story depicted on a short videotape.

The eight tasks prepared specifically for the study were as follows:

1. Core vocabulary preference ($k = 12$). Subjects were asked to complete 12 sentences, for example, "She agreed to _____ a kidney to save somebody's life," and "The drunk _____ over to the bus-stop." Would even very advanced learners opt for core items, like

---

[7]Although I was the supervisor for Spadaro's doctoral dissertation and Lee's master's thesis, the credit for both pieces of research goes to the two students concerned, who worked long and hard on what was difficult work to carry out. Regrettably, neither study has appeared in easily obtainable published form, and given the passage of time since their completion, now seem unlikely ever to do so. My intention here is to enter the major findings into the public record, and thereby alert interested researchers to their existence.

give and <u>walked,</u> as opposed to the educated NS's choice of non-core <u>donate</u> and <u>staggered/stumbled/lurched</u>?

2. Word discrimination (k = 12). Could NNSs identify 12 morphologically plausible, but nonexistent words, like <u>kindwill, nightbreak, walkerby</u> and <u>highbrained,</u> when mixed with 12 real English words?

3. Core overextension (k = 15). Could NNSs identify overextensions of core words, used in one of sets of four sentences, the remaining three reflecting acceptable uses of the items? For instance, <u>pass</u> in:

   a. Bessie passed a relaxing month in Provence.
   b. Twenty years have passed since they last saw each other.
   c. You've got the money you demanded—now pass the hostage.
   d. The whole class passed the weekly test.

4. Multiword unit completion (k = 18). Subjects had to complete three-word units when provided with the first two words, e.g., aches and _____, labor of _____, tie the _____.

5. Multiword unit supply (k = 10). Given one word, subjects had to provide the entire phrase in which that word usually occurred, for example, (gift of the) <u>gab, spick</u> (and span), (off) <u>kilter, beck</u> (and call). (This was generally regarded by subjects as the most difficult of the tests.)

6. Multiword unit correction (k = 25). Subjects had to underline one incorrect word in an idiom used in a sentence and provide the correct word, for example, "I'm afraid you're <u>growling</u> up the wrong tree" (correct: barking), and "The boss likes to throw his <u>size</u> around" (correct: weight).

7. Multiword unit transformation (k = 18). From a total of 18 grammatically correct sentences, subjects had to identify 10 in which "frozen" multiword units had undergone illegal permutations of some kind (active/passive, declarative/interrogative, positive/negative, or changes in word order), as in a–c, and 8 in which the unit was used appropriately in its invariant form, as in d:

   a. Whose eye is she the apple of?
   b. The bush was thoroughly beaten about by her.
   c. Dolores is the party's life and soul.
   d. The kids aren't pulling their weight with the housework.

Internal reliability for the whole test (Cronbach's alpha) was .895, ranging from .635–.922 for the seven subtests.

8. Oral narrative. Subjects produced narratives, typically lasting about 2 minutes, describing the dog's actions in a complicated story after watching a short excerpt from a commercially available comic videotape, *Turner and Hooch*. In addition to providing data on subjects' frequency of use of core and non-core vocabulary—assessed by Spadaro as a percentage of all items used that did not appear in the 1,000-word *Little Language* list (Nation, 1986)—and of multiword units in free production, it was of interest to determine whether four expert judges could distinguish NSs and NNSs solely on the basis of written transcripts of the spoken texts. Raters were not told how many speakers belonged to each category, and were presented with the transcripts in random order.

NNS subjects were divided into three groups according to age of onset of learning (AOL), defined as the "beginning of a serious and sustained process of language acquisition, usually as the result of either migration to an English-speaking community or the commencement of a formal English language program in primary or high school" (Spadaro, 1996, p. 35). Group 1 ($n = 13$) consisted of subjects with an AOL of 0–6, Group 2 ($n = 15$) consisted of subjects with an AOL of 7–12, and Group 3 ($n = 10$) consisted of subjects with an AOL of 13 or older.

Spadaro found no significant between-group differences on the word association task or on Task 1 (Core vocabulary preference), but clear, statistically significant differences (using analyses of variance and post hoc Sheffé tests) between AOL-defined groups on six of the seven other tasks. The NS group always scored highest, NS Group 1 (AOL 0–6) always next highest, and NNS Groups 2 and 3 always lowest and for the most part comparably. The general pattern across all tasks was for the NS group to score an average of 10 percentage points, but never statistically significantly higher than Group 1 (AOL 0–6), and for Group 1, in turn, to score around 10 percentage points higher than Group 2 (AOL 7–12) and Group 3 (AOL 13+), with the latter two groups scoring comparably. The NS Group scored statistically significantly higher than one or both of NNS Groups 2 and 3 on Tasks 2–8, and NNS Group 1 scored statistically significantly higher than NNS Group 3 on Task 4 (Multiword unit completion). The NS Group scored comparably high across all tasks, whereas all NNS groups did considerably better on word-level than phrase-level tasks. Within-group variation in scores (as indicated by higher standard deviations) also increased with increasing AOL. Overall, AOL was a strong predictor of ultimate attainment in lexis and collocation, but no NNS group attained NS norms. To assess the impact of LOR on findings, analyses of covariance (ANCOVAS) were conducted for each task with LOR as the covariate. The effects for AOL remained robust. The only task showing an effect for LOR at all was

Task 4 (Multiword unit completion), where controlling for exposure actually served to accentuate differences between the AOL-defined groups.

Results for individual tasks were as follows:

Word association: Differences among the groups were small and statistically nonsignificant, suggesting that patterns of association among items in the lexicons of very advanced learners ultimately resemble those of NSs.

1. Core vocabulary preference—no significant differences between any groups

2. Word discrimination—NS > Group 2

3. Core overextension—NS > Groups 2 & 3

4. Multiword unit completion—NS > Groups 2 & 3; Group 1 > Group 3

5. Multiword unit supply—NS > Groups 2 & 3

6. Multiword unit correction—NS > Group 2

7. Multiword unit transformation—NS > Groups 2 & 3

Oral narrative: The NS Group produced longer narratives (average: 320 words) than the three NNS Groups (average: 244 words), but neither this difference, nor the negligible ones among groups in their use of core and noncore words, was statistically significant. On a scale of 0–4, depending on how many of four NS raters judged a transcript as the product of a NS, the story-retellings were assigned average ratings as follows: NS Group—2.7; Group 1—2.2; Group 3—1.1; Group 4—1.3.

Spadaro concluded that her results were consistent with the operation of a sensitive period for lexical development with an offset around age 6, visible even in highly advanced learners like those she studied, with syntagmatic and collocational links obtaining between words an important area for continuing research. Whereas advanced NNSs showed no significant preference for using core vocabulary items, Spadaro pointed out that the results on Task 3 (Core overextension) and Task 8 (Oral narrative), and the relatively poor scores on Tasks 6 (Multiword unit correction) and 7 (Multiword unit transformation) all suggest that although the NNSs knew the meaning of core items, they often did not know the limits on their use, that is, they had weaker knowledge of the semantic boundaries and collocational properties of the items concerned.

J. Lee (1998)

Spadaro's findings were broadly replicated in a study by J. Lee (1998) of 15 monolingual NSs of "standard English" and 45 Korean speakers of English as a second language. They were all full-time students at the University of Hawai'i, of similar age (range 20–25) at time of testing; the NNSs had an ESL proficiency of at least 550 on the TOEFL, none being required to take remedial English classes. Again, there were three groups (n = 15 in each case), formed according to AO: 0–6, 7–12, and 13+. Although all subjects had a minimum LOR of 5 years, average LOR among the groups differed considerably: 18.5, 10.8, and 8.1 years, respectively. Also, self-reported daily use of Korean rose sharply with increasing AO across the three NNS groups: Group 1—15.9%, Group 2—37.1%, and Group 3—62.7%, which means that the measures of LOR need to be interpreted cautiously, years of residence for the older groups very possibly overestimating their total exposure relative to the younger groups. Subjects completed a demographic questionnaire and three unspeeded tests, each consisting of 15 items, the whole session taking from 20 to 30 minutes.

Test 1, similar to Spadaro's Task 3 (Core overextension), presented subjects with 15 sets of four sentences, each set using the same verb, and asked them to identify the one sentence in each set in which that verb had been used in a "strange" way—for example, cases of misused verb + preposition, as in "You are always getting on my way," or figurative misuse, as in "The beautiful weather took me to be happy." Test 2 required subjects to supply common verbs to complete sentences with appropriate collocations (e.g., "I've been _____ a diary for over 10 years now," and "After her husband passed away, she got a cat to _____ her company"). Test 3 was a multiple choice test of collocational knowledge, with such items as this:

If you really trust him, you should give him the _____
of the doubt.

a. benefit   b. advantage   c. use   d. merit

Results patterned comparably to those of Spadaro, except that NNS Group 1 (AO: 0–6) performed even better, slightly better even than the NS group overall (a cause for concern), and NNS Group 2 (AO: 7–12) outperformed Group 3 (AO: 13+). Total errors committed by the four groups across all three tests were as follows: NS group—96, NNS Group 1—92, NNS Group 3—244, and NNS Group 3—397. NNS Group 1 (AO: 0–6) scored statistically significantly higher than NNS Groups 2 and 3 on all three tests.

Group 2 scored statistically significantly higher than Group 3 on all three tests. Paralleling Spadaro's findings, within-group variability was higher in groups 2 and 3, as indicated by the higher standard deviations for those groups. Also paralleling Spadaro's findings, an ANCOVA showed that AO remained statistically significantly related to collocation test scores when LOR was partialled out (i.e., between-group differences on the tests were not due to the groups' different average LOR). AO was strongly related to collocational ability, in other words, with the native-like performance of the early starters, and the markedly non-native-like performance of the later starters, both consistent with a hypothesized sensitive period for the acquisition of L2 collocational knowledge closing around age 6. Whereas the differences in reported L1 (and so by implication, L2) use across the three NNS groups may well have inflated between-group differences in test scores, perhaps progressively exaggerating the relatively poorer performance of the later starting groups, the native-like performance of Group 1 in absolute terms remains a striking illustration of the potential of an early AO in L2A.

DeKeyser (2000)

One of several studies lending credence to the existence of a separate sensitive period for L2 morphosyntax, with an offset in the midteens, was reported by DeKeyser (2000), who conducted a modified replication of J. Johnson and Newport (1989). Subjects this time were 57 Hungarian-speaking immigrants to the United States. AO for the sample ranged from 1–40. All had lived in the L2 environment for at least 10 years (mean LOR: 34 years). Average age at testing was 55 (range: 18–81). Subjects completed two tests: a slightly shorter version (k = 200) of J. Johnson and Newport's oral grammaticality judgment (GJ) test (DeKeyser reporting a KR-20 of .91 for the grammatical, and .97 for ungrammatical, items), the new version devised by both removing some of the easier items and adding others targeting known problem areas for Hungarian learners of English, followed by a Hungarian version of the Words in Sentences subtest (a test of grammatical sensitivity) of the Modern Language Aptitude Test (MLAT).

The overlap in GJ scores between subjects with AOs higher and lower than 16 was minimal. The dividing line between the two groups' scores was 180. Only one early AO subject out of 15 scored lower than 180. Only three late AO subjects out of 42 scored above 180. The nonsignificant correlation between AO and GJ scores in the early AO group in this study, compared with a significant −.87 correlation in the J. Johnson and Newport study, DeKeyser suggests, was probably due to the two studies having had very few subjects in the 12–16 AO range (two and five subjects, respectively). To test Bialystok's claim (Bialystok, 1997, 2002; Bialystok & Hakuta, 1999) that test scores in studies like these correlate inversely with AO not because of maturational constraints, but because AO is confounded with age at testing, DeKeyser calculated partial correlation coefficients. With age at test partialled out, the inverse correlation between test scores and AO remained a robust −.54 (p < .001). With AO partialled out, the correlation between test scores and age at testing was a nonsignificant −.13. These results confirm J. Johnson and Newport's findings, and refute

Bialytok's charge. LOR, another potential confound, was not correlated with test scores in DeKeyser's data either. As suggested by Krashen et al. (1979), LOR seems to plays little or no role after the first 5–10 years (see, also, Birdsong & Molis, 2001; J. Lee, 1998; Spadaro, 1996).

DeKeyser reports several correlations between AO and GJ test scores, here summarized in Figure 3.3. Test scores showed that of the few subjects with an AO later than 16 who scored high (over 175 points on the 200-item test), all but one had a high aptitude score (and the exception was a post-doctoral student in natural sciences, implying high analytical abilities, even if not tapped by the aptitude test). DeKeyser claims that what has been lost by late language starters is the younger learner's capacity for *implicit* language learning (an issue to which we will return), and the only way a late starter can achieve native-like abilities, even on a relatively simple test, such as the one in this study, is via use of above-average analytical, problem-solving abilities. Support for this hypothesis comes from the correlation coefficients DeKeyser obtained for relationships between aptitude and GJ test scores, echoing findings by Harley and Hart (1987) for relationships between aptitude and proficiency among early and late French immersion students in Canada. Among subjects with an AO earlier than 16 (n = 15) in DeKeyser's study, there was a nonsignificant correlation of .07. (Harley & Hart obtained a range of −.15 to .09 for early immersion students.) Among subjects with an AO of 16 or older (n = 42), conversely, the

---

- for the whole sample (n=57): -.63 (p<.001) [similar to that of -.77 obtained by Newport & Johnson)

- for AO of 16 or older (n=42): -.04 (n.s.)

- for AO earlier than 16 (n=15): -.26 (n.s.)

- for high aptitude learners (n=15): -.33 (n.s.)

- for low/average aptitude learners (n=42): -.74 (p<.001)

Correlations between GJ test scores and aptitude scores:

- for the whole sample (n=57): .13 (n.s.)

- for AO of 16 or older (n=42): .33 (p<.05)

- for AO younger than 16 (n=15): .07 (n.s.)

FIG. 3.3. Relationships among AO, aptitude, and GJ test scores (DeKeyser, 2000).

relationship was a significant .33 ($p < .05$). (Harley & Hart obtained a range from .41 to .45 for late immersion students.) In sum, all learners in DeKeyser's study with an AO earlier than 16 had achieved native or near-native proficiency, regardless of language learning aptitude. In contrast, only adult starters with above average aptitude had become near-native, as shown by scores on what, despite the presence of some complex structures, remained a relatively simple test when compared with native-like mastery of a full L2 grammar.

DeKeyser obtained interesting differences in the results for different types of L2 structures as a function of AO, differences closely paralleling those found by J. Johnson and Newport (1989). All structures that were clearly classifiable as "easy," such as word order in declarative sentences (except for adverb placement), do-support in yes–no questions, and pronoun gender, showed no AO-related differences in either study. All structures clearly classifiable as "difficult," on the other hand, such as articles, some plurals, and subcategorization, showed strong AO-related effects in both studies. What makes the first group of structures easy and accounts for their insensitivity to AO, DeKeyser argues, is the perceptual saliency of errors involving them, which leads NNSs to notice the gap between their performance and NS norms. This makes the structures amenable to explicit learning by older learners if they have high enough verbal ability with which to compensate for their decreasing capacity to learn abstract patterns implicitly. Young learners, on the other hand, can learn both easy and hard structures regardless of verbal aptitude, because they can utilize their still intact capacity for implicit learning. Instead of just a sizable negative correlation between AO and ultimate attainment, DeKeyser (2000) concludes:

> If the critical period hypothesis is constrained … to implicit learning mechanisms, then it appears that there is more than just a sizeable correlation: early age confers an absolute, not a statistical advantage—that is, there may very well be no exceptions to the age effect. Somewhere between the ages of 6–7 and 16–17, everybody loses the mental equipment required for the implicit induction of the abstract patterns underlying a human language, and the critical [as opposed to sensitive or optimal] period really deserves its name. (p. 518)

DeKeyser, Ravid, and Alfi-Shabtay (2004)

In the second of a valuable ongoing series of studies, DeKeyser, Ravid, and Alfi-Shabtay (2004) reported new data on the effects of AO, language aptitude, and the salience of target linguistic items on performance on Hebrew and English attainment by Russian immigrants to Israel or the United States. DeKeyser et al. administered an oral grammaticality judgment test and a verbal aptitude test to native speakers of Russian, immigrants to Israel or the United States. There were 75 in each sample, at least 18 years old when tested, with LORs of 8 years or more. As is often the case in such studies, there was a decline in achievement over the whole sample, with GJT scores, Age of Testing (AT), and Age on Arrival (AoA) strongly related to one another, making any interpretation suspect. When subjects were divided into three groups, those with AoAs lower than 18, 18–40, and 40 and up, there was a strong inverse correlation ($r = -.67$) for the below 18 group between AoA and GJT scores, with minimal change when AT (which was only moderately related to AoA) was partialled out. Conversely, there was a much lower correlation (–.39) for subjects with AoAs of 18 and above, and this disappeared when the effect for AT (which was strongly related to AoA) was removed. Among subjects with AoA of 40 and above, the negative correlation with test scores was a low –.15, disappearing to close to zero after AT was partialled out. In other words, just as a CPH would predict, there was a marked discontinuity in the data, with a significant decline in test scores until age 17, and no significant decline after that. The patterns for the Israeli sample were very similar.

As was the case in earlier studies (e.g., DeKeyser, 2000), there was no statistically significant relationship between GJT and aptitude scores for the youngest group ($r = .14$), but a significant relationship ($r = .44$–.47) for the older arrivals. Also in keeping with earlier claims by Goldschneider and DeKeyser (2001), there was a significant effect for the (lo, mid, or hi) salience of the target linguistic items: Structures with low salience are harder to learn explicitly and were more problematic for older starters. DeKeyser et al. conclude that their findings are strongly supportive of a CPH for morphology and syntax, and the much stronger effects for language aptitude and target structural salience in the older than the younger cohorts are what would be expected if, as they claim, a loss of ability for implicit learning, and a corresponding shift to explicit learning, is what underlies the observed effects. (Salience, DeKeyser claims, is important for learners of all ages, but probably less so for younger ones.)

Conclusion: Multiple Sensitive Periods

With findings like those of Sibata (1990), Payne (1980), Chambers (1992), Oyama (1976, 1978), and Flege, Munro, and MacKay (1995) showing a loss of ability to acquire native-like ability in a second language or second dialect phonology, beginning around age 4–7, by Hyltenstam (1988), Spadaro (1996) and J. Lee (1998) suggesting a similar pattern for lexis and collocation, and by Hyltenstam (1992), Patkowski (1980, 1982), J. S. Johnson (1992), J. S. Johnson and Newport (1989, 1991), DeKeyser (2000) and DeKeyser, Ravid, and Alfi-Shabtay (2004) implicating the midteens for morphology and syntax, along with those of numerous studies reviewed elsewhere, there would seem to be strong evidence of the existence of maturational constraints on language acquisition. This includes at least one, and probably two or more, sensitive periods in SLA: from birth to 6 to 9 months for categorial perception; from birth to between 4 and 6 or 7 for supra-segmental and segmental phonology, and some lexi-cal/collocational abilities, and from birth to the midteens for morphology and syntax. Yet, such an interpretation and, in some cases, the findings themselves have been challenged by several reputable researchers, so now let us consider the alleged counterevidence to a SPH for SLA.

COUNTEREVIDENCE?

While recognizing clear differences in eventual levels of success related to the age at which learning begins, a small group of scholars, including sev-eral well-respected researchers of this issue, maintain that there are no bio-logical limits on SLA at all. They reject the maturational constraints explanation for those differences on one or more of three grounds. First, they suggest that other learner and/or environmental factors are responsi-ble. Second, they point to patterns in the data from studies of age differ-ences that they allege conflict with one or more hypothesized sensitive period(s) for SLA. Third, they claim to find late learners who have achieved native-like competence in a L2. It is not clear, however, that any of these challenges is sustainable.

Nonbiological Explanations

The unsatisfactory nature of nonbiological explanations for age differences in SLA has been noted before, and so are not detailed again here. DeKeyser and Larson-Hall (2005), Long (1990b, pp. 274–278) and Hyltenstam and Abrahamsson (2003, pp. 563–566), for instance, point out that variation in social/psychological factors (attitude, motivation, etc.), in the characteris-tics of the learner's immediate linguistic environment (input, interaction, etc.), and amount of exposure (as postulated, e.g., by Jia & Aaronson, 2003; Jia, Aaronson, & Wu, 2002), is often as real in child L1A as in adult language acquisition, yet appear to have no effect there. Children, in fact, sometimes have poorer values for the same variables than at least some adult learners (e.g., because older children and adults are better able to negotiate the input they receive; see, e.g., Scarcella & Higa, 1981), yet children outperform adults in ultimate attainment, and age appears to be an absolute barrier to native-like attainment by adults, but not child starters, regardless of how positive the rest of the adult learner's profile. Studies (see DeKeyser & Larson-Hall, 2005, for a detailed review) that have assessed the relative con-tribution of AO and such factors as length of residence (LOR), motivation, and years of formal instruction statistically have found AO, and nothing else, to be a major predictor of ultimate attainment.

General cognitive development (e.g., attainment of Piagetian formal operations) may underlie observed temporary rate advantages in SLA by older children and adults. However, such a one-time change, usually put in the early teens, does not coincide with any of the documented changes in language learning capacity at 6–9 months, 4–7 years, and the midteens, and in any case, could only account for one such decline in ability at most. Large IQ differences have minimal, if any, effect on L1A and show up only on paper-and-pencil-type tests of reading, grammar, and vocabulary in adult SLA, not in oral production, suggesting such measures are tapping metalinguistic abilities, and not language acquisition capacity per se. Again, superior ultimate attainment for child over adult starters in both first and second language acquisition argues against a major role for general cognitive abilities. Newport's (1990) "less is more" hypothesis, similarly, cannot account for multiple sensitive periods, and the posited (in the long term, detrimental) change from morpheme by morpheme to gestalt semantic processing does not appear to have a known independent cognitive correlate or, as might be expected if it did, to alter error patterns or developmental sequences exhibited by child and adult learners.

Problematic Data Patterns

Birdsong and Molis (2001) conducted a replication of J. Johnson and Newport (1989), this time utilizing the original oral GJ task and procedures with 61 NSs of Spanish, 29 of whom had arrived in the United States by age 16 (classified as early arrivals) and 32 of whom had arrived age 17 or older (classified as late arrivals). Mean LOR for the early group was 12.2 years, statistically nonsignificantly different from the mean of 10.5 years for the late group. As with the sample of 46 Korean and Chinese speakers in the original Johnson & Newport study, there was a nonsignificant correlation between AoA and LOR. Subjects in the two studies were comparably (tertiary) educated. The GJ task proved rather easy for the Spanish speakers. There was a ceiling effect among the early arrivals, 28 of 29 scoring 250 or better, resulting in a nonsignificant correlation between AoA and test scores in that group. Conversely, there was a strong inverse relationship ($-.69, p < .0001$) between AoA and test scores among the late arrivals. Both J. Johnson and Newport (1989) and Birdsong and Molis found a strong age effect across the full range of AoA: $-.77, p < .01$, and $-.77, p < .0001$, respectively.

Birdsong and Molis (see, also, Bialystok, 2002; Bialystok & Hakuta, 1999; Hakuta, Bialystok, & Wiley, 2003) claim that their results present three problems for proponents of a sensitive period hypothesis. First, they assert, age effects across the full AoA range in these two studies (and in such studies as DeKeyser, 2000; Flege, 1999; and Oyama, 1976) are inconsistent with a putative cessation of age effects at the end of maturation.

Second, they note, the patterns of decline in test scores differed across the two studies. J. Johnson and Newport found that subjects who arrived by age 7 scored almost perfectly on the test. There was then a linear decline with age from around 8 to 15, after which the distribution of scores was essentially random. In Birdsong and Molis' replication, in contrast, most subjects who arrived by age 16 scored almost perfectly, the decline in performance only starting at around age 17. Third, more of Birdsong and Molis' Spanish-speaking subjects than J. Johnson and Newport's Korean and Chinese subjects had reached mastery of the test items. This, they assert (see, also, Bialystok, 1997; Bialystok & Miller, 1999), suggests onset timing differences for the different language groups, which would be a problem for any sensitive period claim, because such a claim involves putative (non-language-specific) universals.

In response to the first point, a sample in which early arrivals score higher than late arrivals can be expected to produce a negative correlation with age of arrival across the whole sample; there is nothing surprising in that. The sensitive period claim for syntax at stake here is that no subjects beginning L2 exposure after the midteens can attain native-like standards, not that there are no age effects before or after the midteens. Birdsong and Molis' findings are wholly consistent with that claim. Moreover, as Stevens (1999, 2004) has pointed out, several factors associated with increasing age *within adult populations* independently decrease the likelihood of success, and so would be expected to produce a decline in achievement across the life span. For instance, because so many experiences in Western societies (attendance at different kinds of schooling, marriage, family, living arrangements, work, retirement) are age-graded, AoA can often index such relevant factors for SLA as types and intensity of L2 exposure, L2 use, attitude, motivation, and opportunity to learn. Hence, cohorts with the same AA can be expected to exhibit broadly similar attained L2 proficiency at any subsequent AT. Stevens illustrates the importance of this, and of distinguishing AO from "aging" effects, with the study by Hakuta et al. (2003). Hakuta et al. analyzed 1990 U.S. census data, reported finding a steady decline across the life span (from about age 5 to 60) in the level of L2 proficiency immigrants obtained, and argued that a steady decline with no obvious disjunctures constitutes counter evidence to the CPH, which would predict noticeable alterations in the gradient of the slope at offset. They attributed the inverse relationship between AA and L2 proficiency to such *aging* factors as cognitive declines, but Stevens points (2004, pp. 12–13) out that age and aging effects need to be considered as distinct from AO effects.

With regard to the second point, the age at which a decline in scores begins is only relevant (presumably reflecting nothing more than the level of proficiency in the sample in question—much higher in Birdsong & Molis' learners than in J. Johnson & Newport's) if it occurs *after* the posited close of the sensitive period (i.e., in this case, after the midteens) *and* involves late starters scoring comparably with NSs on a test, and a test (certainly unlike the one in question here), with which success truly demonstrates NS competence. Many early starters will fail to achieve native-like competence and they will show that on a test. The sensitive period claim, however, is not that all early starters will achieve native-like abilities, but that only early starters can and late starters can never do so. Similarly, reasonably proficient late starters will do very well on a relatively easy test, such as the one in question, and better than less proficient early starters, but this simply shows they are reasonably proficient, not that they have attained native-like norms, and so again does not constitute counterevidence to a hypothesized sensitive period for syntax. The patterns of decline in studies like these are interesting, and probably worthy of explanation, but the only even potentially relevant counterevidence for the sensitive period hypothesis in either study concerns those subjects who score perfectly, or nearly so, on the test. What is salient about both J. Johnson and Newport's and Birdsong and Molis' results is that all who did so had AoAs comfortably within the putative sensitive period, with the possible exception of one subject in the Birdsong and Molis study who had an AoA of 18 and seems (see Fig. 3.2, panel B) to have scored approximately 270. But then, given the relative ease of the test in question, such a result is untroubling. In fact, on as easy and inadequate a test as this (as a tool for assessing full native-like competence), it would not matter for a sensitive periods claim if numerous late starters had scored perfectly. That would be very different from showing those late starters to have attained native-like abilities. It should also be noted that Birdsong and Molis report that the highest scoring 13 subjects in the late arrivals group in fact had a mean AO (cf. AoA) (i.e., first exposure) of 8.5 years—far lower than the 17-and-older criterion supposed to define this group. Unless the two events are one and the same, as is the case for some immigrants, it is AO, not age of arrival in an L2 environment, that is the relevant factor in the sensitive period hypothesis.

Finally, regarding differences in test scores across L1 groups, the SLA literature supports the notion that language distance affects rate and ultimate attainment (see, e.g., Odlin, 1989; Zobl, 1982), at least where morphology, syntax, and vocabulary are concerned. Thus, it is not surprising to find more NSs of Spanish than NSs of Korean and Chinese doing well on the same test, given the greater typological distance from English of the two Asian languages. Assuming comparable sampling, one would expect an early start to be even more crucial for speakers of Chinese and Korean, and that is what the studies show, because fewer Korean and Chinese subjects overall scored high on the test, despite its comparative ease, and the few who did so began their exposure very early (by age 7). Again, however, this does not constitute counter evidence for a sensitive period claim. In fact, it would be quite easy to find highly proficient Chinese and Korean speakers who could outperform Birdsong and Molis' group of Spanish speakers on the GJ test in question, including subjects who would score almost perfectly despite AoAs of 17 and older. This would prove nothing of interest to the sensitive period debate, simply showing, instead, that some speakers of Korean and Chinese can do better on this GJ test than some speakers of Spanish, and you do not need to start exposure before the close of the hypothesized sensitive period for syntax in order to max out on a test that comes nowhere near reflecting the true complexity of NS competence.

Native-Like Late Starters

Because a native-like accent in a second language or dialect seems so difficult to achieve, more than any other linguistic domain, demonstration of an absence of biological constraints on the acquisition of a second language phonology would undermine claims for sensitive periods in SLA. And there are now those who claim that adult starters can achieve native-like pronunciation in an L2. In a study by Neufeld (1977, 1978), 20 Canadian university students received 18 hours of intensive training in Japanese and Chinese pronunciation, and were then recorded repeating 10 short phrases in each language five times each. The fifth attempts were presented to three NS judges for each language, who then rated the speakers on a 5-point scale. Neufeld reported that 9 of the 20 subjects were judged NSs of Chinese and 8 were NSs of Japanese. In fact, however, the picture was somewhat less rosy. Being rated "native" meant receiving a rating of either 5 ("Unmistakably native with no sign of interference") or 4 ("Appears native with occasional English-like sounds"). Only 1 subject out of 20 really received perfect scores in both languages, and two others only in Japanese. Second, as noted elsewhere (see Long, 1990b, pp. 266–268; Scovel, 1988, pp. 154–159), there were methodological problems with the study. Most obviously, judges were not told, as should have been the case, that they would be hearing tapes of an unspecified number of native and non-native speakers, and given the task of deciding which were which. In reality, there were no Chinese or Japanese NS samples on the tapes at all. Instead, the instructions led them to believe that the samples they would be hearing had been recorded by Japanese and Chinese immigrants to Canada whose L1 pronunciation might exhibit traces of English. In other words, judges were set up to find a good number of NSs in the samples, and did so. Finally, as noted by Bongaerts, Planken, and Schils (1995, p. 36), the production task was to imitate meaningless streams of sound, after four rehearsals, with no attention to meaning or structure required, with the result that subjects could focus entirely on pronunciation. In several ways, in other words, any native-like attainment observed was at best on a tiny sample of an extremely artificial "language-like" task.

In subsequent methodologically superior work, Neufeld (2001) reported a convincing study of the French pronunciation ability of native English-speaking students at the University of Ottowa. On the basis of a 10-minute "semi-formal" conversation with three Francophones, 7 of 18 Anglophone bilinguals with AO for French after 16 were screened into the study as "potentially of French-speaking background." The seven subjects, plus three Francophone controls, then read aloud an 81-word French text seeded with notorious phonological problems for English speakers. Subjects were allowed to rehearse the passage as many times as they liked, and usually after three or four attempts, submitted whichever recording they considered to be their best. The 68 native speakers of the same (Quebec City) variety of French, all weak in English, then rated one of four tapes with different random orders of the 10 text renditions, instructed to designate each speaker as "Francophone" or "non-Francophone." They were told the tapes might include only Francophones, only non-Francophones, or combination of the two. Four of the seven bilinguals achieved ratings statistically nonsignificantly different from those of the three Francophone controls, with 62–65 of 68 raters classifying them as native Francophones. The reading aloud not having involved real conversation with native speakers, Neufeld recognized that the four would not necessarily be able to do as well in that situation. The limited sample, and its "language-likeness" notwithstanding, he continued (2001, p. 194): "Given the difficulty of the task, however, as well as what we observed during the screening interviews, it seems reasonable to suggest that these four NNSs would fare even better during spontaneous communication."

In some of the most carefully conducted research of its type, Bongaerts and associates have reported four studies of supposedly native-like achievement in foreign language phonology by adults identified by experts as exceptionally successful learners of the foreign or second language concerned. First exposure had typically come through high school foreign language lessons, and first intensive exposure at about age 18, through university study-abroad programs. In other words, they were appropriate choices for tests of absolute adult SLA abilities. The basic procedure in each study was for them to be recorded reading aloud phrases or short sentences seeded with notoriously problematic sounds for Dutch speakers, and the tapes to be presented to NS raters. The result in each case was that a small number were judged as performing within the range of NS controls.

In the first study (Bongaerts et al., 1995), 10 Dutch learners of English previously identified as excellent speakers of British English (received pronunciation, RP), 12 additional learners representing a range of proficiency levels, and a control group of 5 NSs of British English (with southern or midlands regional accents) were each recorded (Task 1) speaking for 3 minutes about a recent vacation, and reading aloud (Task 2) a short text, (Task 3) 10 short sentences, and (Task 4) a list of 25 words chosen to include most English phonemes and varying in length from one to five syllables. Subjects performed each task once only, in the aforementioned order, and were not told that their pronunciation would be the focus. Most told the researchers afterward that they had not realized their pronunciation would be evaluated until after the second or third task. Four linguistically naïve NSs of British English (living in York, in the north of England, where accents differ again) rated the four speech samples for accent using a 5-point scale. For Task 1, judges were presented not with the entire 3-minute narrative, but with an excerpt lasting 16–20 seconds chosen by the researchers so as not to include any grammatical or vocabulary-choice errors. Three findings of relevance here were that (a) judges were unable to distinguish the excellent NNSs from the NSs, (b) the NSs' mean score was low (3.94, when 5 represented no accent at all), and (c) 4 of the 10 excellent NNSs received higher ratings than any of the 5 NSs. Bongaerts et al. realized that the judges in their study might simply have preferred prestigious RP to regional accents with which they were not very familiar. This raised questions about the validity of their findings and motivated a replication.

In the second study (Bongaerts, Van Summeren, Planken, & Schils, 1997), 10 NSs of a "neutral" variety of standard British English, 11 excellent Dutch speakers of British English (RP), including 9 from the first study, and 20 Dutch learners of English representing a wide range of proficiency, were recorded reading six sentences aloud ("My sister Paula prefers coffee to tea," "The lad was mad about his dad's new fad," etc.), each sentence three times. There were 13 judges, all NSs of standard British English with no regional accent, 6 of them with linguistic training and 7 without. Told they would be hearing an unspecified proportion of native and non-native speakers of British English (cf. the instructions to raters employed by Neufeld), and using the 5-point scale from the first study, each judge rated a unique tape consisting of two sequences of either the second or third rendition of the same sentence by all 41 subjects, the sequences repeated for all six sentences, for a total of ($2 \times 6 \times 41$) 492 speech samples. Mean ratings were then averaged across judges and samples. Group means and ranges for NSs and NNS, respectively, were 4.84 (4.67–4.94) and 4.61 (4.18–4.93)—a small, but statistically significant difference ($z = 2.82$, $p = .004$, two-tailed)—with only minor differences between linguistically trained and naïve judges. More important was the analysis at the level of individual NNSs, for which Bongaerts et al. applied the standard devised by Flege et al. (1995): NNS subjects are accepted as having spoken with a native-like accent if they receive a mean rating falling within two standard deviations of the mean NS rating. Using this criterion, five subjects in the group of excellent learners passed as NSs. To their credit, Bongaerts et al. achieved this result while correcting the earlier study's problem of varying regional accents, but were concerned that their results (on Dutch learners of English) might not generalize to learners of languages typologically more distant from their L1. More serious than that, one notes, the new findings were based on an even tinier sample of subjects' (rehearsed) performance. Accordingly, a third study was conducted, this time of Dutch learners of French.

In the third study (Bongaerts 1999; Palmen, Bongaerts, & Schils, 1997), using a similar design, 9 exceptionally successful Dutch speakers of French, 18 Dutch learners of French representing a wide range of proficiency levels, and 9 NSs of standard French with a "neutral" accent all read aloud 10 sentences seeded with notorious problems for Dutch speakers, three renditions per sentence, followed by 27 phrases consisting of "Je dis" plus a constant vawel (CV) slot, where C was one of three consonants (p, t, or l) providing varying phonetic contexts for one of nine vowels that followed (pas, ta, la; pu, tu, lu; etc.), the vowels being the focus of interest, due to their well-known difficulty for Dutch speakers. Tapes were rated by 10 judges, all NSs of French, 5 of them linguistically trained, 5 linguistically naïve, using a French translation of the usual 5-point scale for the sentences, and a binary "spoken by a NS/NNS" choice for the CV frames. As in the second study, judges were told they would be hearing speech produced by unspecified proportions of native and nonnative speakers. Using procedures and sets of randomized sequences similar to the second study, ratings were obtained of all (10 × 36) 360 sentences, and of (9 × 36) 324 CV frames per judge. Results for sentences were similar to those in the second study. Ratings of linguistically experienced and naïve judges were again statistically nonsignificantly different from one another (as was also the case with the CV frame ratings) and so were pooled. Group means and ranges for NSs and NNSs, respectively, were 4.66 (4.36–4.86) and 4.18 (3.15–4.88), a difference that was statistically significant ($z = 2.43, p = .015$, two-tailed). Using the same criterion for assessing native-likeness (Flege et al., 1995) as had been employed in the second study, and taking into account the fact that three NSs also had failed to meet criterion on all 10 sentences, three Dutch speakers were identified who had passed as "native-like" in their French pronunciation (1 on all 10 sentences, and 2 on 8 sentences). Results were similar where the CV frames were concerned. The mean percentage of times (and range) the groups of French and Dutch NSs, respectively, were judged to be French NSs were 85.6% (61.1%–95.6%) and 60% (25.6%–93.3%), a statistically significant difference ($z = 2.60, p = .009$). Application of the Flege et al. criterion to individuals resulted in identification of the same three learners as having "managed to attain an authentic, native-like French accent" (Bongaerts, 1999, p. 152).

In the fourth study (Bongaerts, Mennen, & van der Slik, 2000), 30 highly educated longtime residents of Holland previously identified as highly successful learners of Dutch, from a variety of L1 backgrounds and with AAs between 11 and 34, read 10 Dutch sentences aloud three times each, as did 10 Dutch NS controls. The second rendition was presented to 21 NS judges, some with linguistic training and some without, who assigned each a rating using a Dutch translation of the usual 5-point scale. The same pattern of results was obtained, two NNSs this time receiving ratings within the lower range of the NS controls.

Bongaerts' (1999) concluded, "We argue that such results may be interpreted as evidence suggesting that claims concerning an absolute biological barrier to the attainment of a native-like accent in a foreign language are too strong" (p. 154).

Bongaerts recognizes that the native-like pronunciation achieved by a few of the subjects in the four studies appears to be "a fairly exceptional phenomenon" (1999, p. 154), but hypothesizes that in the cases identified, it may have been due to a combination of three factors: "high motivation, continued access to massive L2 input, and intensive training in the production of L2 speech sounds" (p. 155), the last being particularly important. All the advanced learners of English and French had received intensive pronunciation instruction as part of their university training in the languages concerned. Bongaerts reasons that this may have served to develop the finely tuned motor control needed for accurate pronunciation. Also, following Flege's (1995, 1999, and elsewhere) perceptually based theory of foreign accent, he suggests that such instruction may help learners rely less on the categorical mode of speech perception, which children come to do when first establishing the relevant phonetic contrasts in their native language—categories that become stable by age 7—and revert to the continuous mode (see Wode, 1994, and elsewhere), so as gradually to identify the relevant sound cues in the L2. The continuous mode characterizes young children's initial orientation and means that they attend to tiny differences among speech sounds (e.g., intra- and interspeaker and phonetically conditioned contextual variation in the pronunciation of the same phonetic category), making them relatively more flexible and malleable in their search for appropriate phonological targets. In the categorical perceptual mode, older children (and, by implication, adult L2 acquirers) attend only to cues that signal contrasts between categories of sounds (e.g., /b/ and /d/). Once categories become firmly established, Flege argues, learners tend to "filter" new sounds through them, particularly L2 sounds similar to those in the L1.

The key issue, again, is task validity, and hence the generalizability of findings. The justification for use of limited, language-like samples (in phonology studies, at least) is that judgments of pronunciation ability based on anything above isolated words, and especially on natural speech, are vulnerable to bias from cues from other linguistic domains than the one supposedly in focus, most obviously from suprasegmentals, and potentially lexis, collocation, morphology, and syntax. However, to what extent are results obtained using controlled, elicited, often rehearsed, samples of performance in such studies (see, e.g., Bongaerts et al., 1997; Flege et al., 1995; Yeni-Komshian, Flege, & Liu, 2000) acceptable as valid indicators of the same informants' overall L2 abilities? Neufeld, as we saw, was fairly confident that they were, in his 2001 study, at least. Bongaerts' claim is that the non-native subjects rated as native-like in his four studies constitute counterevidence to the hypothesized existence of a biological barrier to adult attainment of native-like pronunciation. I would argue that both claims are too strong.

What both Neufeld and Bongaerts and associates have shown, I believe (and shown with admirable perseverance and meticulous attention to detail), is that a small percentage of an already select pool of exceptionally proficient L2 learners can sound like NSs to judges provided with only limited data on which to base their evaluation. Although it is possible that they could, there is no evidence that those individuals would, pass as natives were even a few minutes of unmonitored spontaneous speech the basis for a judgment. The speech samples on which ratings were based in Neufeld (2001) and the four studies by Bongaerts et al. were tiny, (in four of five cases) rehearsed, and language-like behavior, rather than natural language use.

This is important because some researchers have found non-native speech samples to be rated as more native-like the less language-like the task (see, e.g., Borden, Gerber, & Milsark, 1983; Moyer, 1999; Neufeld, 1988; Tarone, 1983). To illustrate, in a study of 24 English native speakers' German, Moyer found their free production was rated lowest on a 6-point scale; ratings improved progressively across the three other tasks: reading paragraphs aloud, reading sentences aloud, and reading isolated words aloud. Ishida (2004) obtained similar findings with English learners of Japanese in a partial replication of Moyer's study. Put another way, non-native accents are typically more noticeable, the more natural the speech sample.

If the relationship between naturalness, or language-likeness, and accentedness rating is robust, studies like those reviewed and others that have used highly restricted data sets made finding false positives (non-natives judged to be natives) more likely. Studies that have employed global ratings of accent based on larger elicited samples (sentences or paragraphs read aloud) and/or free speech (e.g., Flege et al., 1995; Flege, Yeni-Komshian, & Liu, 1999; Patkowski, 1980; Yeni-Komshian et al., 2000; Yeni-Komshian, Robbins, & Flege, 2001) have found accentedness to increase with AO, and often that native-like accents are not achieved even by learners starting earlier than age 6. When batteries of tasks are employed, as in Ioup, Boustagui, El Tigi, and Moselle (1994), adult starters are able to pass as native-like on some, but not all tests.

The picture is not unambiguous, however, with at least two counter-findings. Flege (1981) obtained comparable accentedness detection rates from judges presented with non-native samples involving reading phrases aloud and spontaneous speech. Thompson (1991) had 36 native speakers of Russian with advanced English proficiency (ACTFL level 3 or better) complete three tasks: reading aloud 20 sentences seeded with problematic sounds for Russians, reading aloud a 160-word passage (not so

seeded), neither with rehearsal opportunities, and 1 minute of spontaneous speech in which subjects described their activities the day of the experiment. Global foreign accent ratings by both eight linguistically
experienced and eight naïve judges were consistently best for the spontaneous speech, and worst for the sentences (with the inexperienced raters
generally perceiving greater accentedness than the more tolerant experienced ones). Finally, Bongaerts et al. (1995, p. 46) report that whereas their
NS and exceptional NNS subjects obtained their highest ratings on the
most monitorable task, reading the word list aloud, neither groups'
performance across Tasks 1–3 differed statistically significantly.

This is clearly an area in need of further research. A factor that may account for some of the contradictory findings is whether or not learners
were able to rehearse the reading aloud tasks. Another is the proficiency
level of the subjects involved, with higher level speakers presumably less
vulnerable to lack of rehearsal opportunities or to deliberately difficult
reading tasks in general. A third might be the relative difficulty and exten-
siveness of all the tasks in a given study. A fourth concerns the precise nature of the rating tasks and outcome measure; are raters asked simply to
identify natives and non-natives, or to grade the non-natives' degree of
accentedness?

To their credit, researchers claiming to have identified exceptional
learners who constitute counterexamples to some version of a CPH in the
limited domains studied have sometimes also noted that the individuals
concerned might not pass muster in other areas, or actually did have
non-native features elsewhere in their L2. (See, e.g.,White & Genesee,
1996, p. 262; Birdsong, 1999, p. 9; Bongaerts, 1999, respectively.) Strictly
speaking, these are admissions that even those exceptional subjects either
might not, or observably did not, constitute counterevidence to a CPH (i.e.,
were not truly exceptional).

A focus on very high-achieving adults, as in the phonology studies, is
certainly needed, but equally insufficient; it is vital that the performance
samples reflect genuine L2 use, and not consist exclusively of tiny rehearsed or edited samples and/or language elicited by tasks that allow or
even encourage monitoring, editing, or use of metalinguistic knowledge.
Some researchers claiming to have found adults who have attained native-like abilities in the L2 have really done no more (or less) than produce
individuals who are able to fool (some) NS judges into making judgments
of nativeness on the basis of inadequate samples of behavior and/or cases
of highly educated, highly analytic learners who are able to score very well
on paper-and-pencil tests of language-like behavior, typically GJ or sen-
tence-combining tasks, for completion of which they have been able to rely
on their explicit, analytic, problem-solving abilities. Even if such measures
tap legitimate domains of competence, they assuredly do not provide data
on which to base a claim of overall native-like attainment. Many people
can perform without error on certain well-defined tasks or within certain

restricted domains, or even with a passable accent for brief stretches, yet they are the first to admit that they are hopelessly non-native-like overall. The same questionable reliance on ratings of tiny domains within L2 abilities is evident in all studies of morphology and syntax that have claimed to find late starters capable of attaining native standards (see, e.g., Birdsong, 1992; van Boxtel, 2005; White & Genesee, 1996). Although valuable work in many ways, the measures used (e.g., grammaticality judgments, acceptability judgments, and sentence combining) often suffer not only from such a narrow focus as to preclude generalizations about native-like grammatical ability overall, but also from allowing subjects to employ metalinguistic abilities.

A study potentially offering more convincing counterevidence for having sampled a much broader, more natural range of language behaviors, is that of Ioup et al. (1994). Ioup et al. administered a battery of tests to two adult female English-speaking learners of Arabic: Laura had received formal instruction, held a doctorate in Arabic, was married to an Egyptian, and had a LOR of 10 years; Julie was a wholly naturalistic acquirer, also married to an Egyptian, with an AoA of 21 and LOR of 26 years. Ioup et al. administered a battery of very difficult tests to the two women, as well as to Egyptian Arabic NS controls: oral production, dialect differentiation (two tests), translation, grammaticality judgment, and interpretation of anaphora. Laura and Julie both performed comparably with the NS controls on the dialect differentiation task, and also on the free production task, according to the ratings awarded by a majority (but not all) of the 13 judges. The GJ and anaphor interpretation tasks revealed some small but measurable deficiencies in both NNSs, however. Contrary to the misleading title of the article in which this study was originally described, as well as the way the findings are often reported in the secondary literature (i.e., as counterevidence to "the" CPH), Ioup et al. do *not* claim to have found such disconfirming cases. They present Laura and Julie as two exceptionally talented and successful L2 acquirers whose ultimate attainment was, nonetheless, measurably non-native-like.

Elsewhere (Long, 2005b) I have closely examined the previous examples and several other studies purporting to provide counterevidence to claims of maturational constraints, in general, and "the" Critical Period Hypothesis, in particular. Each study was found to suffer from one of the following flaws and limitations, at the very least, and often from several of them: confusion of rate and ultimate attainment (see, e.g., Snow & Hoefnagel-Hohle, 1978); inappropriate choice of subjects, either with respect to the L1–L2 contrasts at issue (see, e.g., White & Genesee, 1996) or through inclusion in a sample of subjects learners with too short a length of residence to make them valid test cases for ultimate attainment (Bialystok, 1997; Bialystok & Miller, 1999); problems in the way age of onset (AO) or age of arrival (AoA) was measured (see, e.g., Birdsong, 1992); use of leading instructions to raters (see, e.g., Neufeld, 1977, 1978); assessments based on limited samples of subjects' target-language abilities and/or on "language-like" behavior (see, e.g., Birdsong, 1992; Neufeld, 2001; White & Genesee, 1996; van Boxtel, 2005; and the Bongaerts series discussed earlier); mixing markedly non-native and near-native samples making the latter more likely to sound native to raters, thus producing "false positives" (see, e.g., Bongaerts et al., 1995; and for careful documentation of the dangers of this practice, Flege & Fletcher, 1992; Piske, MacKay, & Flege, 2001); use of questionable (e.g., self-report, including census) data (Hakuta et al., 2003; Seliger, Krashen, & Ladefoged, 1975), and in some cases, clearly unreliable and/or invalid measures, as indicated by such phenomena as non-native subjects outperforming native controls and non-natives scoring comparably with natives due to members of both groups scoring nearly perfectly simply because the test employed was overly simple (see, e.g., Bialystok & Hakuta, 1999; Birdsong, 1992; Birdsong & Molis, 2001; Seliger et al., 1975; van Boxtel, Bongaerts, & Coppen, 2005; White & Genesee, 1996); and faulty interpretation of statistical patterns (see, e.g., Bialystok, 1997, 2002; Bialystok & Hakuta, 1999; Birdsong & Molis, 2001; Hakuta et al., 2003). Whereas late starters with native-like abilities in a foreign language may exist, current published claims to have found them do not appear to be sustainable.

The easiest way of refuting all variants of a CPH is to show native-like attainment by one or more learners first exposed to the L2 after the closure of the alleged period in question in the linguistic domain(s) in question. A distribution of test scores that had no such cases would also show (a) less variance in the ultimate attainment of subjects with AOs earlier than the projected offset, with some probably showing native-like abilities, (b) a noticeable decline in attainment throughout the projected duration of the CP concerned, and (c) less steep a decline/more variability thereafter, due to affective, environmental, cognitive, LOR, AT, and other variables showing effects in the older cohort. If maturational constraints are nonexistent, then it should be easy for opponents of a CPH to produce numerous learners who, despite a late start, have reached native-like levels after living in the target-language environment for several decades. In my view, no one has managed to come up with such a case yet, although many have tried.

TOWARD AN EXPLANATION FOR AGE EFFECTS

The widely documented failure of late starters to achieve native-like proficiency, even when motivation, cognitive abilities, and opportunity are optimal and plentiful, all agree, is one of the most salient facts about SLA. It is a weighty empirical problem, in Laudan's sense, crying out for a solution. The problem is an *anomaly* in the traditional meaning of that term in the philosophy of science for theories (e.g., so-called full access positions), like that of Flynn and Manuel (1991) and Martohardjono and Flynn (1995), which hold that children and adults have the same language learning capacity. Such theories must account for adult failure, but, as far as I can see, simply cannot do so.[8] Age differences are also an *anomalous problem* for the same theories in Laudan's technical sense. Viable rival theories have an explanation for the findings, that is, age differences are *solved problems* for those theories; full access positions, among others, do not. A theory, conversely, holding that adults have a qualitatively or quantitatively diminished capacity would have to account for rare cases of adult success, if they indeed exist, presumably by invoking a more or less mysterious "special talent" for language learning or some genetic abnormality. In the absence of such cases, as I have tried to show is the current situation, the task is to explain adult failure.

Thus far, explanations offered have generally invoked loss of cerebral plasticity (a metaphor), generally tied to one or more neurophysiological changes occurring in childhood (see, e.g., Long, 1990b; Seliger, 1978). The problem with such suggestions is that they are speculative, and putative sensitive period offsets are not known to coincide with key developmental points in processes such as mylenization. Among other things, that is, they have the same weaknesses as the various general cognitive explanations that have been offered, such as the so-called less is more hypothesis (see, e.g., Cochran, McDonald, & Parault, 1999; Kersten & Earles, 2001; Newport, 1990). How, then, are what from the behavioral data seem like robust sensitive periods to be explained? There follows a sketch of a possible explanation.

First, there is abundant converging evidence of language-specific human biology. This is seen in a variety of dissociation phenomena. Thus, the fact that child language acquisition around the globe proceeds at a strikingly similar rate, and to near uniform levels of (native) ultimate attainment, is significant in itself, but made more so for occurring despite considerable variation in the complexity (from an adult perspective) of the languages being learned, which differ typologically and in such features as the richness of their morphology and the regularity of rules in their grammars. The same languages, conversely, present markedly different learning tasks for adults speaking the same L1. For instance, U.S. Foreign Service Institute data show that English-speaking adults require over twice the number of hours of instruction to achieve the same (ILR 2) proficiency level in Arabic, Chinese, Turkish, or Russian, as for French, Spanish, or German (Odlin, 1989, p. 39). Considerable variation in children's general intellectual abilities—as different as three standard deviations below

---

[8]It is noticeable that most opponents of critical period hypotheses avoid the task (see, e.g., Marinova-Todd, Marshall, & Snow, 2000, and for a critique, Hyltenstam & Abrahamsson, 2001). Their approach is typically either to ignore the findings altogether, or else dismiss them as due to adult learners' (alleged) lack of motivation or opportunity, and instead search for cases of success, which if there is no critical period should be plentiful, but are proving to be strangely elusive.

and above the mean—and/or in their linguistic environments also has *relatively* little effect.

Second, normal use of the language-specific capacity appears to be genetically scheduled. In addition to exhibiting roughly similar capacity to make certain kinds of semantic distinctions, and to combine two or more elements to form utterances, in roughly the same sequence and at roughly equivalent ages across the linguistic, individual difference and environmental divides referred to earlier, there is evidence of quite remarkable "catch-up" phenomena in child language acquisition. Isolated or abused children, for example, and hearing children of nonsigning deaf adults, once placed in normal acquisition settings, quickly catch up with age peers and then proceed along with them at the normal rate (see Long, 1990b, for a summary of several such studies).

Third, the availability of the language-specific capacity appears to be constrained, diminishing as the organism matures or disappearing altogether. If first language exposure comes late for adults, for instance, they do not "catch up" or attain native proficiency levels, as shown by the cases of Genie (Curtiss, 1977), who was 13,7 when discovered, and deaf individuals first exposed to a sign language as adults (see, e.g., Newport, 1990). Similarly, the prognosis for recovery from trauma-induced aphasia is well known to deteriorate markedly after the early years.

Where a potential *explanation* for these and related phenomena is concerned, the crucial observation may be that the advantage of an early start continues *after* the closure of the hypothesized sensitive periods. It is not lost when the learner undergoes any or all of the *universal* general cognitive changes hypothesized by some to underlie critical or sensitive periods (in such formulations, usually just one critical period), for example, less-is-more changes in processing abilities, the (alleged) loss of the capacity for implicit learning,[9] or attainment of Piagetian formal operations and accompanying metalinguistic awareness. Young starters undergo the same general cognitive changes as everyone else. Those changes do not affect them, so why should they be what underlie sensitive period(s) offsets in the rest of the population?

The enduring benefit of early language acquisition experience for later language learning capacity are seen in the results of a study by Mayberry and Lock (2003). As measured by a timed grammaticality judgment task and an untimed sentence-to-picture matching task, the L2 syntactic abili-

---

[9]Some experts (e.g., Reber & Allen, 2000, pp. 234–235) deny that the capacity for implicit learning is lost in adults. The results in DeKeyser (2000) may be due to variance in the achievement measure among the early starters being smaller, and it being harder to obtain a significant correlation between language aptitude and AO within that group. Conversely, a statistically significant positive correlation is obtained in the older group, because they vary both in aptitude and obtained proficiency. Also, both aptitude tests (even oral ones) and grammaticality judgment (GJ) tests (which are what DeKeyser's and other studies employ) allow use of metalinguistic abilities to some extent, so in part probably measure the same abilities, meaning some positive association between the two sets of scores is to be expected.

ties (especially for complex grammatical constructions) of deaf adults who had learned either a spoken or a signed language as children were near-native, whereas the abilities of deaf adults who had learned neither were far short of that. Mayberry and Lock note that their findings are consistent with those on the beneficial, often critical, effects of early experience on other biological systems, such as visual perception. (Early visual deprivation alters lifelong visual abilities negatively in animals and humans.) In just the same way, they suggest that "language may be a genetically specified ability but our previous and present results suggest that the development of language capacity may be an epigenetic process whereby environmental experience during early life drives and organizes the growth of this complex behavioral and neurocortical system" (Mayberry & Lock, 2003, p. 382).

The catch-up phenomenon and the benefit of an early start, beyond the occurrence of what some see as potentially negative changes experienced as part of normal cognitive development by all, both suggest that the effect of early exposure to one or more additional languages beyond the L1 is neurophysiological, and a neurophysiological change that is lasting, persisting at least throughout the normal first language acquisition period, which research has shown continues into the early teens for some complex syntax. One possibility is that early richer linguistic exposure leads to the creation of more, and more complex, neural networks before synaptic sheaths harden as part of the mylenization process, making new ones for new languages more difficult to create in older starters. One indication of this may be the more complex dendritic bundles observed in bilinguals and multilinguals than monolinguals (Jacobs, 1988), although it is not clear that that difference is age dependent.

If correct, then the hypothesized explanation is that a *neurophysiological* development, triggered by exposure to two or more languages as opposed to only one, occurring before the close of one or more sensitive periods, and probably with no general cognitive correlate, conveys a lasting advantage on early L2 acquirers—an advantage that persists in adulthood, however adulthood is defined. The potentially crucial observation leading to this neurophysiological enrichment hypothesis is that younger children catch up with, and given adequate opportunity ultimately overtake, older child and adult starters (who set off faster) *after* the supposed maturational constraints take effect. This is consistent with the finding that an AO of 6 or even younger seems necessary for attainment of native-like L1 ASR morphology and syntax, and even then, it is not guaranteed (Mayberry, 1993; Newport, 1990), but for L2 morphosyntax, the window seemingly extends to the midteens (DeKeyser, 2000; J. Johnson & Newport, 1989; Patkowski, 1982), and is simultaneously another possible indication of the influence of exercise on subsequent maturation.

CHAPTER FOUR

Recasts in SLA: The Story So Far

Theorizing and research on the role of negative feedback in SLA has a long and somewhat turbulent history, and scholars today remain divided. Some pedagogues appear to believe that almost all overt "error correction" is beneficial. Some theorists claim that negative feedback plays no role at all (see, e.g., Carroll, 1997; Truscott, 1996, 1999). Scholars who have conducted classroom research on the issue generally suggest that a complex array of linguistic and psychological factors affect its utility (see, e.g., Chaudron, 1987; DeKeyser, 1993; Hendrickson, 1978). Partly inspired by results in first language acquisition, much recent L2 research has focused on the role of implicit negative feedback, and in particular, on the efficacy of so-called corrective recasts.

Work on L2 recasts until now includes over 60 descriptive, quasi-experimental, and experimental studies of their occurrence, usability, and use in classrooms, laboratory settings, and noninstructional conversation. Questions have been raised as to the potential nonsalience and/or ambiguity of recasts, their value as positive or negative evidence, the difficulty of distinguishing acquisition and deployment, among other matters, but results have generally been encouraging.

Researchers have also begun to compare the impact of recasts and more explicit forms of negative feedback on classroom discourse, and—of particular significance for language teaching—the relative utility of models and recasts for language development. Illustrative studies from each of these major lines of work are briefly described and critiqued here, and suggestions are made for the design of future studies. Finally, some implications are drawn for language teaching methodology and pedagogy.

IMPLICIT NEGATIVE FEEDBACK

As recounted in a historical review by Schachter (1991), the role attributed to negative input in learning has varied from one discipline to another and over time, generally being considered greater in psychology, for example, where the construct of interest is usually "negative feedback," than in linguistics, which typically deals in, or eschews, the need for "negative data" or "negative evidence."[1] Its role has also changed over time, declining in importance, for example, when special nativist linguistic theories are in the ascendancy, and vice versa. The supposed unavailability of negative evidence is one of the principal justifications special nativists offer in support of the need to posit a substantial innate linguistic endowment—one constrained in such a way that children's erroneous hypotheses can be corrected on the basis of positive evidence alone (see, e.g., C. L. Baker, 1979). Grimshaw and Pinker (1989) are certainly correct when they note the improbability of corrective feedback being available on each problematic form or construction just when a learner needs it.

Within SLA, whether negative feedback or, indeed, negative evidence of any kind is *necessary* or even *usable* by adults remains controversial (for contrasting views on its role in SLA, see Long, 1996; Schwartz, 1992). Schwartz, for instance, claims that negative feedback perceived by the learner as corrective may affect performance, but cannot permeate underlying competence. As the following review shows, however, there is mounting support from research in both first and second language acquisition for the claim that such feedback does affect competence, *facilitating* language development when it occurs. This is what counts when designing language teaching, where the relevant criterion is efficiency, not necessity, and it is this consideration that has driven most of the intensive research activity on recasts in SLA since the early 1990s.

Of all the many ways negative feedback is delivered in and out of classrooms (for review, see Chaudron, 1977, 1987), *implicit* negative feedback in the form of corrective recasts seems particularly promising. If it can be shown that recasts work, and do so efficiently enough, then teachers in task-based, content-based, immersion, and other kinds of second language classrooms may have the option of dealing with many of their stu-

---

[1]As used in what follows and in most, but not all, of the SLA literature, "negative evidence" refers to information available to the learner as to what is not possible in the L2. It can take many forms, from explicit grammar rules, through over "error correction," to corrective recasts. "Negative feedback," a subset of negative evidence, refers to information learners receive (e.g., in the form of corrective recasts) to the effect that something they (usually just) said or wrote in the L2 was ungrammatical. Negative feedback is contingent on deviant learner performance, in other words; negative evidence may or may not be.

dents' language problems *incidentally* while working on their subject matter of choice, with fewer of the interruptions and other unpleasant side effects caused by traditional overt "error correction" practices.

A *corrective recast* may be defined as a reformulation of all or part of a learner's immediately preceding utterance in which one or more nontarget-like (lexical, grammatical, etc.) items is/are replaced by the corresponding target language form(s), and where, throughout the exchange, the focus of the interlocutors is on *meaning,* not language as object. That is to say, unlike various traditional pedagogic procedures for delivering "error correction,"[2] the "corrections" in recasts are implicit and incidental. This can be seen in two examples, one syntactic and one lexical (both in the form of confirmation checks), in the following excerpt from a conversation between a native speaker (NS) and a Vietnamese child beginning ESL reported by Sato (1986):

NS:	Oh, Mary said that you went to um- you went to a game by the Fever?
Tai:	nou tan hi go yEt
NS:	*You didn't go yet?* To the Fever?
Tai:	wat?
NS:	Did you go to see the Fever play soccer?
Tai:	Yes
NS:	When was that?
Tai:	nat nat nau
NS:	Oh uh- *later?* Oh I see. Who else is going?

(Sato, 1986, p. 36)

As discussed elsewhere (Long, 1996), information about the target language supplied in this manner has several potential advantages from a psycholinguistic perspective over the same information in noncontingent utterances (i.e., as positive evidence, or models). Recasts convey needed information about the target language *in context,* when interlocutors share a *joint attentional focus,* and when the learner already has *prior comprehension* of at least part of the message, thereby facilitating form–function mapping. Learners are *vested* in the exchange, as it is their message that is at

---

[2]"Error correction" appears in scare quotes because, as argued elsewhere (Long, 1977), it is a loaded term. "Correction" is a perlocutionary speech act, implying that a negative feedback move in classroom discourse has its intended *effect* on the learner's underlying grammar, when any experienced teacher knows, and research shows, this is frequently not the case. "Negative feedback" or "feedback on error" are more neutral, more accurate, terms. They describe what a teacher or other interlocutor does, regardless of its effects or lack thereof. Correction is what the learner may or may not do. (Coding speech in terms of its future results also has the highly undesirable side effect of increasing the power of any analysis of discourse, because it assumes the analyst can look forward, not to mention inside the learner's head, when coding current discourse moves.)

stake, and so will probably be *motivated* and *attending*, conditions likely to facilitate *noticing* of any new linguistic information in the input. The fact that learners will already understand all or part of the interlocutor's response (because it is a reformulation of the learner's own) also means that they have additional freed-up *attentional resources* that can be allocated to the form of the response and, again, to form–function mapping. Finally, the *contingency* of recasts on deviant learner output means that the incorrect and correct utterances are juxtaposed. This allows the learner to compare the two forms side by side, so to speak, and to observe the contrast, an opportunity not presented by noncontingent utterances (i.e., models).

As Saxton (1997) stresses, positive evidence (i.e., the occurrence of the correct form; e.g., *didn't go* and *later*, earlier) in ambient, *non*-contingent speech, simply provides instances of what is acceptable in the target language, whereas the same form occurring in a corrective recast simultaneously provides information about what is and is not acceptable. Saxton's Direct Contrast Hypothesis (1997) says, in a nutshell, that corrective recasts (negative evidence) work, and work better than models (positive evidence), because they can inform the learner not only that the form modeled in the recast is grammatical, but also crucially that their own form is ungrammatical. Models (positive evidence) can serve only the first function.

CROSS-SECTIONAL STUDIES OF RECASTS IN SLA

There is a growing body of descriptive, quasi-experimental, and experimental research on corrective recasts in SLA. Most studies to date have been cross-sectional. Some researchers (e.g., Rabie, 1996) have dealt with vocabulary learning, or with both vocabulary and morphology (Iwashita, 1999, 2003), but most have focused on morphological development alone, with English, Japanese, and Spanish the most common source and target languages. Representative studies, often just one or two of several in the category concerned, are referenced in Figure 4.1, in which empty cells reveal where research has yet to be conducted. Much of the work has been couched within the framework of the four-part nativist challenge laid down by Pinker and others for child language acquisition (see, e.g., Grimshaw & Pinker, 1989; Marcus, 1993; Pinker, 1989), and for adult SLA by Beck and Eubank (1991), to show that recasts *exist*, exist in *usable* form, are *used*, and are *necessary*.

Descriptive studies have shown that recasts *exist* in all second language discourse observed so far, whether involving children or adults, in both noninstructional conversation (see, e.g., Braidi, 2002; Brock, Crookes, Day, & Long, 1986; Oliver, 1995; Richardson, 1995; Yamaguchi, 1994) and foreign language, second language, and immersion classroom settings (see, e.g., Doughty, 1994; Iwasaki, 1996; Izumi, 2000; Lyster & Ranta, 1997; Mori, 1998; Moroishi, 2001; Morris, 2002; Muranoi, 1998; Oliver, 2000). Indeed,

Cross-sectional studies	INSIDE CLASSROOMS	OUTSIDE CLASSROOMS
DESCRIPTIVE	R. Ellis et al. (2001), Lyster & Ranta (1997), Morris (2002)	Braidi (2002), Oliver (1995), Richardson (1995)
QUASI-EXPERIMENTAL	Doughty & Varela (1998)	Iwashita (1999), Mackey (1999)
EXPERIMENTAL		Doughty et al. (1999), Leeman (2000), Ono & Witzel (2002), Ortega & Long (1997)

FIG. 4.1. Sample cross-sectional LS recast studies.

descriptive studies of naturally occurring lessons by R. Ellis, Basturkmen, and Loewen (2001), Lyster and Ranta (1997), Morris (2002), Oliver (2000), and Seedhouse (1997), among others, suggest that recasts are by far the most frequent form of negative feedback in classrooms of all kinds.

Outside the classroom, in one of the earliest L2 studies, inspired by work in L1A by Farrar (1992), Richardson (1995) analyzed conversations among 18- to 22-year-olds in 12 NS–NNS dyads for differential NS responses to grammatical and ungrammatical NNS utterances containing errors involving any of eight grammatical morphemes, and NNS use of the grammatical information contained in four different kinds of NS responses to the ungrammatical speech. Richardson found that NSs provided corrective recasts to 54% of ungrammatical utterances, and NNSs imitated 46% of the corrective recasts, as compared with 26% of noncorrective recasts (for similar findings in Japanese as a Foreign Language [JFL], see Yamaguchi, 1994), suggesting that the NNSs were responding at least in part to the negative feedback corrective recasts provide, rather than simply to their imitative component. Also, NNSs were between 2.5 and 4.5 times more likely (cf. L1-acquiring children's two or three times) to imitate/incorporate a grammatical morpheme after corrective recasts containing it than after the three other kinds of response examined (noncorrective recasts, topic continuations, and topic changes). Like the other studies cited, Richardson's findings provide clear evidence that negative feedback exists in NS–NNS conversation outside classrooms, and suggestive evidence that it is both noticed and used by NNSs.

In a larger scale laboratory study, Braidi (2002) also found that recasts occur, and are usable, and approximately one third are used by NNSs even when the criterion for use is the narrow one of immediate incorporation. Braidi randomly assigned 10 adult native speakers (NSs) of English, undergraduate U.S. college students, and 10 adult non-native speakers (NNSs), Japanese students of ESL at the "lower and upper intermediate levels," to form 10 dyads, 7 female–female, and 3 male–male. Each dyad was tape-recorded working on a series of four communication tasks for about an hour: two one-way tasks (the NSs giving instructions so that their NNS partners could match figures displayed on a felt board, and both NSs and NNSs giving instructions for drawing a picture); a two-way, picture-sequencing task, in which each member of a dyad held half the pictures needed to tell a story, pictures that they had to describe in order to determine the correct sequence; and a conversation about the tasks they had performed together. Transcripts of the conversations were first segmented and classified as either one-signal or extended negotiations, the remainder being designated by default as non-negotiated interactions. One-signal negotiations, following work by Varonis and Gass (1985) and Pica (1988, pp. 54–55), were those in which meaning was negotiated satisfactorily with only one signal of comprehension difficulty; extended negotiations were longer (implying greater communication difficulty), involving two or more such signals. Oliver (1995) found that child NSs tended to provide recasts more often in response to "transparent" (less serious) communication difficulties, negotiating more "opaque" instances, and Pica had shown that NNSs modified their output toward NS norms more effectively (making changes to the phonology, morphology, syntax, and semantics) in shorter, one-signal negotiations, the learners tending to limit themselves to semantic changes in extended negotiations. The interactions in Braidi's corpus were then classified using Oliver's (1995) three-part coding system: NNS initial turn, NS response, and NNS reaction, the last simultaneously serving as the initiation of the next three-part sequence.

Braidi found that 880 (35%) of a total of 1,642 NNS initial utterances were incorrect. According to this study, 15% of the incorrect NNS utterances elicited recasts—considerably lower than the 61% for child NS–NNS dyads in Oliver (1995), and the 47% and 40% for adults and children, respectively, in Oliver (2000). Significantly more recasts occurred in extended negotiations, although Braidi notes (2002, p. 35, fn. 19) that their greater length in and of itself offers more opportunities, independent of the communicative difficulty factor. NSs provided recasts more often following multiple-error (17%) than single-error (14%) utterances in one-signal and extended negotiations, another finding contrary to the norm in such studies, for example, 69% of recasts for single-error and 31% for multiple-error utterances in Oliver (1995), where the majority (78%) of multiple-error cases were negotiated rather than recast. The inconsistency of the findings on both overall recasting rate and rates following single- and multiple-error utterances with those of most other studies led Braidi to ask how consistent recasting patterns need to be across interactions to be used. On the other hand, incorporation rates (in the immediately following NNS turn), as noted earlier, closely matched those of previous studies: 10% of all recasts, rising to 34% when an incorporation move by the NNS was both possible (e.g., because the NS did not recast and immediately move on) and sociolinguistically appropriate (e.g., because the recast was not in the form of a clarification request). On this evidence, at least, and with the caveat that these were instructed learners, who may be more accustomed to perceiving NS input as potential linguistic guidance, NSs seem to use recasts as negative feedback despite inconsistencies in patterns of occurrence.

A parallel line of research in classroom settings is well illustrated by a study of negative feedback and uptake in a (Spanish) foreign language classroom by Morris (2002), who examined relationships among error types (morphosyntactic and lexical), feedback types (explicit, recasts, and negotiation moves), and immediate learner repair in conversations in 21 dyads of elementary proficiency students working on a jigsaw task. Whereas negotiation moves (e.g., clarification requests, confirmation checks, and repetition) often constitute recasts, they were distinguished from explicit correction and recasts in Morris' analysis in that they did not provide learners with the correct form (p. 399). Of 152 errors (63% of which were morphosyntactic and 30% lexical), 106 (70%) were followed by corrective feedback of some kind: 87% of the lexical errors and 67% of the morphosyntactic errors. Of the 106 feedback moves, 72 (68%) were recasts and 34 (32%) were negotiation moves. There were no cases of explicit correction. Echoing findings for teacher–student interaction in French immersion classrooms by Lyster (1998a), 91% of feedback moves following morphosyntactic errors were recasts, whereas 70% of those following lexical errors were negotiation moves. The relationship between error type and feedback type was statistically significant: chi-squared (1, 104) = 38.41, $p <$ .0001. Of the 106 feedback moves, 23 (22%) led to (immediate) repair. Of 40 lexical errors that received feedback, 45% were repaired; of 64 morphosyntactic errors that did, only 8% were repaired. Again supporting Lyster's (1998a) findings (discussed later), almost all repairs (96%) resulted from negotiation moves, including 94% of all lexical repairs and 100% of all morphosyntactic repairs, this despite most feedback moves (91%) after the latter having been recasts. Negotiation moves, in other words, were far more effective than recasts at eliciting immediate learner repair. Morris notes (2002, p. 402), however, that immediate incorporation is not the only yardstick by which to evaluate recasts, and that studies (e.g., Mackey & Philp, 1998) looking beyond the speaking turns immediately following feedback moves have found subsequent beneficial effects for recasts on development. This has in fact been a repeated finding in several cross-sectional studies described later (e.g., Mackey, 1999; Mackey & Oliver, 2002), as well as in longitudinal studies by Boom (1998), M. Ishida (2002), and Iwashita (1999).

Confirmation of usability and use cannot be obtained from descriptive work alone, however, because the absence of pretests precludes distinguishing *acquisition* of new knowledge and *deployment* of existing knowledge. Moreover, however implausible it may seem to suppose that subjects would independently happen to learn target linguistic items without exposure to the models or recasts containing them during the generally very limited duration of these cross-sectional studies (most lasting an hour or less), the absence of a control group, strictly speaking, plus the possibility of learning from exposure to target forms in a pretest, also precludes any imputation of causality to the recasts observed.

Clearer evidence that the linguistic information recasts contain is both *usable* and *used* by learners is to be found in quasi-experimental work (e.g., Doughty & Varela, 1998; M. Ishida, 2002) and, especially, true experiments (e.g., Choi, 2000; Doughty, Izumi, Maciukaite, & Zapata, 1999; Iwashita, 1999; Leeman, 2000; Mackey, 1995, 1999; Mackey & Oliver, 2002; Mito, 1993; Ono & Witzel, 2002; Ortega & Long, 1997; Rabie, 1996). Ortega and Long (1997), for example, randomly assigned 30 young adult learners of Spanish as a foreign language to one of four experimental conditions, plus a control group, in a pretest–posttest control group, repeated measures design. Each subject in the treatment groups was provided with six models of one structure and six recasts of a second, with treatments (modeling and recasting), structures (adverb placement and direct object topicalization), and test forms (A and B) crossed and counterbalanced. Both experimental treatments were delivered as student and researcher, separated by a screen, played communication games involving manipulation of objects.[3] Pre- and posttests (picture description and grammaticality judgment) each consisted of 14 items—5 productive or recognition items per structure per test, 2 of them novel, and 4 distractors. The whole session for each subject, including pre- and posttesting and a short debriefing interview, lasted approximately 1 hour. Subjects in the control group took the tests and received a placebo treatment (a semistructured conversation with the researcher in Spanish) during the same period of time. Potential subjects showing any knowledge of either structure on the pretest were eliminated from the study and new subjects introduced, meaning that knowledge displayed by the 30 eventually included could legitimately be interpreted as having been acquired from either the modeling or the recasting they had experienced of the structure concerned.

For a variety of reasons, the grammaticality judgment data were uninterpretable (see Ortega & Long, 1997, for details). On the picture description task, results showed no learning of either structure by the control group (mercifully); no learning of object topicalization in either condition, that structure proving too difficult for all learners; and statistically significantly higher posttest scores on adverb placement for the 12 students who had heard recasts of utterances involving adverb placement than for the 12 who had received

---

[3]There is a tendency in natural conversation for some learners to echo all or part of recasts they receive (behavioral evidence of noticing). The same phenomenon has been observed in classrooms (Ohta, 2000). Probably healthy for language learning (although found nonsignificantly related to subsequent use of targeted interrogative constructions by Mackey & Philp, 1998), this practice would introduce an unwanted production confound in an experiment (as occurred in Mito, 1993), and so was intentionally preempted in this study by having the NS interlocutor, Ortega, swiftly move on to the next item whenever she provided a recast.

models of adverb placement. Two of 12 students who had received models produced one or two tokens (with a maximum individual total score of three) of adverb placement on the posttest. Eight out of 12 subjects who had received recasts of the same structure, conversely, were able to produce (in all but one case) two or more tokens of Verb Adverb Object (VAdvO) on the posttest (with a maximum individual total score of six). Five of the eight subjects who had learned adverb placement through recasts correctly supplied the structure with novel items. Furthermore, in debriefing interviews conducted immediately after the posttest, when asked if they had learned anything new, all eight of the students who had learned the VAdvO structure through recasts were able explicitly and correctly to formulate an explanation of the rule (albeit in lay terms), whereas this was not the case for either of the two (less) successful students who had learned something in the modeling group. Although limited to a majority of subjects and to only one of two learning targets, these findings suggested the potential superiority of recasts to models, at least for salient meaning-bearing L2 structures.

Similar results favoring recasts over models were obtained in a modified replication by Doughty et al. (1999). Doughty et al. employed the same counterbalanced design, but with an additional condition, focused recasts, assessment measures containing more items, increased contextualization of the grammaticality judgment test, and a delayed posttest. In this study, 53 intermediate university students of Spanish were randomly assigned to one of four groups: models, recasts, focused recasts, and control. (The control group received a placebo treatment in the form of a discussion of working conditions for Latin American women.) As in an earlier study by Doughty and Varela (1998, see later), focused recasts consisted of a repetition of the student's utterance with rising intonation, immediately followed by a recast. For adverb placement, for example, compare:

Recast:
(prompt on tape) los sábados [Saturdays]

NNS: Juan bebe la leche los sábados [John drinks milk on Saturdays]
Researcher: Juan bebe los sábados la leche, sí? Mm hmm [John drinks on Saturdays milk, yes? Mm hmm]

Focused recast:
(prompt on tape) los sábados [Saturdays]

NNS: Juan bebe la leche los sábados [John drinks milk on Saturdays]
Researcher: Bebe la leche los sábados? [He drinks milk on Saturdays?] Juan bebe *los sábados* la leche, sí? Mm hmm [John drinks *on Saturdays* milk, yes? Mm hmm]

Subjects in the three treatment groups experienced 10 tokens of each structure, topicalization and adverb placement, instead of six in the Ortega and Long study, while performing somewhat modified versions of the tasks employed in the earlier work. There were eight measures of possible improvement for each group: two structures (topicalization and adverb placement) × two measures (production and grammaticality judgment) × two assessment times (immediate and delayed posttest). Results showed both recast and focused recast groups superior to the control and model groups, subjects in the two recast conditions improving significantly on five of the eight and six of the eight measures, respectively. There was a slight advantage for focused recasts over ordinary recasts, in other words, and once again there was little learning of the more difficult topicalization structure in any condition; subjects receiving focused recasts also improved slightly more there, even if not to anywhere near full target-like performance.

In a classroom study, using a quasi-experimental intact groups design with pre- and posttests, Doughty and Varela (1998) followed two middle school teachers of ESL content-based science over a period of approximately four months. Both teachers were recorded teaching six simple science experiments as part of the regular content-based science curriculum, each experiment taking one or two weeks to complete, to a total of 34 students ranging from age 11 to 14. Experiments 1, 5, and 6 served as the pretest, posttest, and (after a two-month interval) delayed posttest. One teacher provided no explicit grammar instruction whatsoever, his class (n = 13) serving as the control group. During work on Experiments 2, 3, and 4, the second teacher provided her students (n = 21) with consistent negative feedback, often in the form of focused recasts, on nearly all errors in the use of two structures, simple past and past conditional (e.g., "I thought the earthworm would die") when reporting (first in writing, and then orally) predictions the children made before carrying out the experiments. Both teachers taught content only, with no attention to language as object, during the two-month period between the posttest and delayed posttest. The focused recasts in the treatment group typically consisted of repetition of the deviant learner utterance with rising intonation, followed immediately by a corrective recast that was always delivered with falling intonation. In the case of the written reports of the experiments, errors involving the target structures were circled, and written recasts juxtaposed (procedures, it should be noted, that are both more explicit than what is normally understood by "corrective recast"). Changes in the students' use of the target structures were analyzed in three ways: shifts to target-like use (TLU), changes that showed improvements while still falling short of the full target version, and declines in non-TLU, all three applied to both their written reports and transcriptions of their oral reports on the posttest and delayed posttest, resulting in a total of six measures. The control group showed essentially no change on five out of the six measures on the posttest, and their one slight, but statistically significant, improvement in interlingual uses in the written reports had disappeared by the time of the delayed posttest. The treatment group, on the other hand, showed large, statistically significant gains on all six measures, and (despite no treatment of language errors in the interim) maintained five of the six improvements on the delayed posttest two months later; only the initial gain for TLU in the written reports was no longer statistically significant.

The need to match target structures to learners' developmental stages when evaluating the role of recasts (as in all effect-of-instruction work) is well illustrated in a study by Mackey (1995, 1999). Mackey randomly assigned 34 adult ESL learners into four experimental groups and a control group. Two treatment groups participated in task-based conversation with a NS designed to focus on English question formation—one group predicted to be developmentally ready and another unready to acquire the target interrogative structures on the basis of their current developmental stage. A third treatment group observed such conversation, and the fourth participated in prescripted versions of the task (where a NS mostly read premodified directions to them), which subjects could not negotiate. Mackey found that only learners who actively participated in fully negotiated conversation and who were developmentally ready for the target structures developed statistically significantly, also producing significantly more higher level structures, and with the improvement showing up not immediately, but on the delayed posttests, one week and one month after the treatment. The observers, the prescripted, and control group subjects changed very little. In a second study, Mackey and Philp compared ESL learners who received interactionally modified input while completing tasks designed to create contexts for the use of specific target forms, one group of whom experienced intensive recasts as part of those sessions. Results suggested that for more advanced learners, interaction with recasts was more beneficial than interaction alone in increasing production of higher level morphosyntactic forms, whereas recasts were not as effective with less advanced learners.

In a modified replication of Mackey's study, Mackey and Oliver (2002) assessed the impact of recasts and negotiation moves on the development of interrogatives by children, age 8–12, from a variety of L1 backgrounds learning English at an intensive ESL center in Western Australia. In this study, 22 children were randomly assigned to either an experimental (interaction and feedback) or control (interaction) group. Treatments, pre- and posttests utilized a mix of spot-the-difference, story completion, picture placement, and picture sequencing tasks designed to elicit similar ranges of question forms. Each child interacted with Oliver for 30 minutes while working on the tasks on seven separate occasions over a five-week period: the pretest session, one treatment session per day for three days, an immediate posttest on the following day, a delayed posttest one week later, and a final delayed posttest three weeks after that. The 11 children in the interaction and feedback group asked and answered questions about the tasks and were provided with negotiation and recasts as needed during their treatment sessions. The 11 children in the interaction control group performed the same task-based activities, but (following the system utilized by Pica, 1994, and Gass & Varonis, 1994) with the researcher's input premodified, based on the interaction and feedback provided to the children in the experimental group. Care was taken to script similar amounts and types of input and equivalent numbers of opportunities to hear and ask questions. The difference was that children in the interaction control group had to complete the tasks without the interactional feedback children in the experimental group received—specifically, without recasts or clarification requests using question forms. Eight of 11 children in the experimental group showed sustained stage development (operationalized as production of two or more different question forms at a higher level in the Pienemann hierarchy on at least two tasks on at least two of the posttests), as compared to only three of 11 children in the control group, a significant difference (Fisher's exact – .0211, $p <$ .05). Unlike Mackey's (1999) results with adults, the stage improvement was apparent on the immediate posttest.

Although far from complete and showing some variation, the picture emerging from the aforementioned and other studies (described later) as to the effectiveness of recasts is quite favorable. In general, the L2 findings parallel those from child L1A research (see, e.g., N. D. Baker & Nelson, 1984; Farrar, 1990, 1992; Saxton, 1997; Saxton, Kulscar, Greer, & Rupra, 1998), except that, if anything, older (L2) learners appear to notice recasts more efficiently than do children (perhaps due to heightened metalinguistic awareness), giving additional cause for optimism about their likely effectiveness for adult SLA. As noted earlier, Richardson's subjects imitated 46% of corrective recasts, and in a laboratory study of task-based NS–NNS conversation by Yamaguchi, Iwasaki, and Oliver (1999), Australian university students of JFL incorporated over 60% of the negative feedback provided. Adults' ability to notice recasts likely varies with certain situational factors, however, as suggested in a study by Philp (1997, 1999, 2003), which defined noticing, following Robinson (1995a, p. 318), as "detection with awareness and rehearsal in short-term memory," operationalized as subjects' ability for immediate cued recall when prompted by the researcher/interlocutor knocking twice on the table between them. Philp found higher proficiency learners more likely to notice recasts than lower proficiency learners by that measure, and learners at all levels better able to notice and recall shorter than longer recasts, simple than complex recasts (recasts with one change better than recasts with three), and recasts involving changes in morphology better than changes to syntax. As is also the case with the L1A findings, there is some initial experimental evidence that recasts can be more effective than models for grammatical development in the short term (Doughty et al., 1999; Iwashita, 1999; Leeman, 2000; Mackey, 1999; Ortega & Long, 1997), although, as with some other research findings on the effect of instruction, it is not clear that the advantage will always be maintained over time.[4] There is also some evidence that the positive impact of recasts is not limited to lexical item learning (e.g., particular verbs forms subjects encounter in an experimental treatment), but induces pattern learning as well. Several of the studies cited (e.g., Doughty et al., 1999; Ortega & Long, 1997) have been careful to include novel items in posttests in order to test for generalization of learning, and generalization of pattern learning was a principal focus of a study by Choi (2000).

Along with work by Ayoun (2001), Choi's is one of the few studies to date to have examined the effectiveness of recasts in the written mode. This study randomly assigned 36 adult elementary learners of ESL (22 Koreans and 14 Japanese), who were recent arrivals in Hawai'i (maximum LOR of six months) to one of two groups: recast and control. Data collection, which was conducted individually, took about 90 minutes for each subject and began with a 15-minute pretest on the irregular past tense forms of nine real verbs. After pilot-testing six irregular past tense patterns with native speakers of English, Choi targeted three tokens of each of three semiproductive classes in her study with non-natives (ring, sing, spring; bend, lend, spend; and bleed, feed, lead) and, based on the phonological properties of each pattern, nine novel verbs (*kend/kent, crend/crent, nend/nent; ling/lang, ning/nang, tring/trang; and keed/ked, cheed/ched, yeed/yed*). Stem forms were given in parentheses in two stories, and subjects had to fill in blanks on these and a variety of distractor items. This was followed by two 30-minute Internet web chat sessions using a program (*Yahoo! Messenger*) that allows interactive synchronous communication, with both parties able to see previous lines they had written. Subjects read two stories in their native language and were asked to retell them to the researcher in English via the computer with the help of picture and word cues. The researcher asked questions or confirmation checks to help subjects retell the stories or to elicit the nine target irregular past verbs (only real verbs were used in the treatment), but provided corrective recasts on their use of the target forms (and no other forms) only to the experimental group, as in:

Researcher: What did Peter do to him?
Subject: He *leaded* the stranger to shopping center

---

[4]It is arguable that undue importance is attached to the need for delayed posttests in this and other areas of effects-of-instruction SLA research. The durability of new learning—obtained from recasts or any other source—is primarily a function of the intensity of continued exposure to the items concerned. Thus, although delayed posttests can be important for capturing delayed effects of instruction (see, e.g., Mackey, 1995, 1999), the most important test of the relative efficacy of (in this case) models and recasts in producing *acquisition* is their initial impact, as measured by an immediate posttest. This is not to be confused with immediate impact in the sense of incorporation of linguistic forms in learners' immediate responses to recasts, either forced or echoic, which may have little or nothing to do with acquisition.

Researcher: He *led* the stranger to the shopping center? How nice
                   of him!

Similar errors by subjects in the experimental groups were ignored, as in:

Researcher: Why did Peter fall down?
Subject: and he *bleed* a lot of his knee
Researcher: Oh, no!
Subject: I see a dog besides him
Researcher: What happened to the dog?

Both groups produced 162 tokens of the target verbs; the recast group received recasts in 114 cases (70%), and the control group received none. The session ended with a 10 to 15-minute fill-in-the-blanks production posttest consisting of the same items and distractors as the pretest in a slightly modified version of the story lines.

The recast group's mean score on the nine real irregular verbs targeted in the treatment improved statistically significantly from 3.50 on the pretest to 5.78 on the posttest, and statistically significantly more than that of the control group, which barely changed (3.87 to 4.00).[5] Unlike the real verbs, the nine novel irregular verbs only appeared in the pre- and posttests. The results were similar. The recast group's mean score on the nine novel irregular verb forms improved statistically significantly from 1.67 on the pretest to 3.83 on the posttest, and statistically significantly more than that of the control group, which merely rose from 1.72 to 2.22. Finally, if recasts were effective, as they had been, in promoting generalization of the patterns, then they should also have produced an unlearning effect on regularization of novel verbs. This was indeed the case. The mean number of regular forms produced by the recast group decreased statistically significantly from 4.9 on the pretest to 2.3 on the posttest, and statistically significantly more than that of the control group, which remained virtually the same, moving only from 4.89 to 4.67. Task-based interaction in synchronous written communication with intensive recasts had been effective in both lexical item learning and pattern learning, at least where inflectional morphology was concerned, whereas (as Choi notes, 2000, p. 59), an equal number of opportunities for the control group simply to produce the target forms, without negative feedback (i.e., output alone), had not resulted in either.

Additional cross-sectional classroom and laboratory-type studies are clearly required, but there is also an urgent need for longitudinal studies. It is impossible to know how stable and durable any effects of recasts (or

---

[5]For ease of exposition, subclass differences are not reported here, nor later for novel verbs.

models) may be or, especially, the extent to which the cross-sectional findings are generalizable without such longitudinal work.

LONGITUDINAL STUDIES OF RECASTS IN SLA

In what appears to have been the first of only four longitudinal[6] classroom studies to date (see Fig. 4.2), Boom (1998) examined the effects of recasts over time on nine elementary-level ESL students in Hawai'i. Boom recorded their conversations with one or more other students (baseline data), then with himself (the teacher), during which he recast some of their utterances (treatment), and then again with from one to four (mean 2.4) other students after talking to the teacher (posttest and delayed posttests), all over a 3-day period while they repeatedly retold the same story about the worst accident they had experienced. Boom then conducted a very detailed qualitative analysis of the transcribed conversations in which he followed the fate of all grammatical targets subject to recasts, both simple and complex (i.e., treating one, or two or more, forms, respectively), and of "good" or "poor" quality. Poor quality recasts were those he judged to have suffered from having been provided with too much delay, spoken too softly, with needlessly changed components so as to prompt a yes–no response, or with insufficient wait-time.

The nine students received a total of 77 recasts while telling Boom their stories; of these, 51 were simple and 26 were complex, and 57 were "good," and 20 were "poor." Also, 41 of the 51 simple recasts were "good" and 10 were "poor"; 16 of the 26 complex recasts were "good" and 10 "poor." In addition, 36 (47%) of the immediate learner responses to the 77 recasts involved incorporation, and 41 (51%) did not. There was virtually no difference in incorporation rates immediately following simple and complex recasts. However, incorporation was considerably higher following "good" (51%) rather than

Longitudinal studies	INSIDE CLASSROOMS	OUTSIDE CLASSROOMS
DESCRIPTIVE	Boom (1998), Loewen & Philp (2005)	
QUASI-EXPERIMENTAL		M. Ishida (2002), Iwashita (1999)
EXPERIMENTAL		

FIG. 4.2. Longitudinal L2 recast studies.

---

[6]Although it took place over just 3 days, the study was longitudinal in the sense that subjects experienced repeated treatments (in the form of intensive recasting) during that period, accompanied by repeated observations of treatment effects.

"poor" (35%) recasts. When Boom looked at incorporation in subsequent conversations, he found evidence suggesting that uptake is higher than indicated by immediate incorporation alone (see earlier discussion). Despite the absence of contexts for some forms in later retellings, the incorporation rate for "good" simple and complex recasts rose from 52% to 71%, and for "poor" recasts from 35% to 55%. Combined immediate and later incorporation rates for individuals varied from 22% to 88% (mean of 47%). There were less happy findings, too, Boom is careful to point out, including cases where students reverted to their original deviant form, used it in variation with the recast version, or produced new deviant forms.

Boom also analyzed how the deviant forms recast during the conversation with the teacher had been used in conversations with other students that preceded it, if used then. Where the recast deviant form had also been the one used in prior sessions, the immediate or later incorporation rate was 62%. And, when the prior form used varied between both the deviant form and that experienced in the recast, the rate was 75%. In the few (nine) instances where the prior form was the same as that in the recast, eight (89%) were incorporated immediately or later. As Boom notes, these data are consistent with the idea that recasts are most effective when a learner has something approaching the correct form-meaning mapping in their L2 representation (Mackey, 1999). Among several other analyses Boom conducted, one focusing on relationships between incorporation following recasts and target linguistic categories showed (with a caveat about small sample sizes) that recasts of phonological, lexical, irregular past, and prepositions produced the highest incorporation rates (ranging from 64% to 100%), and articles and regular past produced the lowest (33% and 38%, respectively). Overall, information in 65% of "good" recasts were incorporated, as compared with 45% of "poor" ones.

Like Boom, Loewen and Philp (2005) probed the relative effectiveness of recasts with different features in a longitudinal classroom study. Theirs was a far larger database, consisting of transcripts of 17 hours of meaning-based ESL lessons involving 12 teachers and 118 "intermediate" students, mostly from East Asia, in a private language school in Auckland. The relative frequency of recasts, elicitations, and metalinguistic feedback was quantified, together with student uptake following the three types of feedback. Students' subsequent performance on the particular items on which they had received corrective feedback was assessed using individualized immediate and delayed posttests, in which they had to make oral corrections of the deviant items that had originally led to the feedback. Of 465 "form-focused episodes" examined by researchers, 228 (49%) involved recasts, 172 (37%) involved the provision of explicit information about the problematic linguistic form, and 65 (14%) involved follow-up elicitations of responses from the learners. As indicated by posttest results, all three types of feedback, including recasts, were roughly comparably effective. On the immediate and delayed posttests, respectively, recasts were effective 53% and 50% of the time, metalinguistic feedback 65% and 49% of the time, and elicitation 75% and 59% of the time.

Of particular interest, Loewen and Philp examined the relative effectiveness in two areas, uptake and accurate posttest scores, of recasts with different characteristics. Successful uptake was found to be more likely when recasts were characterized by atypical stress (realized by pitch, additional pausing, or emphasis), declarative intonation, single changes (Boom's "simple" recasts), and multiple feedback moves. Accurate posttest scores for the targeted items were more likely when recasts had been delivered with interrogative intonation, shortened length, and only one change. More such finer grained work is needed. It is labor intensive, but has the potential both to inform classroom practice and to improve understanding of how recasts work. Findings would be easier interpreted in all such studies, however, if pretest data on targeted items were available; without them, it is impossible to tell whether recasts and the other forms of negative feedback with which they are compared are differentially effective in improving the chances of acquisition, on the one hand, or deployment of latent knowledge.

In one of the most important studies of recasts to date, Iwashita (1999) investigated the role of task-based conversation in the acquisition of Japanese grammar and vocabulary in non-native speaker–native speaker (NNS–NS) interaction, and in particular, examined the effects of different interactional moves (models and recasts) made by the NS conversational partners on this development. There were two studies: one cross-sectional and one longitudinal. A quasi-experimental (pretest, treatment, posttest and delayed posttest) design was used for both. In the cross-sectional study, 55 young adults learning Japanese as a foreign language at an Australian university were randomly assigned to treatment and control groups. All subjects took the same pretests of their knowledge of two grammatical structures, a locative-initial sentence construction and the -*te* form (an inflectional morpheme used with the auxiliary verb *iru/imas* or *aru/arimas* to indicate progressive aspect and state after an action was taken or something took place, depending on the verb) and 24 concrete nouns and verbs. Control group subjects then participated in 30 minutes of free conversation with a NS partner. Treatment group subjects performed three communication tasks with a NS for the same period. There followed immediate and delayed recognition and production posttests (one week later) for all subjects. Results showed that task-based conversation with a NS conversational partner facilitated short-term development of both grammar and vocabulary, with naturally occurring recasts statistically significantly related to an improvement on one target structure (the verb morpheme), but not the other. No relationships were found between NS and NNS interactional moves and vocabulary learning, except for "requested translation model" (confirming findings for vocabulary by Rabie, 1996).

For the longitudinal study, five of the same subjects were followed over a 12-week period during which they met with a NS conversational partner once a week for an hour to perform a variety of communication tasks. After Week 8, three of the five subjects also received intensive recasts of whichever of two new structures (specificative genitive, and adjectival phrase) was by then known to be harder for them. Findings showed that the continuous treatment over 12 weeks had a positive short-term and long-term impact on the development of whichever of the two new grammatical structures was targeted for each learner, and also on 55 vocabulary items, the latter improving continuously throughout the 12-week period. Intensive recasting positively affected development of the targeted structure for all three subjects receiving the treatment, but this was in each case accompanied by a temporary decline in accuracy in their use of the control structure (perhaps, Iwashita suggests, resulting from confusion due to the similarity of the two structures in some semantic domains, e.g., colors).[7] The two subjects not receiving intensive recasts, meanwhile, improved slightly on one of the structures, the specificative genitive, but not as much as the subjects receiving recasts of that structure, whose accurate use of it improved by approximately 50% immediately after the first intensive recast session and stayed at that level or better from then on, including up until the last delayed posttest six months later. Accuracy by the two control subjects, conversely, never exceeded 45%. Although remaining higher than before the treatment, vocabulary scores gradually declined over the series of posttests.

In a third longitudinal instructional study, M. Ishida (2002) employed a time-series design to examine the effects of intensive recasting on the acquisition of Japanese aspect morphology, *-te i-(ru)*, by three English-speaking learners and one Chinese-English bilingual learner in their fourth or fifth semester of Japanese instruction. Of eight 30-minute semistructured conversational sessions between each subject and the researcher over a period of four weeks, the first two served as pretests, the next four for the recast treatment, and the final two as posttests. The durability of any effects was addressed through a ninth session with one of the English-speaking subjects and the Chinese-English bilingual seven weeks later. The frequency of recasts of the target structure varied among the four subjects because (deliberate, but from the subjects' viewpoint, seemingly natural) provision was not controlled, depending instead on the frequency of subjects' spontaneous attempts to use nonstative verbs to express different aspects with or without the use of *-te i-(ru)*.

Analyses of change over time at the level of both individual and group showed significant increases in the accuracy of *-te i-(ru)*, from pretest means of 37% and 35% TLU in Sessions I and II; to treatment session (Sessions III–VI) means of 56%, 50%, 53%, and 59%; and posttest means (Sessions VII–VIII) of 65% and 60% (percentages rounded from those in M.

---

[7]Viewed in a more positive light, this could be further evidence of generalization, or productivity, of learning from negative feedback and, in turn, of its impact on underlying competence, not just performance.

Ishida, 2002, p. 24, Table 1).[8] TLU increased rapidly once recasting began in Session III, and stayed at or above the improved level even when the frequency of recasts dropped markedly from Session VI on. The total number of recasts provided to each learner correlated significantly with the degree of increase in that learner's TLU ($r = .96$, $p < .05$). Whereas all four learners' resultative use of *-te i-(ru)* benefited from recasting, improvement in the progressive and habitual uses varied according to each subject's developmental readiness for instruction, echoing findings by Mackey (1999). A one-way ANOVA with repeated measures showed a significant main effect for the recast treatment; the increases in group TLU means from the two pretest sessions to the four treatment sessions, and to the two posttest sessions, were both statistically significant ($F = 11.80$, $df = 2, 6$, $p < .05$, $h2 = .80$, $b = .92$). There was also a slight, but statistically nonsignificant, improvement from treatment sessions to posttest. As assessed in data on two subjects from Session IX, the improvements were durable in that mean TLU scores for each, although slightly lower than their posttest scores, were still much higher than their pretest scores.[9]

SUMMARY

In sum, in both cross-sectional and longitudinal studies, recasts have been shown to *exist* and to exist in relatively high frequencies in all classroom and noninstructional settings observed so far (although not to occur for any and all structures when needed, of course). Like children acquiring their L1, child and (seemingly, to an even greater extent) adult

---

[8]Learners' resultative use of *-te i-(ru)* with punctual verbs showed the greatest improvement in each learner's data, regardless of the number of recasts of that function, and was more accurate than their progressive use of the structure with durative verbs or habitual and perfective uses (M. Ishida, 2002, p. 35). This result differs from that of previous studies, all of which have found durative activity verbs marked accurately for aspect first, not resultative aspect and punctual verbs. M. Ishida (2002, pp. 39–44) attributes this in part to the kinds of obligatory contexts for different *-te i-(ru)* constructions created by her elicitation tasks, in part to her use of the arguably more valid accuracy (TLU) measure and a type count, rather than the frequency distribution analysis and token count (vulnerable to effects of task and of the discourse segment in which certain aspect markers and lexical aspect classes tend to be used) of previous L1 and some L2 work, and in part to the varyingly difficult processing demands of the different uses of the target structure, as judged by Processability Theory (Pienemann, 1998). Most resultative subcategories of *-te i-(ru)* are processable at lower levels of Pienemann's hierarchy, and so easier learned, whereas most progressive subcategories require information exchange between phrases and clauses or between main and subordinate clause.

[9]The subject with higher retention was taking a fifth semester of Japanese instruction at the time of the delayed posttest, whereas the subject whose scores were somewhat lower had not been taking Japanese for the previous six weeks. Once again, the suspicion is that the durability of instructional effects—in this case, of recasts—is largely a function of continued exposure, making delayed posttest scores less interesting, and certainly a less direct measure of acquisition, than the results of immediate posttests.

L2 acquirers notice the negative feedback corrective recasts contain, as evidenced by the higher proportion of corrective than noncorrective recasts they echo in whole or in part, as well as by the higher proportion of corrective recasts than other kinds of moves (e.g., topic continuations or changes) that they imitate. Pretest, posttest, experimental, and quasi-experimental studies have shown that the feedback in recasts is *usable,* and that learners can (not, will always) indeed *use* it. In some studies, at least, implicit negative feedback in the form of recasts has been found more effective in promoting durable interlanguage development than an equivalent amount of positive evidence in the form of noncontingent models of the same structures or lexical items. No studies have found models superior. Immediate incorporation of the feedback in a learner's next utterance is an unreliable measure of effectiveness, given that discourse constraints often preempt the possibility of repair in the immediately following turn, especially in classroom settings, and also because studies show that effects are sometimes delayed.

Although clearly not *necessary* for acquisition, recasts appear to be *facilitative,* to work better than models, and to do so incidentally, without interrupting the flow of conversation and participants' focus on message content. This last feature is an important advantage for teachers and students in task-based, content-based, sheltered subject matter, bilingual, and immersion classrooms. It means they can concentrate on nonlinguistic curricular content, their main concern, without worrying that language development will be impeded if they do not resort to intrusive, explicit "error correction" of traditional kinds. In some work, at least, recasts appear to be as effective as more on-record, interventionist forms of negative feedback, such as elicits and the provision of metalinguistic information about deviant production.

The jury is still out on recasts in SLA. In particular, more research is needed on the relative effectiveness of recasts and models, and of recasts and various explicit "correction" procedures. However, results thus far, of which those described previously are a small but representative sample, roughly parallel those for child L1A, and are encouraging.

THE SKEPTICS

Amidst the constrained optimism expressed by most L1A and L2A researchers working on the issue, Lyster (1998a, 1998b, 1999; Lyster & Ranta, 1997) has repeatedly drawn attention to two potential problems with recasts in classroom discourse. First, echoing an argument used by nativist critics of any role for negative feedback in L1A (see, e.g., Marcus, 1993), he has shown that the function of recasts can often be ambiguous (e.g., as between confirmation, paraphrase, and "correction"; Lyster, 1998b). Second, he has reported that whereas recasts (55%) were by far the most prevalent form of negative feedback provided by teachers in transcripts of a total of 18 hours of four content-based (maths, science, social studies, and language arts) immersion lessons for 9- and 10-year-olds studied by Lyster and Ranta (1997), they elicited relatively few instances of what Lyster and Ranta refer to (misleadingly, as will become clear[10]) as immediate "uptake," and fewer instances of such uptake, proportionately, than five other types of negative feedback that make up what Lyster calls "negotiation of form." Together, these accounted for the other 45% of negative feedback: Elicitation (14%), Clarification requests (11%), Explicit correction (7%), Metalinguistic feedback (8%), and Repetition (5%). Teachers used recasts to respond to 72% of grammatical and 64% of phonological errors, but negotiation of form to respond to 55% of lexical errors. (Similar findings have been reported by Lyster, 1998a; Morris, 2002, as described earlier; and for six Japanese as a foreign language classrooms, by Moroishi, 2001.) Because ambiguity and uptake are both important considerations when evaluating any form of negative feedback, including recasts, it is important to examine the evidence on which Lyster's arguments are based and the arguments themselves.

In useful descriptive studies of French immersion lessons at Grades 4 and 6, Lyster (1998a, 1998b) has documented the fact that the function of recasts in classroom discourse *can be ambiguous,* just as it can in talk outside classrooms.[11] For instance, the immersion teachers he observed tended to react similarly to correct and incorrect student utterances. There is no doubt Lyster is correct. Additional empirical support is to be found in subsequent stimulated recall studies by Roberts (1995) and Mackey, Gass, and McDonough (2000). Roberts asked three volunteers to view a 50-minute videotape of a beginning-level college Japanese lesson in which they had been students, to note down the meter reading every time they thought the teacher had been correcting someone, and to identify the nature of the error. The students noticed an average of one third of 27 full recasts, and 43% of 38 partial recasts (focusing on the segments of student utterances containing an error), which Roberts identified independently using a transcript of the

---

[10]Lyster and Ranta's work contains several conceptual confusions: "focus on form" (see, e.g., Long & Robinson, 1998) is equated, successively—and wrongly in each case—with "negative feedback" (p. 38), "form-focused instruction" (p. 38 and p. 42), and "analytic language teaching" (p. 42), "recast" is equated with "paraphrase" (p. 46); and implicitness is treated as an optional characteristic of recasts (p. 47).

[11]In a benchmark study of negative feedback some 20 years earlier, also conducted in immersion classrooms, Chaudron (1977) noted that "in many cases the teacher assumes that his correct model is automatically perceived, and he neglects to insure its 'intake' by the learner with new elicitative acts" (p. 43). The potential ambiguity of negative feedback, both implicit and explicit, in language classrooms has been noted by many observers, including Allwright (1975), Allwright and Bailey (1991), Calvé (1992), Fanselow (1977), Long (1977), Netten (1991), Nystrom (1983), Roberts (1995), Schachter (1981), and Seedhouse (1997).

lesson.[12] Similarly, Mackey et al. observed that whereas adult learners of ESL and Italian as a foreign language perceived recasts of their lexically and phonologically deviant utterances as negative feedback, they were very poor at spotting morphosyntactic recasts, which made up 75% of all recasts in the corpus.

Ambiguity certainly can and does arise; however, there is evidence from both the first and second language acquisition literature that learners are able to perceive a sufficient proportion of recasts as recasts in order to benefit from them. For instance, children acquiring their first language have been observed to imitate a corrected morpheme two or three times as often after corrective recasts than after any other kind of parental response providing positive evidence (Farrar, 1992), suggesting that they are able to differentiate corrective recasts from other responses at considerably better than chance levels. As noted earlier, similar findings have been obtained in L2 work by Richardson (1995), Oliver (1995), and Yamaguchi et al. (1999), with adults, if anything, appearing to be more sensitive to negative feedback than children.

In an early descriptive classroom study, Doughty (1994) found that in six hours of lessons for beginner level university learners of French, nearly 60% of teacher feedback took the form of recasts (68% on single-error utterances), the other main alternatives being clarification requests (23% on single-error utterances) and repetitions. Learners repeated 61 (22%) of 284 recasts, but only four of 173 repetitions, suggesting that they perceived the implicit corrective function of at least some of the recasts, and the contrast between the correct reformulations and their own deviant versions. (Learners also sometimes repeated other kinds of teacher feedback, however.) A finding of 22% seems low, but as noted elsewhere, the interactional structure of most teacher-fronted classroom discourse often preempts student responses to recasts, repetitions or otherwise. Even in Lyster's own study (Lyster, 1998b), 31% of recasts produced "uptake," as compared with only 5% of simple repetitions of correct learner utterances, and in the stimulated recall study by Mackey et al. (2000) referred to earlier, learners often *used* feedback (34% of incorporations) they claimed not to have perceived.

There is some suggestive evidence that it is subtle prosodic and extralinguistic cues, such as facial expressions, which help with the disambiguation (Haig, 1995), although the fact that written recasts have also been

---

[12]The three subjects in Roberts' study might have been expected to recognize *more* feedback than during the original lesson itself for having been primed to do so, and due to their direct access to the video of the lesson. (In a related study, Slimani, 1992, had students fill out an "uptake sheet" at the end of a lesson, with some "noticing" inevitably being lost because filtered through students' memory of what had transpired.) On the other hand, Roberts' subjects may also have missed some instances of feedback while noting down counter numbers and the nature of the errors concerned. Although told they could stop the tape and review segments for clarification, Roberts reports (1995, p. 169) that none of the students in fact exercised the option. Success rates might be higher in a study in which subjects were obliged to put the tape on "pause" each time they made written notes.

found effective (Ayoun, 2001; Choi, 2000) means that verbal and immediate visual cues cannot be essential. Loewen and Philp (2005) found the ambiguity of classroom recasts was greatly reduced by phrasal, prosodic, and discoursal cues teachers provided. Lyster (1998a) has suggested that in classroom conversation, the corrective function of recasts (as distinct from the confirmative function of noncorrective repetitions) may sometimes be signaled to learners by a teacher's "additional signals, such as waiting longer or looking at students in ways that invited uptake" (p. 67). Such cues would not be apparent in conventional transcripts. The ambiguity issue has been further addressed by Doughty (2003), who suggests that potential confusion arises if teachers provide negative feedback on any and all errors, as Lyster and Ranta's immersion teachers apparently did, and ambiguity can be reduced through the use of "focused" recasts. Focused recasts can provide negative feedback that is consistent, intensive, addresses fewer targets, and targets that are in intonational focus, perhaps alerting students thereby to their intended corrective, rather than purely confirmatory, function.

In sum, whereas the function of some recasts can undoubtedly be ambiguous, as Lyster points out, research findings show that the issue is neither serious enough nor pervasive enough in and of itself to negate the utility of recasts for either first or second language acquisition, in or out of classrooms. In both contexts, child and adult learners alike perceive recasts for the grammatical information they contain often enough for their impact to be more beneficial than models, and teachers can, if they so desire, use focused recasts to increase the salience of their intended corrective function. It may well be, however, that the risk of ambiguity is greater in immersion classrooms, which Lyster studied, and in some task-based or content-based lessons, where the focus is firmly on meaning, than in the communicatively focused (ESL or foreign language) language classrooms where some of the studies reported earlier were conducted and where learners, especially adults, are likely to be oriented toward language as object, and so potentially primed to perceive corrective recasts for what they are. At least occasional use of focused recasts may be required in the former cases (for useful discussion, see Nicholas, Lightbown, & Spada, 2001, p. 749).

Lyster's second concern, his skepticism about the relative utility of recasts based on a comparison of immediate "uptake" following recasts and other more explicit feedback moves, is less well founded. To interpret either the potential ambiguity of some recasts or Lyster and Ranta's (1997) finding that immediate "uptake" by French immersion students was more frequent following more explicit forms of negative feedback as indications that recasts are either ineffective or less effective than various forms of "on record" correction is unwarranted for several reasons. First, there were no data on effectiveness in Lyster's or Lyster and Ranta's research, which was purely descriptive, lacking any pre- or posttesting. Second, where *immediate* uptake is concerned (not necessarily to be equated with acquisition, as becomes clear), defined as incorporation of the input in the turn immediately following its provision, an important methodological finding of Oliver's study (Oliver, 1995) of negative feedback in the conversations of child NS–NNS dyads engaged in problem-solving games was that NNSs incorporated 10% of all recasts, but over 33% when given the opportunity and when it was discoursally appropriate to do so. *Immediate* incorporation was often impossible, Oliver (1995) showed, due to a NS continuation after a recast 16% of the time, or inappropriate (e.g., because recasts were in the form of yes–no questions) 55% of the time. Braidi (2002, p. 30) obtained very similar findings with adult NNSs: an immediate incorporation rate of 10%, rising to 34% after adjusting for possibility and appropriateness of response. In a study of child and adult ESL classrooms, teachers left no chance for learners to respond after fully one third of the recasts they provided (Oliver, 2000, p. 144).

Oliver's observation is crucial because it shows that NNSs may notice and use a substantial proportion of the feedback they receive in dyadic, task-based conversation, much more than is revealed through immediate incorporation, the only measure Lyster and Ranta apply. How much truer this must be in immersion classrooms, where curricular subject matter (e.g., history) is being dealt with through the medium of the L2. As documented by numerous studies over the years (see, e.g., Hoetker & Ahlbrand, 1969; Swain, 1985), the quality and structure of what is typically very heavily teacher-dominated classroom discourse can provide learners with relatively few opportunities for speech at all, let alone for immediate incorporation (i.e., in the very next utterance, following a feedback move of linguistic information conveyed implicitly), because the chances are high that the teacher, who controls interaction, will him- or herself continue, switch topic, or switch student.

The cognitive maturity and motivation of 9- and 10-year-old children, moreover, may also have been a factor in Lyster's data. Using Lyster and Ranta's narrow definition, R. Ellis et al. (2001) found uptake was a much higher 72% following recasts in 12 hours of ESL lessons by two teachers in a private English language school in Auckland. The students in the New Zealand study, R. Ellis et al. note (p. 311), were mostly adult Asian learners who were paying for their classes and were motivated to improve their English.

Also relevant are findings by Ohta (2000) in a longitudinal qualitative study of seven college students of Japanese as a foreign language. Ohta showed that the learners' private speech (oral language addressed softly by students to themselves, captured on tape through small lapel microphones[13]) frequently constituted what Lyster would call uptake, but would not be included in an analysis of Lyster's type, among other reasons, because it was usually not addressed to the teacher, not part of audible full-class conversation, and more often than not *vicarious* and incidental, taking the form of responses in private turns to teacher recasts directed at the whole class or to other students, and sometimes coming several turns beyond the recasts. Ohta

---

[13]It is possible that awareness that they were being observed, due to the presence of the lapel microphones, may have encouraged atypically high frequencies of echoic private speech by Ohta's subjects.

(2000) concludes that "private speech provides powerful evidence of the mental activity triggered by the noticing of contrasts between ill-formed and correct utterances. The efficacy of recasts should not be doubted based on the presence or absence of an overt oral response" (p. 66).

In general, there is no reason to expect that recasts—or any other form of feedback, including explicit procedures, for that matter—will always have *immediate* "corrective" effects, especially after exposure to single tokens of a target form, and least of all as measured by spoken production, which is often one of the very last indications of change in an underlying grammar, whether induced by recasts or otherwise. In fact, several studies (e.g., Boom, 1998; Gass & Varonis, 1994; Mackey, 1995, 1999; Mackey & Oliver, 2002; Mackey & Philp, 1998) have shown just the opposite (i.e., delayed effects). As experienced language teachers know, a learner's ability to echo a teacher's model utterance on command is notoriously unreliable as an indication that the structure involved has really been learned; it is all too often no more than "language-like" behavior. Self-correction on demand, when no teacher model is presented, is more suggestive of genuine improvement, but again should not be confused with unmonitored production, when the learner's focus is on meaning not language as object, and at most indicates potentially improved accuracy in deployment of existing knowledge, not acquisition of new knowledge (see later). Empirical evidence against attributing too much importance to immediate incorporation (as exhibited in oral production), moreover, is to be found in Mackey and Philp's (1998) findings that intensive recasting resulted in production of more complex question types, despite learners not repeating the recasts or reformulating their output at the time, and in Iwashita's finding (Iwashita, 1999) that whether or not learners' L2 Japanese vocabulary scores improved as a function of type of conversational experience depended on the type of NS interactional move, not the NNS response type. As the title of Mackey and Philp's (1998) work suggests, learners' immediate responses to recasts are quite likely to be red herrings.

A third problem with Lyster's "uptake" argument involves the nature of the comparison on which it is based. As used in the L1A (and most L2A) literature, a recast is a discourse move that is by definition *implicit* (not "generally implicit," as Lyster & Ranta, 1997, p. 47, state), designed not to interrupt speakers' focus on message, and is often immediately followed by speech by the party providing the recast that continues or changes the topic, thereby making the learner's immediate production of the correct form(s) impossible. Conversely, four of the five moves with which Lyster and Ranta compared recasts (i.e., Explicit correction, Metalinguistic feedback, Elicitation, and Repetition—of the student's erroneous utterance in isolation, usually with stress to highlight the error) were overt, and all four, plus the fifth, Clarification request (the only other implicit feedback move) were designed to *oblige* students to (try to) self-correct or (in the case of Explicit correction) to incorporate a teacher's correction before continuing with their own message. Is it any wonder, therefore, that students attempted to repair their deviant utterances when their teacher responded with such things as (examples directly from Lyster & Ranta, pp. 46–48, or based on others provided there): "You should say X" (Explicit correction), "Pardon?" (Clarification request), "Not X. Can you find your error?" (Metalinguistic feedback), "It's a ...," "How do we say X in French?" or "Can you say that another way?" (three kinds of Elicitation), or "*Le* girafe?" (Repetition)? Given the rules of unequal power, teacher-controlled, classroom discourse, they had little choice. Assessing the relative effectiveness of those five moves and of recasts, therefore, by the proportions of each that elicited immediate student "uptake" produced predictable findings, but findings that are, at best, only marginally relevant to evaluating the role of recasts in SLA.[14]

A fourth problem with Lyster's position concerns the definition of uptake employed by Lyster and Ranta, indeed their use of the term at all, which they recognized had until then been employed with a "very different sense" (1997, p. 48) in the applied linguistics literature. Lyster and Ranta (re-)defined "uptake" as

> a student's utterance that immediately follows the teacher's feedback and that constitutes a reaction in some way to the teacher's intention to draw attention to some aspect of the student's initial utterance (this overall intention is clear to the student although the teacher's specific linguistic focus may not be).... There are two types of student uptake: (a) uptake that results in "repair" of the error on which the feedback focused and (b) uptake that results in an utterance that still needs repair (coded as "needs-repair"). (p. 49)

The second part, (b), of the "needs repair" definition is crucial. Elsewhere (1997, pp. 50–51), Lyster and Ranta explain that "needs repair" includes six categories of student response to negative feedback: Acknowledgment (e.g., "Yes"), Same error (repetition by student of his/her original error), Different error (response that neither corrects nor repeats the original error, but makes a different one), Off target (response that circumvents the teacher's linguistic focus altogether), Hesitation (exactly what the word implies), and Partial repair (response that includes a correction of only part of the initial error). In

---

[14]Nicholas et al. (2001, p. 739) report that similar patterns to those observed by Lyster and Ranta (1997)—with recasts by far the most frequent form of negative feedback provided by teachers, but producing less immediate student uptake than other, more explicit forms—have been found in two studies unavailable to me by Panova (1999) and Lochtman (2000). To the extent that the two additional studies employed the same analysis, such results offer support for the robustness of Lyster and Ranta's findings, but not their validity. According to Nicholas et al. (p. 740), going beyond immediate incorporation, a third study by Havranek (1999), also unavailable to me, found recasts less likely than more explicit treatments to be associated with accuracy on tests of features that had received negative feedback during eight high school and three university classes. One would need information on such matters as the relative frequencies of the various feedback moves, the learnability of the target forms for the students concerned, and the relationships between those forms and the feedback types before being able to evaluate Havranek's results.

other words, uptake as used by Lyster and Ranta for evaluating feedback moves included both success (defined, questionably, as immediate echoing of a teacher's utterance) and failure (defined, equally questionably, as absence of such a student response). That is to say, Lyster and Ranta's definition potentially included *any* student oral response to a feedback move, even hesitation, repetition of the same error, or something completely unrelated to the feedback, as "uptake." According to their own criteria, in other words, their evaluation of feedback moves was based not on their (apparent) effect on acquisition, but on whether or not the same student spoke next, or had the opportunity to do so, regardless of what he or she said, if anything. For reasons already noted, this has little or nothing to do with effectiveness, but everything to do with the rules of classroom discourse.

In this light, Lyster and Ranta's Table 3 (1997, p. 54), reproduced here as Table 4.1, takes on a very different meaning from that attributed to it by the researchers themselves. Based on the percentages in the first two columns in Table 4.1, it could just as easily (if equally invalidly) be argued that Recasts were more successful than three out of five of the other feedback moves (Elicitation, Clarification request, and Repetition) on the grounds that, unlike those three moves, Recasts produced higher percentages of "repair" than "needs repair." In other words, focusing on apparent acquisition and/or more accurate deployment of existing knowledge (Column 1) instead of, as Lyster and Ranta did, the "no uptake" percentages (Column 3) allows for a very different interpretation, albeit one with no greater validity than that preferred by the researchers.

TABLE 4.1
Uptake Following Teacher Feedback

	Repair	Needs Repair	No Uptake
Recast (n = 375)	66 (18%)	49 (13%)	260 (69%)
Elicitation (n = 94)	43 (46%)	51 (54%)	0 (0%)
Clarification request (n = 73)	20 (28%)	44 (60%)	9 (12%)
Metalinguistic feedback (n = 58)	26 (45%)	24 (41%)	8 (14%)
Explicit correction (n = 50)	18 (36%)	7 (14%)	25 (50%)
Repetition (n = 36)	11 (31%)	17 (47%)	8 (22%)

Note. From "Corrective feedback and leaner uptake," by R. Lyster and L. Ranta, 1997, *Studies in Second Language Acquisition, 19*(1), p. 54. Copyright © 1997 by Cambridge University Press. Reprinted with permission from Cambridge University Press.

Elsewhere, Lyster and Ranta claim (see, also, Lyster, 1998a, pp. 190–191) that the fact that some of the alternative types of feedback moves do *not* provide the correct model (unlike recasts) is an advantage for language acquisition, in that self-repair without the help of a model forces learners to confront their errors more actively and allows them to "automatize the retrieval of target language knowledge *that already exists in some form*" (1997, p. 57, emphasis added). Recasts, conversely, engage learners less actively, they assert, and "there is little evidence that they can actually notice the gap ... between their initial use of nontarget forms and the teacher's reformulation, given the ambiguity of recasts from the classroom learner's perspective" (1997, p. 57). This reasoning is open to challenge. First, acquisition of new knowledge is the major goal, not "automatizing" the retrieval of existing knowledge, even for the minority of language acquisition researchers who subscribe, as Lyster and Ranta appear to, to some variant of a skill-building theory of SLA. Thus, absent a model of the correct form, their preferred feedback types can only help if the learner already knows the correct target item (i.e., can only assist deployment, not acquisition; and even then, not necessarily do so any better than recasts). Only learners who already "know" the correct form can repair successfully; for the rest, feedback moves that demand immediate second efforts may merely create further embarrassment through exposing their lack of knowledge publicly again. Second, for reasons explained earlier, ambiguity of classroom recasts is not a given. Third, to say that there is little evidence that learners can notice the gap between their utterances and recasts is to ignore research findings in first and second language acquisition, including, but not only, those reviewed and referenced earlier.

Finally, Lyster and Ranta boldly assert (1997, p. 54) that "none of the [alternative] feedback types stopped the flow of classroom interaction." However, sequences like those they cite to exemplifying their various feedback categories show this claim to be only trivially true. Interaction of *some* kind continues, to be sure, but often only with the interlocutors' attention shifted from communication to language as object, the original thread having been interrupted to address an error of some kind. To take just two of several obvious examples, this is clearly the case with Explicit correction (Lyster & Ranta, 1997, p. 46):

| Student: | La note pour le shot. |
| Teacher: | Oh, pour la, oh, pour ça. Tu veux dire pour la piqure. Piqure. Oui? |

or with Metalinguistic feedback (Lyster & Ranta, 1997, p. 47):

| Student: | Euhm, le, le éléphant. Le éléphant gronde (sic). |
| Teacher: | est-ce qu'on dit le éléphant? |

One of the reasons for research interest in recasts in SLA, although by no means the major one, is precisely that *if* recasts turn out to be sufficient (and better yet, efficient) as a means of delivering negative feedback, their implicit and genuinely unobtrusive qualities will allow teachers and learners to continue their joint focus on meaning (e.g., the substance of task-based or content-based curricula, including immersion education), while still dealing with linguistic problems. Whatever their merits as facilitators of language development, recasts really are implicit and do not interrupt communication. Conversely, even *if* more explicit alternatives are eventually found to work, or even to work better, than implicit feedback of some kind,[15] it will be at a cost to coverage of tasks, curricular subject matter, or other syllabus content. There will also be a need, incidentally, for anyone suggesting that explicit treatment of target structures is more effective than implicit treatments of some kind to explain how such treatments can be used to handle anything more than *simple* grammatical, lexical, or pragmatic problems.

In addition to their inevitable disturbance of classroom communication, explicit treatments may well have a crucial psycholinguistic drawback. Based both on theory and converging lines of experimental findings in L1 work on memory and speech production, Doughty (1999, 2003) reports that there is reason to believe that interruption of their attempts at communication in order to divert learners' focal attention to form impedes form–function mapping. Conversely, attracting roving attention to linguistic form while leaving remaining selective attention engaged in processing meaning shows promise. More promising still, Doughty reports, provision of feedback immediately *after* error commission allows comparison in working memory of the recast and the utterance that triggered it, thereby facilitating mapping.

In sum, although providing a useful reminder of the need for caution, particularly in the early stages of a research program, and especially when preliminary results are encouraging, and although he may eventually turn out to be right, Lyster's concerns seem to be unwarranted at this stage. This is not to say, of course, that the case for recasts, or for the superiority of recasts to models or to other forms of negative feedback, has been definitively made—far from it. Among other unresolved issues is the possibility that recasts (or implicit negative feedback of any type) work better for certain classes of target linguistic forms, and less effectively for other classes

---

[15]Occasional reports in the SLA literature suggesting a superiority for explicit instruction of various kinds (see, e.g., DeKeyser, 2003; Norris & Ortega, 2000) need to be treated with caution, for at least two reasons. Studies comparing explicit and implicit instruction of any sort, including negative feedback, have tended to focus on simple grammatical targets only, and to have been of short duration (typically no more than two or three hours, sometimes less), both factors favoring explicit treatments.

of items than more explicit treatments of learner error (an issue discussed further later).

A more recent challenge to the optimism about recasts has come in the shape of doubt that they are successful because of the negative evidence they provide. Leeman (2000, 2003) argues instead that recasts work because they provide *enhanced salience to positive evidence*. Leeman compared the absolute and relative effectiveness of three treatments—models, recasts, and enhanced positive evidence—for the learning of Spanish gender and number agreement on nouns and adjectives by 74 English-speaking learners randomly assigned to one of the three treatment groups or to a pure control group. Enhanced saliency was operationalized as increased (unnatural) stress and intonation (in models delivered in the form of directions for placing objects in a picture) highlighting the grammatical features proven problematic for particular learners during a prior task. For example (Leeman, 2000, p. 205), a learner who had produced an adjective, *big*, modifying the word for *apple*, a feminine noun (*manzana*) in Spanish, with the incorrect masculine ending -*o* during Task 1 (**La manzana rojo esta en la mesa*) received that item with the correct feminine ending -*a* accentuated in a direction they heard during Task 2:

La	manzana	rojA		esta	en	la mesa
The (fem.)	apple (fem.)	red (fem. + stress)		is	on	the table

The recast and enhanced positive evidence groups (but not the group receiving unenhanced models) outperformed the control group on both immediate and delayed posttests (comprising 50% training items and 50% novel combinations), leading Leeman to conclude that recasts work because of the enhanced salience they bring to the positive evidence they contain, not because they constitute negative evidence.

There are at least two problems with this argument. First, Leeman's utterances containing enhanced input differed from recasts in three ways: a lack of contingency, artificial prosody, and greater (although still low) explicitness. If naturally occurring recasts provide added salience to the positive evidence they contain, it is salience accruing from their contingent status in discourse, as immediate reformulations of deviant learner utterances, plus such factors mentioned earlier as greater learner investment, attention, and available processing resources at the moment they are received. In other words, advantages accrue from differences in the learner's underlying psychological state, not in the way the input is presented to him or her, and the ensuing opportunity for cognitive comparison with the deviant utterance, not from artificial stress that can only occur of the speaker's focus has shifted from meaning to form, in which case we are no longer talking about recasts at all. Thus, what Leeman's study actually shows (apart from providing more evidence that recasts work better than normal models) is that *on-record corrective feedback* of the sort common in traditional forms-focused classrooms, delivered at a distance from the original deviant utterances in the form of unnatural, non-contingent models (the enhanced positive evidence condition), can produce as much learning as implicit corrective feedback, delivered incidentally, unobtrusively, in the form of recasts (for some categories of simple grammar, at least)—not that recasts work because they provide enhanced input rather than negative evidence.

A second problem for Leeman's position is the findings of a study by Ayoun (2001), in which written recasts produced statistically significantly greater improved development of a target-like complex aspectual distinction between two French past tenses (*passe compose* and *imparfait*) than a traditional explicit grammatical treatment, and greater, although not statistically significantly greater, improvement than written models. In a pretest, posttest design, in Week 1, a total of 145 second, third, and fourth semester university students of French completed a pretest consisting of a two parts: a 24-sentence grammaticality judgment and correction task, and a written composition about the best birthday party they had ever attended. Ayoun then classified the students as of low, mid, or high proficiency, based on their combined score on the two tasks, and blocking on proficiency, randomly assigned them to one of three conditions: model, recast, or grammar. Each week for the next four weeks, the model and recast groups read a different story with illustrations on a computer screen. Subjects in the model condition were shown a sentence corresponding to each illustration for three seconds (e.g., in French, *She played the guitar all afternoon long*; preemptive positive evidence) and were then asked to respond to a related question (e.g., in French, *What/she/to play?*). They typed in their answer, conjugating the verb in one of the past tenses, pressed the return key, and received the next illustration and model sentence on the screen. Subjects in the recast condition were given basic sentence elements describing an illustration immediately above them (e.g., in French, *She/to play/___ all afternoon long*), typed in their answer, conjugating the verb in one of the past tenses, pressed the return key, and were then exposed to the correct French answer for three seconds: *Elle a joué de la guitare tout l'après-midi (She played the guitar all afternoon long)*—implicit negative feedback or additional positive evidence, depending on the accuracy of their response. The grammar group read traditional grammar-based lessons on the screen and did a practice activity, usually in the form of a short passage replicating the stories the other two groups were reading (positive evidence), and were then shown the answer key (negative feedback or more positive evidence, depending on whether their answers were correct). There were progress tests immediately after the first three treatments sessions (Weeks 2–4): a translation from English to French, a grammaticality judgment test, and a preference task. The posttest for each group took place immediately after their fourth treatment session (Week 5).

It consisted of a second written composition, but on a different topic from that of the pretest.

All three groups improved statistically significantly from pre- to posttest. Averaging across the three proficiency levels in each case, the recast group improved most (+39%), followed by the model group (+33%) and the grammar group (+28%). The recast group performed significantly better than the grammar group: $t(272) = 2.552$, $p = .011$, although (with a Bonferroni-adjusted alpha of .017) not statistically significantly better than the model group: $t(272) = 2.033$, $p = .043$. The written modality precludes any possibility that recasts worked as well as models in Ayoun's study because of the enhanced salience Leeman claims they bring to the positive evidence they contain, and means they must work for other reasons (i.e., as negative evidence) in that modality, at least.

Finally, a third objection to the work on L2 recasts raised of late concerns the allegedly unduly narrow definition of "corrective recast" as a response to *ungrammaticality* in learner output, and by extension, the allegedly overly narrow focus of SLA research on recasts on form, not meaning. Mohan and Beckett (2001) argue that an analysis based on such a definition (i.e., where the focus is on negative feedback on *ungrammatical* learner output) is less revealing (about form–meaning connections) than one that treats as recasts cases where (positive or negative) feedback modifies *grammatical* output in order to expand a learner's "meaning potential," to use a Hallidayan term, as in the following exchange: Student: To stop the brain's aging, *we can use our bodies and heads* ... Teacher: So, we can prevent our brain from getting weak *by being mentally and physically active?* (2001, p. 37). They point out, correctly, that this teacher utterance would not be considered a recast under the traditional analysis because the preceding learner utterance was grammatical and because what the teacher did was not correct grammar but "edit discourse" (p. 138), or as they later put it, provide a "semantic paraphrase" (p. 138). Hallidayan systemic-functional linguistics can handle the link between form and meaning that the traditional analysis is, they assert (p. 152), unable to address.

In fact, examples like those Mohan and Beckett cite from content-based ESL classrooms have frequently been studied by both first and second language acquisition researchers, who code them (operational definitions vary) as *semantic repetitions, reformulations, paraphrases, expansions, growth recasts,* or *recasts* (as distinct from *corrective recasts*) because they have *different* functions (see, e.g., Bohannon, Padgett, Nelson, & Mark, 1996; Nelson, 1987; Speidel & Nelson, 1989; VanPatten, Williams, Rott, & Overstreet, 2004). Further, whereas Mohan and Beckett's appeal to systemic-functional grammar succeeds in including a vast additional set of utterances within the category of recasts, it is not clear what explanatory insight is gained by ignoring their structural and functional differences. Moreover, criticizing studies that focus on recasts in L2 *grammatical development* because they do not also focus on other impor-

tant aspects of SLA is like criticizing studies of car engine reliability because they do not also consider safety records in collisions, or, for that
matter, some studies of functional aspects of L2 acquisition or use for not
also addressing the development of grammatical accuracy. Some studies
do one, some the other, some both. The particular insights into
form–meaning connections in language *use* offered by systemic-functional linguistics are real and valuable, but they come at a steep price in
such areas as (lack of) generative potential. The theory itself has little to
say about how language is *acquired* (e.g., about how a learner comes to
distinguish between acceptable and unacceptable forms). Such limitations probably account for why Halliday's system, 40 years on, remains
ignored in all but a minority of the world's linguistics departments, and
is virtually unheard of in research on language *acquisition.*

RECASTS AND PERCEPTUAL SALIENCE

Whereas findings on the effectiveness of recasts have been generally positive thus far, several issues remain unresolved. In particular, as noted earlier, there are indications that implicit negative feedback may be
differentially effective for certain classes of structures or forms. There are
several hints of this in the L2 recast literature—for example, the findings
by Ortega and Long (1997, p. 367) and Doughty et al. (1999) that recasts improved Spanish learners' adverb placement, but not the same learners' use
of clitic pronouns, and the suggestion by Leeman (2001, pp. 274–275) that
Spanish number agreement may have benefited more than gender agreement from recasts and enhanced positive evidence in her study for always
occurring in word-final position (whereas gender agreement does so vari-
ably) and for being more semantically transparent and phonetically substantial.

More generally, the importance of *perceptual salience* for acquisition has
been recognized in the SLA literature for some time (see, e.g.,
Bardovi-Harlig, 1987; Goldschneider & DeKeyser, 2001; Sato, 1986). Sato
(1986), for example, noted that the two Vietnamese boys she studied
showed little development in their use of lexical or inflectional past time
marking over their first 10 months in the United States, despite abundant
conversational experience. She suggested that the relative acoustic imper-
ceptibility of inflectional past time markers, plus the fact that past time reference is often easily recoverable from context or communicated via
temporal adverbials and use of interlocutor scaffolding, meant that
interactional opportunities were of less help with such features than with
linguistically more salient ones: Conversation was *selectively facilitative* of
acquisition.

The relationship between the saliency of linguistic targets and the relative utility of models, recasts, and production-only opportunities was the

primary focus of a carefully designed cross-sectional study by Ono and Witzel (2002) of the acquisition of four (supposedly) comparably learnable morphemes by 42 young adult Japanese learners of English. Ono and Witzel note that saliency is hard to define. It can be a function, among other things, of the frequency of a target form, whether the form is syllabic or asyllabic, stressed or unstressed, contracted or uncontracted, regular or irregular, bound or free, word/sentence-initial/-final or string-internal, meaning-bearing or communicatively redundant, semantically transparent or opaque, and combinations of those qualities. The target forms selected for their study were plural -s, past -ed, progressive -ing, and third person possessive pronouns, all of which fall within the same developmental stage (Stage 2), and require the same type of (lexical) processing, according to Pienemann's Processability Theory (Pienemann, 1998). Of the four, plural -s and past -ed were considered less salient, and progressive -ing and third-person possessive pronouns more salient, on the bases of phonetic substance, syllabicity, sonority, and bound/free status (see Ono & Witzel, 2002, pp. 25–29, for details considered in calculating and quantifying the relative salience of the four learning targets).

The 42 subjects, all recruited from beginner level ESL classes in Honolulu, were randomly assigned to one of three groups of 14, two experimental input groups and a production-only control group, in a pretest, posttest, control group design. The pretest consisted of two picture-description tasks, each designed to provide nine different production opportunities for each of either the two salient or two nonsalient morphemes. In the treatment phase, with targets and treatments crossed such that each of the four morphemes were treated with both recasts and models, subjects in both input groups received recasts of 15 different tokens of each of two morphemes (or confirmation models in the event that they produced target forms correctly), 15 models of the other two, and equal production opportunities for all four, while they worked to help a NS partner (one of the researchers) complete two information gap/puzzle-completion tasks. The production-only group was given the same number of production opportunities of the four forms, but no input in the form of models or recasts, while performing the same tasks. The posttest consisted of two more picture-description tasks, designed to elicit a total of 24 different tokens of the four morphemes; of those, six were carried through from the pretest and treatment tasks, nine from the treatment tasks only, and nine were novel items to assess learning (generalization) at the level of type. (See Ono & Witzel, 2002, for a detailed description of the materials and procedures in what was a very complex study.)

The whole procedure was tape-recorded and the tapes transcribed. The data from the pretest, treatment, and posttest for all groups were coded for number of obligatory contexts for the four morphemes, correct–incorrect suppliance in those obligatory contexts, suppliance in nonobligatory contexts, and misformations (*mouses, beeses, sitted, was/were paint, fixeding, stoling, her's, his/her* for *their*, etc.) in obligatory contexts. For the (experimental) input groups, in addition, recast, uptake (what turned out to be relatively few NNS repetitions of all or part of recasts containing the targeted forms), and positive input frequencies were calculated. Overall interrater reliability for coding of the four morphemes was 98.7% (k = .97). Adjusted targetlike use (ATLU) scores were calculated for each morpheme at the level of type.[16] With alpha set at .05, a three-way (3 × 2 × 4) repeated measures ANOVA was conducted with Treatment group (three levels) as the independent variable, Test and Morpheme as the two within-subject, repeated measures factors, and Morpheme ATLU (four levels) as the dependent variable. Because initial results showed Morpheme to be a significant factor, a two-way repeated-measures (2 × 3) ANOVA was conducted for each morpheme, with Treatment as a grouping factor and Test as a repeated measures factor. With results for this analysis significant for possessive pronoun, a one-way (1 × 3) analysis of covariance (ANCOVA) was carried out, with Pretest as the covariate, Treatment as a grouping factor, and Posttest ATLU as the dependent variable. For the two latter analyses, alpha was set at .01, with a Bonferroni adjustment to maintain an experiment-wise alpha of .05.

Ono and Witzel found that all three groups performed similarly on plural -s on both pre- and posttest, making comparable gains. With the other three morphemes, there was a clear advantage for recasts over models and production-only opportunities in one case, and suggestions of an advantage in two. On possessive pronouns, the recast group outperformed the model group statistically significantly, and the production-only group nonstatistically significantly. There were nonsignificant trends in the same direction—recasts producing higher posttest scores than models or production-only opportunities—for past -*ed* (where the recast group started with the lowest pretest score, but finished with the highest posttest score, and the control group showed little improvement) and progressive -*ing* (where the recast group showed the highest gain score, although not the highest posttest score). The positive results for -*ing* and possessive pronouns, as compared with the findings for plural -s, provided some support for the hypothesized greater effectiveness of recasts with salient learning targets, but interpretation of gain scores (and attainment of statistical significance) was made difficult by sometimes sizable differences in pretest ATLU scores among the three

---

[16]ATLU was calculated using the following formula (notation slightly modified from that in Ono & Witzel, 2002, p. 54):

$$ATLU = \frac{(2 \times \#correct\ SOC) + (\#mis - formations\ in\ OCs)}{(2 \times \#correct\ OCs) + (2 \times \#S\ in\ non - OCs)}$$

groups.[17] Ono and Witzel (2002, pp. 80–81) are careful to point out, moreover, that the positive impact of recasts on past -ed, although difficult to interpret for the same reasons, is potential counterevidence to the saliency hypothesis.

Whether saliency and/or other qualities of target forms influence the effectiveness of different sorts of negative feedback clearly merits further research. Knowing which classes of problematic target language features can be addressed successfully via implicit negative feedback and which, if any, require more explicit treatment would be both theoretically important, because it could help explain how recasts work, and pedagogically useful. Is it possible to predict differential effectiveness accurately as a function of saliency? And given that language *learning* is the matter at hand, will a psycholinguistically based classification of target features, rather than one based on purely linguistic contrasts between particular L1–L2 pairs, be successful, with the advantage that it will be usable cross-linguistically?

METHODOLOGICAL ISSUES

Researchers designing studies of the role of recasts in SLA face the difficulty (especially, but not only, in true experiments) of (a) preempting a metalinguistic focus, and (b) allowing sufficient input and time for specific learning effects to become apparent, while (c) maintaining control of the linguistic environment, compounded by (d) the usual problems in research on any procedure for providing focus on form. Those include the need to match target structures to control structures of comparable learnability and to learners' current proficiency and processing abilities (see Lightbown, 1998). In addition, there is a need to produce reliable and valid outcome measures sensitive enough to detect treatment effects that do not necessarily result in development to full target-like grammatical control, a process that may take longer than most experiments allow.

The following are 11 more specific considerations when designing future research on negative feedback in general, and on recasts in particular:

1. Definitions of recasts (and of other forms of negative feedback)—corrective/noncorrective, simple/complex, focused/other, complete/partial, etc.—should be clear, consistent, and operationalized (ideally, standardized across studies).

2. Researchers need to be sure to distinguish acquisition from deployment. Spanish and Japanese studies reported by Inagaki and Long (1999)

---

[17]The fact that the control group started with highest pretest scores, and the recast group with the lowest for -*ing,* and the lowest by a small margin with possessive pronouns, meant that larger gain scores were easier for the recast group. Also, there was something of a ceiling effect for the control group with past -*ed* and, especially, progressive -*ing.* Thus, it was difficult to distinguish clearly between treatment effects and those from preexisting differences among the groups on those morphemes.

and Long, Inagaki, and Ortega (1998) illustrate both success and partial failure, respectively, in this regard. One solution to the problem is to screen subjects into a study, so that there is no preexisting knowledge of target items at all. However, this can be costly in terms of subjects and time, and tends to apply easiest at elementary proficiency levels and with easier learning targets. It also risks underestimating the effectiveness of recasts because the evidence on psycholinguistic readiness (e.g., Mackey, 1999) suggests that learners benefit more when they are already beginning to produce a target item. Identifying subjects with low TLU of more advanced learning targets, so as to allow sufficient potential for measurable improvement, can be labor intensive, but may be the only viable alternative.

3. It is necessary to time provision of feedback appropriately. At the macrolevel, this concerns matching subjects with targeted linguistic items, and the notion of *learnability* (Pienemann, 1984, and elsewhere). Its importance is illustrated by Mackey's findings on the use of recasts for acquisition by her "readies," but not by her "unreadies" (Mackey, 1995, 1999) and M. Ishida's (2002) results for differential learning of various functions of her target Japanese structure. Useful proposals on how to achieve this matching successfully during communicative language teaching using Pienemann's (1998) Processability Theory are described in Dyson (2000), and may lend themselves to the design of experiments, as well. It also means matching learning targets with one another, as best exemplified to date by Ono and Witzel (2002). At the microlevel, the issues Doughty (2003) has raised about the precise moment at which feedback is provided—just before, as an interruption during, simultaneous with, or immediately contingent on, processing—become both the object of study (levels of the independent variable) and a way of operationalizing recasts. Doughty's review of the L1 experimental psycholinguistics literature suggest that results will vary according to which of these options is chosen.

4. Use of stimulated recall can help ascertain whether or not subjects actually perceive recasts as corrective feedback. This is a feature of some recent work, and is important for its potential to provide evidence that a treatment was actually delivered, in the sense of "noticed" (Schmidt, 1990, and elsewhere), for theories that hold noticing to be necessary for acquisition. For a thorough exposition of stimulated recall procedures, see Gass and Mackey (2000).

5. There is a need for more studies in the written modality, the work by Ayoun (1998), and Choi (2000), and part of the study by Doughty and Varela (1998), being two of very few such examples to date. The written mode holds greater potential for precise manipulation of degrees of saliency of target items. Also, evidence for the efficacy of written recasts is especially important for those responsible for designing distance language instruction programs.

6. There is a need to determine the durability/stability of change achieved via recasts. Only a few studies to date (e.g., Boom, 1998; Doughty & Varela, 1998; Doughty et al., 1999; M. Ishida, 2002; Iwashita, 1999; Loewen & Philp, 2005; Mackey, 1999) have employed delayed posttests. The use of time-series designs (for an overview, see Mellow, Reeder, & Kennedy, 1996), as in Ishida's and Iwashita's longitudinal studies, is promising, but not all longitudinal data on recasting will meet the rather rigorous statistical requirements for such studies (for discussion, see Saxton et al., 1998). That said, for reasons stated earlier, the importance of demonstrating lasting effects for recasts or any other (intentional or unintentional) instructional event may be somewhat overstated in the SLA literature (see footnotes 5 and 9).

7. There is a need to ascertain the robustness of findings, for example, for learners of different ages (Oliver, 1998, 2000), on different task-types (Haig, 1997; M. Ishida, 2002; Izumi, 2000; Rabie, 1996; Richardson, 1995) and, especially, for different categories of linguistic targets (Boom, 1998; Iwashita, 1999; Oliver, 1995; Ono & Witzel, 2002). By way of illustration, a finding by Izumi (2000) that recasts were generally less frequent in task-based conversation with little inherent focus on form underscores the importance of work attempting to predict the types and qualities of talk generated by different task-types. And, to reiterate, the issue of classes of problematic target features more or less susceptible to treatment via implicit negative feedback is a particularly important topic for those concerned with both language acquisition and language instruction. It is quite possible that future research will support what current findings already suggest: Recasts or other delicate, unobtrusive forms of corrective feedback work satisfactorily for some linguistic targets (e.g., meaning-bearing items) better than others, but that more explicit, more intrusive intervention is required for communicatively redundant, acoustically nonsalient forms.

8. The reliability and validity of outcome measures of the effects of recasting are a problem largely ignored in the literature on recasts to date, as in so much SLA research. For example, Lyster and Ranta's use of immediate production as a measure of uptake produced very different findings from those in Mackey's study, which employed delayed posttests. Similarly, findings based on rather blunt measures of zero-to-target change (e.g., Ortega & Long, 1997) and those using more sophisticated interlanguage-sensitive, or developmental, measures (e.g., Doughty & Varela, 1998) need to be compared.

9. The generalizability of negative feedback effects needs to be ascertained. Do recasts affect only narrowly the particular items recast, or, productively, other items in that class (see, e.g., Doughty et al., 1999; Ortega & Long, 1997), and does the scope of change vary depending on the kinds of linguistic items involved? The most direct test of the generalizability issue

to date, the study by Choi (2000), produced very positive results, but it is only one study and was conducted in the written modality.

10. Research is needed on the relative effectiveness of positive and negative evidence (e.g., models vs. recasts) in general, and of implicit and explicit negative feedback in particular (Carroll & Swain, 1993; Carroll, Swain, & Roberge, 1992), and of each for "easy" and "hard" learning targets. Care must be taken not to repeat the mistakes of some initial work on the relationship between age of onset and second language achievement. Early studies of that issue tended to be short-term, laboratory experiments, some lasting just a few minutes or hours, and employing paper-and-pencil tests. As Krashen et al. (1979) pointed out, results favoring adults over children were erroneously interpreted as showing that older learners were better than younger learners, when in reality they were simply faster in the early stages of a new language, especially if taught and/or tested in a manner suited to their more advanced general cognitive development. Now, there is a likelihood that short-term studies of negative feedback on easy target items will tend to favor explicit approaches, and this needs to be considered when interpreting results. Implicit negative feedback, such as corrective recasts, is more likely to be successful than explicit "error correction" when applied in long-term treatments of hard learning targets.

11. Finally, and perhaps most important of all in the long run, understanding must be sought of the mechanism(s) underlying the putatively greater effectiveness of negative feedback, especially recasts, compared with positive evidence. Consider, for example, the very different explanations offered by the Rare Event, Cognitive Comparison Hypothesis (Nelson, 1987, and elsewhere), the Direct Contrast Hypothesis (Saxton, 1997), and the "positive evidence with enhanced saliency" thesis of Leeman (2000). Nelson claims (e.g., 1987, p. 314) that a relatively infrequent set (less than 10%) of adult responses to child speech are *potentially* useful for development, and of those, a relatively rare subset that the child selects are what actually produce it. These "growth recasts" present challenging linguistic input strings following a child's utterance (deviant *or* grammatical) while preserving the meaning of that utterance—strings that are stored by the child and compared with similar previously stored exemplars. It is the salience of the input provided by such recasts, and by mismatches noticed through their comparison with previously stored strings, that makes them so useful for acquisition Nelson maintains, not the status of many of them as negative evidence.

Whereas Nelson predicts benefits from children comparing new structures with previously stored exemplars of "a similar sort" (i.e., potentially removed in time and somewhat different in kind), Saxton (e.g., 1997, p. 155; see, also, Farrar, 1990) emphasizes the importance of immediately contingent negative feedback (i.e., of recasts' corrective function). The juxtaposition of child utterance and adult reformulation is held to increase the likelihood of the child perceiving the *contrast* between child and adult version of the *same* utterance, and of the contrast in turn providing the basis for children perceiving the adult version as a correct alternative to their own. Leeman, as discussed earlier, considers (immediate) recasts' potential negative evidentiary function irrelevant, claiming instead, like Nelson, that it is the enhanced salience they bring to the positive evidence they contain that produces results.

As an alternative to these three, I again offer my own rather more complex explanation, restated here for ease of comparison. Recasts work, and work better than models, for certain types of linguistic targets at least, because information about the target language supplied in the form of negative feedback has several potential advantages from a psycholinguistic perspective over the same information in noncontingent utterances (i.e., as positive evidence, or models). Recasts convey needed information about the target language *in context*, when the interlocutors share a *joint attentional focus*, and when the learner already has *prior comprehension* of at least part of the message, thereby facilitating form–function mapping. Learners are *vested* in the exchange, as it is their message that is at stake, and so will probably be *motivated* and *attending*, which are conditions likely to facilitate *noticing* of any new linguistic information in the input. The fact that learners will already understand all or part of the interlocutor's response (because it is a reformulation of the learner's own) also means that they have additional freed-up *attentional resources* that can be allocated to the form of the response and, again, to form–function mapping. Finally, as Saxton claims, the *contingency* of recasts on deviant learner output means that the incorrect and correct utterances are juxtaposed. This potentially allows the learner to compare the two forms side by side, so to speak, and to observe the contrast, an opportunity not presented by (noncontingent) models.

PEDAGOGIC IMPLICATIONS

In addition to its potential psycholinguistic advantages, the implicitness of recasts makes them the least intrusive of the many possible procedures for delivering negative feedback (see Doughty & J. Williams, 1998b, for a detailed review of other options), and thus one with great potential for allowing teachers and students to focus on content (tasks, curricular subject matter, etc.) uninterrupted, while still dealing with language problems, but doing so incidentally. The fact that recasts occur as responses to learner-initiated messages also means that they fit well with a learner-centered classroom methodology in general, which is independently desirable. Models, in contrast, assume teacher-dominated classroom discourse (or incidental exposure) in addition to their other disadvantages from a psycholinguistic standpoint.

There is some evidence that recasts, like instruction in general, are differentially frequent and effective (certainly not a magic wand), depending on setting, learner age, proficiency, and type of L2 structure, all discussed earlier, as well as developmental stage and task. The need to match instructional targets to stage of learner development (Dyson, 2000) was demonstrated in the studies by Mackey (1995, 1999) and Mackey and Philp (1998). Where task is concerned, Iwashita (1999) found task-based conversation improved subjects' performance on three Japanese target features more than free conversation. Izumi (2000), however, observed that in the context of an object-assembly task, negative feedback was more likely when the learner's utterance was crucial for task completion. Utterances serving the discourse functions of identification and location of a picture, for example, elicited more negative feedback than those describing details of the picture. Izumi noted that such findings suggest the importance of the information structure of pedagogic tasks for creating the most natural opportunities for negative feedback, and for focus on form in general.

If there is a difficulty with the use of recasts as one important means (not the exclusive means, of course) of delivering grammatical information, it is in the basic modification required to the classic three-part exchange structure that numerous studies have shown to be so firmly entrenched in classroom discourse (see, e.g., Hoetker & Albrand, 1969; Sinclair & Coulthard, 1975). The traditional structure is perfectly suited for teacher-dominated conversation and for the provision of models:

Teacher: (Initiation)	What's the capital of the United States?
Students: (Response)	Washington, D.C.
Teacher: (Feedback)	Good

The joint focus, moreover, is on accuracy and forms (characterized by heavy teacher use of display questions and evaluation moves), not meaning. Recasts, conversely, can by definition occur only when the joint focus is on meaning:

Teacher:	What's the meaning of that tattoo?
Student:	It mean a fan this band.
Teacher:	It means you're a Chumbawumba fan? My goodness! A really serious fan!

or when roles are reversed:

Student: (Initiation)	Japan export more computers in 1985

Teacher:	Japan exported more than the U.S.?
(Response)	
Student:	Right Japan exported more
(Feedback)	

There is very little research on how to accomplish such a fundamental change, but what little has been reported (see, e.g., Long, Adams, McLean, & Castanos, 1976; Long et al., 1984; Long & Crookes, 1987; Nunan, 1987) suggests that it will require one or more of the following: explicit instruction for teachers in the use of referential questions, provision of materials (pedagogic tasks) of kinds that promote such discourse, use of more varied classroom organization (especially small group work), familiarity on the part of teachers with basic findings in SLA research, and a corresponding recognition on their part of the need to adopt new, supportive rather than directive, roles for parts of lessons, at least. Needless to say, such a fundamental reorientation will not be achieved overnight.

Part III
Practice

CHAPTER 5

Texts, Tasks, and the Advanced Learner

In an era of rapid globalization, there is growing recognition of the importance of foreign language abilities, especially "advanced" proficiency in a language. In many parts of Europe (the Netherlands, Belgium, Switzerland, and Scandinavia being prime examples), advanced knowledge of one or more additional languages has been routine for large sections of the population for many years. Recognition of its value is something new, however, at least as far as governing elites are concerned, in what has traditionally been the devoutly monolingual English-speaking world. In the United States, for example, the proficiency levels required to satisfy a college language requirement, typically after four semesters of obligatory study, are fairly low. The knowledge obtained (i.e., whatever survives longer than 48 hours after the final examination) is rarely enough even to satisfy basic tourist needs, and it is certainly inadequate for a career involving sustained use of the language concerned.

Recently, however, and especially since September 11, 2001, government departments, nongovernmental organizations (NGOs), corporations, militaries, diplomatic services, universities, research scientists, academic communities, and individuals alike have been waking up to the fact that advanced abilities are important, with the need for proficient speakers of less commonly taught languages especially critical. U.S. military personnel, diplomats, and other government employees who have attained the traditionally required ILR-2 level (roughly equivalent to ACTFL Advanced), which is *higher* than that needed for the typical college language requirement, have consistently been found unable to function adequately in the field. As a result, there is now considerable activity aimed at learning how best to produce adults who can perform at ILR-3 and beyond. Several federally funded projects (e.g., the University of Maryland's Center for the Advanced Study of Language, CASL, and the National Foreign Language Initiative, NFLI), have been designed to develop a new knowledge base and new national "Flagship" language teaching programs eventually capable of bringing tens of thousands of government employees up to speed.

Lagging behind these developments, unfortunately, is much real understanding of the fact that language proficiency advanced enough to satisfy career requirements is largely synonymous with knowledge of language use in specialized discourse domains. Similarly, there is little awareness of the fact that teaching and learning languages for specific purposes (LSP) involves more than substituting another four semesters of general purpose courses, or as I believe they deserve to be called, language for no purpose (LNP) courses, with a diet of so-called authentic texts.

The inadequacy of LNP has long been clear from studies like Jacobson (1986) of the problems of undergraduate non-native speakers of English conducting an experiment in the physics laboratory at a U.S. university. The problem was not so much a lack of general English proficiency, Jacobson reports, as it was students' inability to use their linguistic knowledge to do such things as assemble apparatus following written instructions, and then to run an experiment working cooperatively in a group with other students (i.e., the *tasks*). My own experience is that many international students arriving at U.S. universities have done well on tests of grammar, vocabulary, and general reading ability, such as the TOEFL, yet they are unable to function adequately in academic settings important to them. Impressionistically, the reverse is also true: Many individuals can function successfully in academic (vocational and professional) contexts despite having scored relatively low on the same tests.

Operating successfully in academic and workplace settings means being able to accomplish the *tasks* involved, with pragmatic abilities often more important than grammatical knowledge, as traditionally measured. Yet, the major consistent modification in LSP course design and materials development has been the substitution of LNP *texts* about nothing in particular with texts about subject matter in students' cognate academic, professional, or vocational field. Although a step in the right direction, there are several problems with texts of any sort as the starting point in the design of language teaching materials, especially—but not only—where adults, advanced courses, and LSP are involved.

TEXTS AND TASKS

Texts are frozen records of someone else's prior task accomplishment. A reading passage describing a chemistry experiment in a text-based program, for example, reports what someone else did in a laboratory one day.

In language teaching materials, such texts are often written in a very different forms from those that learners will encounter in real chemistry textbooks or professional journals.[1] This is mainly because language teaching materials, even content-based ones, are at best realistic examples of insider-to-outsider, specialist-to-non-specialist speech or writing, whereas the subject-specific discourse learners need to be able to handle is insider-to-insider, specialist-to-specialist communication. Moreover, language students usually have no reason to be reading the passage that day, or at all, any more than they need to read about omnipresent John and Mary going for another walk in the park and the other trivia of text-based LNP textbooks. Where methodology is concerned, teachers typically exploit both LNP and LSP texts (or think they do) by highlighting grammatical structures exemplified in them, and drawing attention to new vocabulary items. There are serious psycholinguistic problems with such an approach.

Thirty years of modern SLA research has repeatedly demonstrated that learners do not acquire grammatical structures or lexical items on demand, incrementally, one at a time, or in the order in which they happen to be presented by teacher or textbook. Instead, with some modifications due to L1 influence (see, e.g., Jansen, Lalleman, & Muysken, 1981; Zobl, 1982), they acquire structures in roughly the same order, regardless of instructional sequence or classroom pedagogic focus (see, e.g., R. Ellis, 1989; Lightbown, 1983; Pienemann, 1984). Within many structures, they traverse seemingly universal, immutable interlingual sequences, make errors as an apparently required part of the learning process, and often exhibit U-shaped and zigzag, not linear, developmental paths. Learning is not a one-step, sudden, categorical, parameter-resetting process either; it is gradual, cumulative, and often partial and incomplete. There is increasing evidence that even seemingly native-like end-state grammars in fact diverge from those of true native speakers in subtle ways (see, e.g., Sorace, 2003).

These and other findings motivate rejection of the traditional grammatical syllabus and accompanying methodology, or what I call "focus on forms." Focus on forms attempts the impossible: to impose a pre-set, external linguistic syllabus on learners, riding roughshod over individual differences in readiness to learn, even within classes of students with the same overall "proficiency." It is psycholinguistically untenable. What needs to be recognized is that most text-based instruction is simply a variant of structurally based teaching at the sentence level, the main difference being that target code features are first presented embedded in larger

---

[1]Texts in language teaching materials bear little resemblance to genuine target discourse samples learners encounter in the world outside classrooms. Every study in which language teaching materials—even supposedly LSP materials—and genuine texts have been compared has found the former to be unrepresentative in important ways (see, e.g., Barlett, 2005; Selinker, 1979; M. Williams, 1988).

units, content-area texts, before being isolated for teaching. It is still traditional focus-on-forms instruction, and suffers from the same psycholinguistic invalidity as overtly grammar-based courses. There is the same improbability that linguistic items the texts happen to contain will accidentally constitute appropriate one-step learning targets for a particular set of students on a given day. The students, after all, were unknown to the language teaching materials writer, or in the case of a genuine text, to the original author. It is guaranteed, conversely, that at least some items will be unsuitable for those students.

SLA research has also shown, however, that appropriately timed formal instruction helps. Instructed learners make speedier progress than naturalistic acquirers, for example, and may achieve higher levels of ultimate attainment in certain specifiable cases (for findings on the effects of instruction, see, e.g., Doughty, 2003; Long, 1983a, 1988; Norris & Ortega, 2000; Pica, 1983). As demonstrated by the successes of Canadian French immersion programs, students can learn much of a target language this way, but it is also clear from data from the very same programs that no amount of comprehensible input alone will result in target-like attainment. The French immersion students sometimes achieve receptive abilities statistically nonsignificantly different from those of monolingual age-peers, but continue to make a wide range of basic morphological and syntactic errors in their spoken and written production after as many as 12 years (Swain, 1991). Despite having heard literally tens of thousands of examples of French determiners and nouns marked correctly for gender, 18-year-olds continue to make errors in those areas. Mere exposure, even when the input is mostly comprehensible, is not enough. It is logically impossible, moreover, to "unlearn" L1 options in the absence of evidence in the input about their impossibility in the L2. This situation potentially arises whenever structural possibilities in a given L2 grammatical domain (e.g., adverb placement in English) constitute a subset of those in the L1 (e.g., Spanish; White, 1987). The same may be true of less marked L1/more marked L2 relationships (see, e.g., Schachter, 1990), especially if the L2 structures are perceptually nonsalient and/or communicatively redundant. Such research findings and arguments, and those of positive rate effects, rule out the radical alternative to a focus on forms, an exclusive "*focus on meaning*," advocated by Krashen, among others (see, e.g., Krashen, 1985, 1993; Krashen & Terrell, 1983).

For these and other reasons, I have argued (see, e.g., 1991, 2000; Long & Robinson, 1998) for an alternative to both focus on forms and focus on meaning that I call "*focus on form*." MP 6: Focus on form, the sixth of 10 methodological principles in Task-Based Language Teaching (TBLT; see Doughty & Long, 2003a), involves briefly drawing students' attention to problematic linguistic targets, when certain conditions are met, in context, in an otherwise communicatively oriented lesson. It can help learners "notice" items in the input (in the sense of Schmidt, 2001, and elsewhere) that otherwise may escape them, as well as mismatches between the input and deviant forms in their output, especially when there is no resulting communication breakdown that might serve the purpose.

A critical factor, in two senses, is timing. First, focus on form must be responsive to learners' current developmental stage to be effective. Put another way, the forms brought to learners' attention must be "learnable" in Pienemann's sense (see, e.g., Pienemann, 1984). Thus, in Task-Based Language Teaching (see, e.g., Long, 1985b, 1998; Long & Crookes, 1992, 1993b; Long & Norris, 2000), it is recommended that teacher intervention be triggered by evidence of difficulty with the targeted features as learners work on communicative tasks. The intervention should be constrained, however, by teachers' (conscious or unconscious) judgments as to the potential target forms' learnability (hence teachability) at the time. Focus on form attempts to respond to a learner's internal syllabus, and so is more likely to be psycholinguistically coherent. Student difficulty serving as a trigger for intervention means learners indirectly control the timing of focus on form to harmonize with their developmental readiness to learn.

Second, unlike focus on forms (and contrary to what is sometimes mistakenly implied in the applied linguistics literature), focus on form is, by definition, *reactive*, and not proactive. As a result, learners' underlying psychological state for focus on form and focus on forms is very different, and far more conducive to learning. In the case of focus on form, at the time a new form is presented (e.g., as a corrective recast, moments after a failed attempt to express or decode meaning for lack of, or misuse of, the code feature concerned), its meaning and function are likely already to be understood by the learner. This simplifies the learning task, and means that attentional resources are freed up. In focus-on-forms instruction, conversely, with no objective need for them, learners are suddenly confronted by new forms and their equally unknown functions and meanings, simultaneously. Another advantage of focus on form is that, because learners have a present felt need to communicate, coupled with awareness that they need help, they are more likely to be attending to the form in the input.

Not surprisingly, focus on form (MP 6) is amassing considerable empirical support as a methodological principle for language teaching well beyond TBLT, where it originated (see, e.g., Norris & Ortega, 2000, for a statistical meta-analysis of over 40 studies comparing focus on forms, form, and meaning). This is so despite the often unrecognized built-in advantage for focus on forms in the experimental literature to date. Incidental and implicit learning typically require longer to work, and are especially useful for hard targets. However, due to the constraints under which researchers usually operate when conducting true experiments, most comparative studies to date have focused on the acquisition of easy linguistic targets in short-term laboratory studies.

As noted earlier, focus on form is one of a set of 10 putatively universal *methodological principles* in TBLT (see Doughty & Long, 2003a), each realizable using a wide, potentially infinite, range of *pedagogical procedures*. Selection among the latter is a local matter, a function of such factors as proficiency level, learner age and literacy, and mode of delivery. Thus, to deliver MP 6, Focus on form, a classroom teacher might choose to employ a range of implicit and explicit devices—from input flood and input enhancement, through recasting and on-record error "correction," to input processing, explicit grammar rules, and the so-called Garden Path technique (for detailed discussion, see Doughty & J. Williams, 1998).

In addition to lending themselves to psycholinguistically more defensible instruction, there are several other advantages for tasks over texts in course design. One of considerable practical importance is that tasks, knowledge, and performance standards, not linguistic units of any kind, are the ways in which work is commonly conceptualized in almost all walks of life, as shown by descriptions of occupations, jobs (within occupations), and announcements for particular positions. See, the *Dictionary of Occupational Titles* (U.S. Department of Labor, 1991) or *The Soldier's Manual of Common Tasks* (U.S. Army, 1994), job descriptions in corporate personnel offices and union contracts, alike, or any current listing of job openings in education, the government, the military, the business sector, and elsewhere. The use of tasks in this manner is an important advantage whenever a needs analysis is conducted—the first stage in the design of a TBLT program, as it should be for any serious specific purpose program design, at any proficiency level.

Where good task-based descriptions are available, as they often are, the first of the two major stages in NA (identification of target tasks) is already done. Even when not readily available, task-based information is relatively easily obtained, and with greater reliability, from insiders. Domain experts, or people who do a job or train others to do it, often know very little about the language required for a job, but are usually very good at explaining what the work consists of.[2] Because they are not applied linguists, they do so, naturally enough, in terms of tasks, knowledge, and performance standards—not grammatical structures, notions, functions, or any other linguistic unit of analysis. Needs analysts, on the other hand, typically know very little about the specialized academic, vocational, or professional domain concerned. They can identify the language required (the second major stage in NA, collection of samples of target discourse surrounding target task accomplishment), however, once they understand what the work consists of (i.e., the tasks their learners will encounter in their target discourse domain).

As with needs analysis, so in classroom instruction, (pedagogic) tasks are the relevant level of analysis. Unlike "approach," "method," or "technique," for example, task is known to be a meaningful unit around which teachers can plan, deliver, and recall lessons (Shavelson & Stern, 1981;

---

[2]See Long (2005a), for an empirical study of the needs of airline flight attendants that demonstrates this.

Swaffer, Arens, & Morgan, 1982). Tasks are also meaningful and motivational units from the students' perspective. They lend themselves to courses characterized by problem solving and learning by doing. Such active student involvement tends to sustain student attention longer than linguistically focused lessons, however innovative. Practical hands-on experience with real-world tasks brings abstract concepts and theories to life and makes them more understandable. New knowledge is better integrated into long-term memory, and easier retrieved, if tied to real-world events and activities.

An important precursor to such ideas was the notion of "integral education." It was the guiding principle for all libertarian educational philosophy and practice, exemplified in the writings and experimental schools of Charles Fourier, Paul Robin, Madeleine Vernet, Sebastian Faure, Leo Tolstoy, and Francisco Ferrer, among others, and subsequently in the educational philosophies of such writers as Dewey, Goodman, Holt, Illich, and Freire. Faure's La Ruche (The Beehive), founded in 1904, is a famous example. In a rational, liberating, noncoercive, coeducational environment, "problem" children rejected by the traditional French education system learned mathematics, science, and other academic subjects effectively through operating an on-site agricultural cooperative producing eggs, milk, cheese, vegetables, and honey, and then selling them in nearby Paris to help support the school.[3]

TBLT is an example of learning by doing, and of integral education, at several levels. It aims to equip learners to meet their present or future real-world communicative needs, as identified through a task-based learner needs analysis. Then, inside the classroom, instead of studying the new language as object in order to use it to communicate at some late date, *students learn language through doing pedagogic tasks.* Almost all pedagogic tasks have a "hands-on," problem-solving quality designed to arouse learners' interest and hold their attention. Following taped street directions from a native speaker by tracing out a route on a road map of Barcelona is more likely to prepare learners to find their way when lost there than studying a narrative "reading passage" describing the route that someone else took from A to B or a "dialog" showing someone asking for and receiving directions. As the findings of the study by Jacobson (1986) suggest, assembling apparatus and conducting a chemistry experiment following spoken or written instructions is more likely to prepare students for laboratory work as part of a degree program at an English-medium university than linguistically focused study of a reading passage describing someone else doing so, let alone study of "general purpose" texts. Learning to make a particular kind of social, business, or emergency medical telephone call through acting one out, as in a role play, and/or making a real one to given specifications, in a task-based program is very different

---

[3]For English-language histories and rich sources of references on integral education, see Avrich (1980, pp. 3–68), Shotton (1993, pp. 1–32), and, especially, Smith (1983, pp. 18–61).

from listening to, or reading, a "dead" script of someone else's effort in a text-based program. Actually *doing* a task, or initially, a simple version thereof, is more relevant, comprehensible, and memorable than reading about someone else doing it.

Focusing lessons on texts, in contrast, as in most content-based language teaching, means studying language as object, not learning language as a living entity through using it and experiencing its use during task completion. Learners need to learn how to do a task themselves. Acquiring L2 knowledge tightly related to tasks similar to those that learners will encounter in their target discourse domains increases the likelihood of learning being successfully generalized to those domains. A basic law of transfer of training is that the closer a training task is to a transfer task, the more likely the training is to transfer.

In sum, tasks have several advantages over texts as the starting point for course design, and the second methodological principle of TBLT is MP 2: "Use tasks, not texts, as the unit of analysis." The advantage of tasks over texts is especially (but not only) obvious for advanced adult learners, whose needs are usually fairly easily identified in terms of target tasks. This is part of the reason for the growing interest in TBLT (e.g., for the design of the federally funded U.S. National Flagship programs mentioned earlier). TBLT has considerable potential for facilitating needs analysis, producing courses designed systematically to be relevant to learners' precisely specified communicative needs, for developing functional foreign language proficiency without sacrificing grammatical accuracy, and for harmonizing the way languages are taught with what SLA research has revealed about how they are learned.[4] It would be wrong to present task-based instruction of any kind, including TBLT, as a panacea. There are problems, to which we now turn.

SOME PROBLEMS WITH TASKS

A number of problems arise when task is selected as the unit of analysis, one of which is *sequencing*. This issue arises, of course, but is rarely addressed scientifically, regardless of the kind of syllabus used. The solution implicit or explicit in most grammatically based materials is some intuition-based and question-begging notion of *linguistic complexity*. Beyond some obvious differences (sentences containing relative clauses are "harder" than equational "NP copula NP" strings, etc.), the linguistic complexity criterion quickly gives out. Is this type of relative clause more complex than that one (for speakers of language X learning language Y)? Are

---

[4]By no means do all so-called task-based courses offer these advantage, it should be noted, and none to date do so that I am aware of in the commercial publishing sector. Most, like much writing in support of "task-based learning" in the literature, are task-based in name only, tasks providing thin cover for covert grammatical, notional-functional, or lexical syllabuses of some kind.

relative clauses more complex than conditionals, or the subjunctive more complex than the past perfect? Another possibility is *utility*, or coverage (*disponibilite*): Most "useful" structures come first. Again, intuition rules, and one might ask, "Most useful for whom?" The same problems afflict notional-functional materials. Should sequence be taught before duration, requests before apologies, or sequence before requests? And, if so, is the answer altered by the structural and/or lexical realizations of the notions or functions selected for early presentation within target language X or Y or across languages X and Y? In some recent lexically based materials, corpus-based frequency data are employed, with texts in early books in a series such as COBUILD written using the X00 most frequent words (in non-domain-specific, general corpora). Although at least having some empirical basis, the problems with this approach include the fact that there is no reason to expect any particular text to conform to mean word frequency data, that frequency will vary by (specific purpose) discourse domain, and that grammatical structures in so-called lexically based materials are still sequenced intuitively. None of these criteria have much to do with learnability, moreover, and all pertain to units of analysis that are ruled out on psycholinguistic grounds.

My own solution in TBLT is not to attempt to sequence either target tasks or target task-types (i.e., the final *product* in a task-based syllabus) on analogy with native-like grammatical structures. Rather, the focus should be on steps in the learning *process*, instantiated in *pedagogic tasks*, the initially simpler, progressively more complex approximations to target tasks on which students and teachers work in the classroom. It should be possible to sequence pedagogic tasks rationally in terms of (inherent, unchanging, and objectively measurable) pedagogic *task complexity*, with *task difficulty* (which varies as a function of the interaction of a given task complexity with attributes of specific learners, such as their L2 proficiency) modifiable as needed by alterations to *task conditions* (the circumstances under which the pedagogic tasks are carried out, e.g., with or without task familiarity or planning time). By working through a series of pedagogic tasks, learners can build up the abilities needed eventually to perform the *target tasks* identified by the needs analysis, to the standards required. A promising model of relationships among task complexity, task difficulty, and task conditions, and of all three to interlanguage accuracy, complexity, and fluency, has been offered by Robinson (2001a, b, 2003). Robinson defines task complexity in two ways, with one dimension involving resource-directing elements of a task, and the other dimension constituted by resource-depleting task demands.

It *should* be possible to sequence pedagogic tasks rationally, and to identify the characteristics of tasks that predict complexity, as well as the effects of task complexity, difficulty, and conditions on interlanguage use, but the jury is still out. These are all currently areas of intensive research in SLA. To date, researchers have had only mixed success at predicting interlanguage accuracy or complexity from putative pedagogic task complexity (see, e.g., Gilabert Guerrero, 2004; Kong, 2002; Y.-G. Lee, 2002; Robinson, 1995b, 2001b; Skehan, 1998). Worse, this work has been conducted with what should have been relatively easy tasks to grade, mostly having to do with concrete, low inference dimensions suggested nearly two decades ago (Long, 1989), such as a here-and-now versus there-and-then orientation, the number of options available or choices to be made when completing a task (e.g., selecting aircraft seats in economy and/or business class, aisle and/or window, or on this or that flight), the number of elements involved (e.g., cars and pedestrians in each of a series of three pictures depicting a traffic accident), and the degree of difference (in size, shape, color, etc.) between similar elements (see, e.g., Y.-G. Lee, 2002). It would undoubtedly be harder still to sequence more abstract pedagogic tasks, such as three versions of a political speech, a treaty negotiation, or a sales pitch. As frequently happens in the early stages of a new line of work, moreover, several methodological problems have weakened the studies thus far. For example, whereas expert raters typically agreed unanimously on the relative complexity of different versions of tasks to be used in experiments before a study began, some subjects in the studies themselves (see, e.g., Y.-G. Lee, 2002) occasionally perceived the whole task differently and/or took short-cuts that had the effect of simplifying what was supposed to be a more complex version.

While waiting for the research to bear fruit, TBLT course designers draw on findings to date, and add theoretical motivation from the SLA and applied linguistics literatures. They are then obliged to blend the two with a combination of knowledge from accumulated teaching experience and what remains most materials writer's only source: intuition. Figure 5.1 shows the structure of a module of TBLT materials developed for first semester students in a federally funded demonstration project on TBLT for the teaching of Korean as a foreign language at the University of Hawai'i (Long, Doughty, et. al., 2003) The results of a needs analysis (Chaudron et. al., 2005) had revealed that over 90% of learners had already visited and/or intended to travel to Korea for a variety of reasons. The first module developed for one group of students (near beginners) comprised a series of seven pedagogic tasks motivated by the target task, "Following street directions." The eighth pedagogic task listed in Figure 5.1 is under consideration for development. (*Prototype Directions Module* provides a rationale and illustrates the process of pedagogic task development in English. This template was used to develop the Korean materials. For further details, see Chaudron et al., 2005; and for a video demonstration of the module in classroom use, Long, Kim, Y.-G. Lee, & Doughty, 2003.)

Another unresolved issue (again, as with all syllabus types, not just task syllabuses) is *transfer* of learning. As the language assessment literature attests, little is known about how far, if at all, learners' ability to perform one

Target task: Following street directions

Pedagogic tasks:

1. Listen to numerous samples of target discourse surrounding target-task completion, i.e., genuine examples of Korean NSs giving directions.

2. Listen to fragments of elaborated directions while tracing them on a very simple, 2-D map. Within this task, the fragments increase in complexity.

3. Listen to ever more complex fragments while tracing them on a more complex, 3-D map, periodically answering questions like *"Where are you now?"*

4. In collaborative pairs, read scripted (first pair) and follow (second pair, collaboratively) directions on a simple map.

5. Using real maps of Seoul, listen to elaborated target discourse samples and follow routes already marked on the map with colored lines.

6. Given a starting point, follow an unknown route, with periodic comprehension checks like *"Where are you now?"* along the way, and at the end.

7. Do the same as in PT 7, but in one "go," i.e., without breaks or comprehension checks along the way, but labeling the building/space/etc. on the maps at the end of each route as evidence of having successfully reached the destinations.

8. Virtual reality map task. Using video from the target location and audio of the target discourse, complete a simulation of the target task. (This can be used as the exit test if the physical location of the learners is not in the target community.) For a Spanish prototype, see, e.g., En busca de esmeraldas <http://marta.lll.hawaii.edu/enbusca/> (Gonzalez-Lloret, 2003).

FIG. 5.1. Pedagogic task sequencing in a demonstration TBLT module.

task predicts their ability to perform another. How close do the training and transfer tasks need to be? Is it possible to test the underlying *construct* and assume that success with one or more tasks based on it indicates capacity to perform (any?) other such tasks, or must learners' performance on each target task be assessed separately? The answers to these questions have implications far beyond testing alone (and beyond task-based performance testing alone). Where course content is concerned, for example, the further abilities generalize, the fewer the target tasks that will need to be included in course materials. Theoretically, should no generalization occur, it would be necessary to write series of pedagogic tasks for each target task, which would clearly be uneconomical in terms of time, effort, and funding. For discussion of these and related issues, see Bachman (2002); Mislevy et al. (2002); Norris (2002); and Norris, J. D. Brown, Hudson, and Yoshioka (1988). Once again, transfer of training is a (hidden) issue for all course designers, no matter the type of syllabus employed. The fact that most are unaware of it or ignore it does not absolve advocates of task-based syllabuses from finding a solution.

A third issue concerns *types of target discourse samples*, specifically, optimal types of modifications to make to L2 input to which students are exposed. Although tasks are the unit of analysis in TBLT, and the starting point for materials writing, many target tasks either contain or result in texts. TBLT often involves texts, too, therefore, but not as ends in themselves. Students are exposed to, and create, relevant samples of target language discourse when those are natural components, or products, of doing pedagogic tasks. The question arises, therefore, as to what sorts of spoken or written texts they should encounter and create, when, and how. Of the three problem areas noted, this is the one where most progress has been made.

Both genuine (so-called authentic) texts and the most popular alternative, linguistically simplified ones, suffer from serious disadvantages as data for language learning. Except when used at very advanced levels, *genuine texts* (originally spoken or written by and for native speakers, not intended for language teaching) impede learning by confronting learners with large amounts of unknown language (new vocabulary, complex syntax, etc.) without compensatory devices to facilitate comprehension. They present too dense a linguistic target, due to the lack of redundancy. The traditional "solution" to this problem is linguistic simplification. *Simplified texts* improve comprehension through use of shorter sentences and restricted vocabularies and grammars. However, they tend to result in stilted, basal-reader-type input, with the typical materials writer's desire for them to be free-standing and self-contained resulting in their also lacking in implicitness, open-endedness, and intertextuality, among other features of natural discourse. They impede learning, also, by modeling unnatural *usage* (e.g., noncollocations), not *use* (Widdowson, 1972), and—a critical flaw—by removing from the input many of the very items to which learners need to be exposed if they are ever to learn them. Fortunately, there exists a third alternative, with considerable promise: *elaboration.*

Elaboration is an approach to improving the comprehensibility of spoken or written texts that grew out of research findings on "foreigner talk discourse" in the 1970s and 1980s. Contrary to what was asserted by some

SLA theorists at the time, studies showed that, aside from use of slower rate of delivery and shorter utterance length, both of which improved comprehensibility, native speakers (NSs) *simplified* their speech rather little. Instead, they succeeded in getting their message across to non-natives (NNSs) mostly by means of discourse-level alterations, seemingly made with different degrees of awareness, which helped non-native interlocutors cope with quite complex (retained) vocabulary and syntax. The *interactional structure* of NS–NNS conversation was modified during *negotiation for meaning* (more so on some kinds of tasks than others, e.g., closed and two-way tasks) by more frequent use of such devices as simple and brief treatment of conversational topics, a here-and-now orientation, confirmations, (exact or semantic, self- and other-, complete or partial) repetitions, reformulations, confirmation checks, comprehension checks, clarification requests, and various other kinds of scaffolding (e.g., decomposition, lexical switches, a NS preference for yes–no or or-choice over *wh* questions, and NS acceptance of unintentional NNS topic switches). (For data and reviews of the literature, see Gass, 2003; Long, 1983b, 1983c, 1996; Wesche, 1994.) Similar findings hold for NNS–NNS conversation (Pica, Lincoln-Porter, Paninos, & Linnell, 1996).

Elaboration in materials design involves adding redundancy and regularity to a text, and often more explicit signaling of its thematic structure, followed by gradual removal of the "crutches" the modifications provide as learner proficiency increases. *Redundancy* is achieved by such devices as repetition, paraphrase, provision of synonyms of low frequency lexical items in appositional phrases, a preference for full NPs over pronouns, and more overt marking of grammatical and semantic relations already retrievable from context (e.g., use of optional Japanese particles to mark topic, subject, object, directionals and locatives). *Regularity* is attained through such devices as parallelism, more frequent use of canonical word order, retention of optional constituents, for example, subject pronouns in pro-drop languages, full NPs instead of anaphors, and matching order of mention to order of occurrence (*The plane took off before the family reached the airport*, in preference to either *The family reached the airport after the plane took/had taken off* or *When the family reached the airport, the plane had taken off*). Greater *explicitness* of logical relationships often involves use of (optional) overt marking of grammatical and semantic relations, mentioned earlier, and the addition of intra- and intersentential linkers, such as *but, so, however, although, therefore, on the other hand, as a result*, and *whereas*. Several of these processes and features can be seen in the sample texts in Figure 5.2.

With the exception of slower rate of delivery, including use of pauses (Blau, 1990, 1991; Griffiths, 1992; Kelch, 1985) and macro-markers (i.e., signals or meta-statements about major propositions or transition points in a lecture, e.g., *What I am going to discuss next is X*, or *That was the reason why X*; Chaudron & Richards, 1986; but see, also, Dunkel & Davis, 1994), single

---

Genuine (NS-NS) version

The advent of the personal computer is often claimed to be of great social significance. The widespread availability of word-processing, for example, has supposedly had a major impact on the productivity of those who have traditionally made their living at least in part from the pen, or in recent years, from the typewriter ...

Simplified version

This is the age of the personal computer. People usually say the computer is very important for society. Word-processing, for example, is easy for everyone. Many people have to write with a pen or a typewriter as part of their work. Word-processing, people think, increases the amount of writing ...

Elaborated version

The advent, or arrival, of the personal computer is often claimed to be of great significance for society. For example, word-processing is easily and widely available to everyone. This widespread availability of word-processing has caused a major increase, people think, in the amount of work, or productivity, of a certain group of people. The group whose productivity has supposedly been helped in this way is those people who have always traditionally made their living, that is, earned money, at least in part from writing, either with a pen, or in recent years, with a typewriter ...

FIG. 5.2. Computer literacy for everyone?

adjustments are alone usually insufficient to improve the overall comprehensibility of whole passages or lecturettes (Blau, 1982; Parker & Chaudron, 1987). In concert, however, elaborative devices have usually been shown to improve the comprehensibility of both spoken and written input significantly, or at least not significantly less than linguistic simplification, and without its harmful side effects. Both simplification and elaboration facilitate comprehension most for students at lower levels of proficiency (Blau, 1982; Long, 1985a; Tsang, 1987), but there is evidence that elaborated input can aid reading comprehension (Oh, 2001) and listening comprehension and incidental vocabulary acquisition (Urano, 2000) among relatively more advanced learners as well; some studies have found that elaboration assists higher proficiency students more (see, e.g., Chiang & Dunkel, 1992). Perceived comprehension of elaborated spoken discourse is also higher (Long, 1985a). Elaboration achieves its positive effects despite producing what are often very considerable increases in utterance/sentence length, syntactic complexity, and overall text length. As assessed by standard readability measures, the difficulty of elaborated texts in some studies is several grade levels higher than that of the simplified equivalents, and often higher even than the original NS baseline versions. To illustrate, the descriptive statistics for the computer literacy texts are shown in Table 5.1.

Despite elaboration's effects on overall text length and readability, subjects exposed to elaborated input in many of some 20 studies of listening and reading comprehension to date (for review, see Chung, 1995; Kim, 1996, 2003; Oh, 2001; Silva, 2000; Urano, 2000; Yano, Long, & Ross, 1994) have demonstrated improved comprehension, and often comparable (statistically nonsignificantly different) levels of comprehension to groups exposed to simplified versions of the same texts (e.g., R. Brown, 1987; Oh, 2001; Pica, Doughty, & Young, 1986; Tsang, 1987; Yano et al., 1994). Subjects in simplified and (less often) elaborated conditions have also statistically significantly outperformed students confronted with the genuine (baseline) versions in many cases.

To illustrate, Yano et al. had 483 Japanese college students read 13 passages (ranging in length from a short paragraph to two pages) in one of three versions: genuine, simplified, or elaborated. Comprehension, assessed by 30 multiple-choice items, was highest in the simplified group, but not statistically significantly higher than in the elaborated group, despite the fact that the elaborated passages were (a) 16% more complex in words per sentence, 60% longer, and nearly one grade level harder in readability than the genuine texts; and (b) 125% more complex in words per sentence, 50% longer, and six grade levels harder in readability than the simplified texts. Subjects in all three conditions had the same amount of time to complete the reading task and comprehension test. Type of text was found to interact with type of comprehension task: replication, synthesis, or inference. Performance on inference items was best among readers of elaborated texts. Yano et al.'s results, including the interaction effect for

TABLE 5.1
Descriptive Statistics for the "Computer Literacy" Texts

	NS	Simplified	Elaborated
Words	55	52	98
Sentences	2	5	4
s-nodes	4	8	10
Words per sentence	27.5	10.4	24.5
s-nodes per sentence	2	1.6	2.5

elaboration and question type, were replicated in a study with Korean secondary school learners of English as a foreign language by Oh (2001). Retention of the original propositional content was also best in elaborated texts (Long & Ross, 1993), a finding with especially significant implications for educational systems operating through the medium of a second language, as it suggests that, unlike simplification of teacher speech or textbook language, elaboration need not result in serious dilution of curriculum content over time.

In a later study, Urano (2000) had three randomly formed groups of 10 college-age Japanese learners of ESL read 10 English sentences presented to them on a computer screen in one of three versions: baseline (NS), lexically simplified, and lexically elaborated. A fourth group viewed 10 distractor sentences for an equivalent time period. Reading comprehension was measured by mean reading time and comprehension questions on each sentence. A surprise vocabulary test in two sections, form recognition and meaning recognition, assessed incidental vocabulary acquisition. Urano found that both lexical simplification and lexical elaboration produced significantly improved comprehension, as shown by a (shorter) mean reading time than was required by those in the baseline condition. Incidental vocabulary acquisition, as assessed by the form recognition measure, was greater for higher proficiency students in the elaborated than in the baseline condition, whereas lower proficiency students did better with the simplified sentences than those in the baseline group. Incidental learning was small across all conditions, however, probably due to a single exposure to each target lexical item being insufficient.

In a listening study, Toya (1992) provided brief training in the recognition of six devices (first identified by Chaudron, 1982, in a study of elaboration in teacher speech) used to provide implicit and explicit explanations of lexical items, and then compared the effects of implicit (IE) and explicit (EE) explanations (two kinds of elaboration) of unknown vocabulary items on the acquisition of those items. In the study, 109 Japanese university students listened to two texts three times each, taking a receptive test of the target items' meanings after each exposure, and a delayed posttest, 4 weeks later. In each text, one third of the 12 target lexical items received IE, and one third EE, while the remaining items were left unelaborated, as in the original, items and treatment being rotated and counterbalanced in the three forms of each text. Understanding of the target items was found to improve with each exposure, and pretest to delayed posttest gains were significantly greater in all three conditions. The EE version, however, produced statistically significantly higher scores than both the IE and baseline versions (although that difference had all but disappeared by the delayed posttest, presumably due simply to lack of exposure to the items during the intervening period). The more explicit explanatory devices (definition, naming, and description) appeared to induce more noticing of the targets than did the implicit devices (apposition, parallelism, and paraphrase),[5] but perhaps also resulted in something more like intentional learning, compared with the more incidental IE condition.[6] The beneficial effects of elaboration were clear, nonetheless. In a subsequent listening study, Derwing (1996) showed that EE instructions were significantly better comprehended by 12 Korean high school EFL teachers than unelaborated and excessively elaborated versions. Also, the EE, IE, and unelaborated versions were significantly better comprehended than the excessively elaborated versions by 74 "high-intermediate" and "advanced" EFL college students from various L1 backgrounds, and by 19 Japanese students attending high school in Canada.

As measured by EFL students' ability to position utensils on drawings of a kitchen, R. Ellis, Tanaka, and Yamazaki (1994) found significantly greater comprehension of directions in the form of an interactionally modified text (in the making of which learners had been allowed to request clarifications and confirmations), than of either a baseline (NS) or premodified (NNS) version. Vocabulary acquisition was also greater in the interactionally modified condition than in the other two. In a follow-up analysis of several features of the directions, R. Ellis (1995) found "range," the number of different directions in which a target item occurred, to be positively correlated with vocabulary learning, and length of definition and number of defining characteristics (i.e., something akin to excessive elaboration) negatively correlated.

As noted, elaboration achieves roughly comparable improvement in comprehension to simplification in studies like these, despite subjects in the elaborated conditions having to handle significantly longer texts containing significantly more complex input, and do so in the same amount of time. In laboratory studies, greater complexity and length is not a problem, because they are typical by-products of elaboration that *disfavor* the hypothesis. They need not muddy pedagogical waters, however. *Modified elaboration*—essentially, elaboration, followed by the one form of simplifi-

---

[5]The following were two of the target lexical items (underlined here) and explanation types [EE] or [IE]: (a) "But since they [the Greeks] could not dive into the waters, they could not lay bare these secrets. Lay bare means to make things know." [EE] Or: "But since they [the Greeks] could not dive into the waters, they could not lay bare these secrets, or make these secrets known." [IE] (b) "And they also learned how not to contaminate the oceans. You know, when the water is contaminated, it is dirty and polluted." [EE] "And they also learned how not to contaminate the oceans, or not to make the ocean dirty." [IE] The possibility that EE might have worked better due to the (natural) tendency for target items to be repeated in EE seems not to have been realized, because and item-by-item comparison of posttest means showed that five items whose EE did *not* involve such repetition produced equivalent improvements over IE to those that did.

[6]Toya (1992, p. 94) notes that knowing they would be tested only on the vocabulary items, and not on overall comprehension of the passages, may well have led subjects to concentrate on the former and pay little attention to the latter. This strategy would have disfavored IE, whose effectiveness resides largely in the impact it has on improving overall comprehension of target forms in context.

cation found typical of NSs in the original foreigner talk research, reduction of utterance or sentence length—will deal with the unwanted side effects of pure elaboration (see Fig. 5.3 and Table 5.2).[7] Elaborated texts employed as target discourse samples in TBLT courses, and texts in those courses created by learners as they work on progressively more complex approximations to target tasks, are both authentic in two ways. They are relevant input for the learner because, based on genuine target discourse samples for the tasks concerned, and they are psycholinguistically realistic, in that they are input processable by, and output processed by, the learner.

The crucial thing to note about all the comparative findings on comprehension, to reiterate, is that elaboration does its work *without* bleeding the

---

1. *Genuine (NS-NS baseline) version*

Because he had to work at night to provide for his family, Paco often fell asleep in class.

2. *Simplified version*

Paco had to make money for his family. Paco worked at night. He often went to sleep in class.

3. *Elaborated version*

Paco had to work at night to earn money to provide for his family, so he often fell asleep in class next day during his teacher's lesson.

4. *Modified elaborated version*

Paco had to work at night to earn money to **provide for** his family. As a result, he often fell asleep in class next day during his teacher's lesson.

provide for means   a. educate
                                        b. leave
                                        c. support

FIG. 5.3. Paco sentences.

---

[7]"Provide for" is shown enhanced in the modified elaborated version to indicate another option that has sometimes been found to improve vocabulary development in modified materials (see Chung, 1995; Kim, 2003), input enhancement. A similar effect can be achieved in listening materials by added stress and/or a brief "priming" pause before key meaning-bearing lexical items.

TABLE 5.2
Descriptive Statistics for the Paco Sentences

	NS	Simplified	Elaborated	Modified Elaborated
Words	18	19	27	29
Sentences	1	3	1	2
s-nodes	4	4	5	5
Words per sentence	17	6.33	26	14.5
s-nodes per sentence	4	1.66	5	2.5

input of items to which students must be exposed if they are to progress. Genuine texts retain those items, but are usually too complex for all but "advanced" learners, and so largely unusable as input for acquisition. The undeniable improvement in comprehension that simplification achieves comes at a high cost where language acquisition is concerned—removal of many, usually most, of the learning targets. Elaboration, conversely, retains almost all unknown material, meaning that new language is available for acquisition.[8]

In sum, elaboration of listening and reading comprehension materials is one practical application of naturalistic and laboratory SLA research in the 1970s and 1980s on the characteristics of foreigner talk discourse (i.e., language use by native speakers communicating with non-natives). *Elaborated texts* achieve almost as great an increase in comprehension as simplified ones, but do so without impeding acquisition. Comprehension is improved through adding redundancy (eight types of repetition, paraphrase, etc.) and transparency (clear signaling and marking to increase topic saliency, reversion from subject-predicate to topic-comment constructions, matching order of mention to chronological sequence of events, preference for a here-and-now orientation, etc.) and—especially, but not only, in spoken texts—by slower rate of delivery, and where interactional discourse is concerned by frequent use of clarification requests, comprehension checks, and confirmation checks. Retention of unknown linguistic targets (new vocabulary and syntax, collocations, etc.) means learners are exposed to them—yet with comprehension, due to the elaboration—exposure that is essential if the forms are to be learned, the new forms mapped

---

[8]See Chaudron et al. (2005) for a detailed description of the design and production of some elementary-level Koren TBLT materials, including elaboration of target discourse samples, from task-based needs analysis to classroom implementation.

onto their meanings and functions. Texts should be presented to learners not as found objects for study, as in text-based programs, but rather as a natural component of doing *tasks*.

MP 3: "Elaborate input" is theoretically motivated and sufficiently supported empirically to merit its status as another of the 10 methodological principles in Task-Based Language Teaching (see, e.g., Doughty & Long, 2003a; Long, 2006). Listening (and reading) comprehension materials, from political speeches, through telephone conversations, to academic lecturettes, should be elaborated and not simplified. Elaborated texts are almost as good for comprehension as simplified versions and better for language learning, which is a program's primary concern. Traditional belief in the value of so-called authentic *text*-based language teaching needs rethinking.

CHAPTER SIX

SLA: Breaking the Siege[1]

This chapter summarizes, and responds to, three broad accusations made against SLA research in recent years. The charges are sweeping enough: sociolinguistic naiveté, modernism, and irrelevance. It then identifies some structural problems that weaken SLA as an embryonic discipline, as shown not so much by the charges themselves as by the reception they have been given in some quarters. The discussion wraps up with one or two suggestions concerning how some of the structural problems could be remedied.

THE CHARGES

Against a background of three decades of steady growth and reasonable success, the field of SLA has recently been loudly criticized from a number of quarters and these criticisms have been entertained in scholarly journals. Several charges have been leveled, mostly by individuals outside the field, at work in SLA in general, and at named individuals in particular. Three of the most frequent are: sociolinguistic naiveté, modernism, and irrelevance (at least, irrelevance for language teaching). The three charges are sometimes made separately, but are also (in the first two cases, especially) often confused and conflated. The chapter attempts to summarize

---

[1]I thank Catherine Doughty and Kevin Gregg for useful comments on an earlier draft of this chapter. Neither agrees with everything that follows, or, of course, is responsible for any remaining errors of fact or interpretation.

two representative critics' arguments in each case as fairly as possible, letting their own words speak for them, and then shows that most of the accusations are themselves naïve and irrelevant, albeit potentially very damaging, nonetheless, which means that they need to be addressed. It is important at the outset to grasp the *scope* of the charges: Even when specific individuals or studies are targeted as examples of the problems critics perceive, it is often the field or SLA as a whole that is under siege.

SOCIOLINGUISTIC NAIVETÉ

A number of writers, most notably Firth and Wagner (1997), have criticized SLA research in the most sweeping terms for "ignoring social context" (see, also, Firth, 1996; Tarone, 1997; Wagner, 1996, and, especially, the important and more constructive work of Rampton, 1987, 1995, 1997a, 1997b, 1997c, and elsewhere). By this, Firth and Wagner mean such things as the following: (a) SLA researchers should take account of the fact that learners, including participants in SLA studies, have social identities in life (e.g., "father," "friend," or "business partner," in addition to those of "NS," "NNS," and "learner")—categories about which Firth and Wagner, like others (e.g., Davies, 1991), are highly skeptical; (b) acquisition often takes place in contexts in which little or no access to NSs is available[2]; (c) conversational norms vary, so there is no standard way of speaking that is modified for learners, casting doubt on strong claims for the role in acquisition of certain kinds of experiences with the target language; and (d) (surely uncontroversially) it can be unwarranted to generalize findings from experimental to natural settings. Firth and Wagner's criticisms are ostensibly aimed at "discourse" studies in SLA. However, as suggested by the title of their article (Firth & Wagner, 1997) in a special issue of *the Modern Language Journal*, their target is much broader. Any ambiguity as to what they really have in mind is dispelled in the very first lines of their abstract:

> This article argues for a reconceptualization of SLA research that would enlarge the ontological and empirical parameters of the field. We claim that methodologies, theories and foci within SLA reflect an imbalance between cognitive and mentalistic orientations, and social and contextual orientations to language, the former orientation being unquestionably in the ascendancy. (Firth & Wagner, 1997, p. 285) and in an early footnote: "our critique of SLA is based on the view that the field has core interests, theoretical predilections, methodologies, and basic assumptions. It is this SLA 'core' that has the focus of our attention here." (p. 296, fn. 1)

---

[2]"NS," "NNS," and "learner" are categories that Firth and Wagner alternately condemn and utilize themselves.

Firth and Wagner, it transpires, believe SLA researchers should give up their preoccupation with what goes on in the learner's mind, with what Rampton (1987, p. 49) refers to as the space between speakers and their interlanguage grammar. The focus, they assert, should shift from such linguistic and "mentalistic" matters as input, innate knowledge, cognitive factors, linguistic processing, mental representations of L2 grammars, and mechanisms and processes in interlanguage (IL) change, where it is now, to a "more balanced" treatment of cognitive and (largely unspecified) social factors. This will correct the "general methodological bias and theoretical imbalance in SLA studies that investigate acquisition through interactive discourse" (1997, p. 288). Note, incidentally, that a major source of confusion in Firth and Wagner's reasoning is their tendency (e.g., 1997, pp. 287–288) to equate all "cognitivist" work in SLA with the narrower meaning of "cognitive" in studies conducted within a UG framework, of which they are highly critical. This is unfortunate and very misleading. UG SLA-ers may have the single most coherent research program (some would say the only one) and some of the best minds in the field, but most cognitively oriented SLA-ers are *not* UG-ers. They include general nativists, for example (I believe), all the cognitive-/social-interactionists whom Firth and Wagner attack in their article, and literally hundreds of other "cognitively oriented" researchers who are not mentioned by them, presumably because they work predominantly with interlanguage, rather than conversational, data. Firth and Wagner's misrepresentation continues, despite the error having been pointed out explicitly (Long, 1997b, p. 322, fn. 2). In an attempted response to their critics (Firth & Wagner, 1998), they explained: "In our view, SLA seems to be dominated by Chomskian thinking to such a degree that others' frames of reference for the understanding of language and cognition have become inconceivable" (p. 92). They may have become "inconceivable" to Firth and Wagner, but clearly not to SLA researchers. The 1998 PacSLRF in Tokyo, for instance, was fairly typical of the larger SLA conferences in that it included a small minority of (roughly 10) UG-motivated papers amidst numerous others (over 100) from various cognitive perspectives. These included a day-long symposium called "Cognition and SLA," which consisted of nine papers by prominent figures in the field on such topics as attention, sentence processing, automaticity, aptitude, focus on form, and incidental and intentional learning, not one of them operating within a generative framework.

It is clear that Firth and Wagner really have in mind much more than simply a "more balanced" view, given such statements as the following:

As part of this examination, we discuss the status of some fundamental concepts in SLA, principally nonnative speaker (NNS), learner, and interlanguage. These concepts prefigure as monolithic elements in SLA, their status venerated and seemingly assured within the field. We claim that, for the most part, they are applied and understood in an oversimplified manner, leading, among other things, to an analytic mindset that elevates an idealized "native" speaker above a stereotypicalized "nonnative," while viewing the latter as a defective communicator, limited by an underdeveloped communicative competence. (1997, p. 285)

The predominant view of discourse and communication within SLA, Firth and Wagner assert, is: "individualistic and mechanistic, and ... fails to account in a satisfactory way for interactional and sociolinguistic dimensions of language. As such, it is flawed, and obviates insight into *the nature of language, most centrally the language use* of second or foreign language (S/FL) speakers" (p. 285, emphasis added). The field is said to privilege settings in which the L2 is widely spoken or taught by NSs, and to ignore those in which few, if any, participants are natives. This means, for example, that SLA should be studied, or should have been studied (more often) in societies like India, Nigeria, or Singapore, where English and other languages may serve as lingua francas, or in foreign language settings when, for example, English is used as a means of communication by a Dane and a German discussing a business deal on the telephone. By (allegedly) ignoring such settings, and "while the field in general perpetuates the theoretical imbalances and skewed perspectives on discourse and communication" (p. 296), Firth and Wagner assert, SLA will not realize its "potential to make significant contributions to a wide range of research issues conventionally seen to reside outside its boundaries" (p. 296). They recognize "the growing number of SLA studies, mainly of an ethnographic nature, that are socially and contextually oriented" (p. 286), but contend that "most tend to take the formal learning environment (i.e., the S/FL classroom) as their point of departure. Thus, although S/FL interactions occurring in non-instructional settings are everyday occurrences (e.g., in the workplace), they have not, as yet, attracted the attention of SLA researchers" (p. 286).

Firth and Wagner and others are quite correct in pointing out that few published studies to date have focused on acquisition in what is here loosely called lingua franca environments, or situations in which "nonstandard" or "nativized" varieties have been involved, although there have been some (see, e.g., Fraser Gupta, 1994; Sato, 1990; Siegel, 2003; Warner, 1996; M. Williams, 1988). Rather than being the result of theoretical myopia or methodological imbalance, however, I suggest that this is simply a reflection of the situations in which, and the constraints under which, most SLA researchers work. Also, the force of Firth and Wagner's criticism could only increase if they were to suggest the kind of new insights about SLA they envisage from studies in such environments. This is not to say the research could not be motivated, but simply that they have not done so. With respect to the alleged paucity of research in naturalistic settings, on the other hand, one can only assume Firth and Wagner are either unfamiliar with, or dissatisfied with, the publications of work in naturalistic (noninstructional) settings by the likes of Clyne (1977), Huebner (1983), Meisel et al. (1981), Sato (1990), Schmidt (1983), Terrell (1990), and Watson-Gegeo (1992), among many others. Note that a common criticism of SLA research from Firth and Wagner and other members of the "discourse community" is that too many studies are conducted in classrooms, and there are not enough that take place in naturalistic settings. As we shall see, the "irrelevance community" argue that SLA research has little or nothing to say to language teachers because researchers conduct too much of their work in naturalistic settings and not enough in classrooms.

Research in sociolinguistics, Firth and Wagner note, has "irrefutably established and documented [a] reflexive relationship between *language use and social context*" (1997, p. 293, emphasis added). And who would deny it? They continue: "Language is not only a cognitive phenomenon, the product of the individual's brain; it is also *fundamentally a social phenomenon*, acquired and used interactively in a variety of contexts and for myriad practical purposes" (p. 296, emphasis added). Some *would* deny that. But assertion and counterassertion will get us nowhere. What Firth and Wagner need to show for their criticisms to have substance is *which* social dimensions of language use and social context allegedly ignored by SLA researchers play an important enough role in SLA to justify reorienting the field to a "more balanced" consideration of "both cognitive and social factors." Indeed, perhaps to whet our appetite, they could provide data showing how even *one* of the social dimensions to which they allude has any influence on acquisition (as opposed to use) at all. This they signally fail to do. Instead, what they offer are lengthy re-analyses of brief excerpts from conversational data treated in "mainstream" discourse analysis studies, the results of which (if one accepts the validity of the re-analyses, which the original researchers generally do not, judging from the responses to Firth and Wagner's article by those criticized, published in the same issue of *the Modern Language Journal*, and by Gass, 1998) is that the L2 speakers might occasionally have meant something different in one or more of their utterances, and this might have been appreciated if the original researchers had taken more contextual information into account. Even *if* the re-analyses are accepted as valid, nowhere do Firth and Wagner say what the import of any of this even might be for *acquisition*. It is impossible to falsify an existence claim, that is, in this case, for SLA researchers to prove the *irrelevance* of context, however defined, to acquisition; it is up to Firth and Wagner to show that context *is* relevant. Nowhere do they provide evidence to that effect. This did not, however, give them pause before bringing a sweeping indictment of the field. Nor did it preclude their article being published in a major journal.

Quite apart from the complete absence of evidence from Firth and Wagner, here or elsewhere, that SLA is indeed "flawed," as they claim, since when has the "nature of language" or the "language use" of L2 speakers been the explanandum for SLA? Is SLA really supposed to be concerned with language, and "most centrally" with L2 use, as they assert that it should be, or with L2 learning? The answer, surely, is clear: As Kasper (1997) underscores in the title of her trenchant response to Firth and Wagner, "'A' stands for acquisition." The same point is made by Poulisse (1997), Gass (1998), and Long (1997b) in their replies. Few researchers would deny the *potential* importance of the interactional and sociolinguistic context in which SLA occurs, least of all the individuals Firth and Wagner criticize most strongly as representative of the mainstream, many of whom, paralleling work in L1A, have spent years studying the putative effects on acquisition of modified input, output, feedback, task-type, and various kinds of negotiation opportunities, in conversations between learners and NSs, and among NNSs themselves (for review, see Gass, 1997, 2003; Long, 1996; Pica et al., 1996).

Theories of (S)LA differ, of course, in the significance of the role they attribute to the linguistic—let alone the social and sociolinguistic—environment, and researchers also differ in their interpretations of the empirical findings to date. Some (e.g., Grimshaw & Pinker, 1989) view linguistic input to the learner as degenerate and underspecified; others (e.g., Bohannon, MacWhinney, & Snow, 1990) see it as tailored for acquisition in various ways. Some view negative evidence and negative feedback (e.g., in the form of recasts) as nonexistent, unusable, unused, or nonuniversal (and thus nonessential), or irrelevant for competence, in any case; others think they have shown that such feedback is available and can be at least facilitative of acquisition (Doughty & Varela, 1998; Mackey, 1999; Oliver, 1995; Ortega & Long, 1997, and see chap. 4 in this volume). Some schools within SLA, particularly some groups within the UG camp, are highly skeptical of this latter work on theoretical grounds (see, e.g., Schwartz, 1993), and given the well-documented resilience of the human language learning capacity in child L1A, even in cases of severe linguistic deprivation, theirs is surely a very reasonable starting hypothesis. But the point here is that, as Eckman (1994) argued in connection with a similar debate over research on the role of variation in SLA, it is an empirical matter, not one to be settled a priori by fiat by the UG-ers, by the cognitive-interactionists, or in the present case, by the new champions of social context. I suggest, moreover, that the same standards apply to anyone—whether working inside the field or, like Firth and Wagner and some other critics, mostly outside it—who claims that SLA should or should not focus on a broader array of social factors (e.g., on other social identities of speakers than "NS" and "learner," such as "father," "friend," or "business partner"), that researchers should or should not use this or that methodology in discourse studies (Firth and Wagner favor Schegloffian conversational analysis), or should or should not adhere to this or that theory. Instead of dismissing all past work as "narrow" and "flawed" and simply *asserting* that SLA researchers should therefore change their database and analyses to take new elements into account, Firth and Wagner should offer at least some evidence that, for example, a richer understanding of alternate social identities of people currently treated as "learners," or a broader view of social context, makes a difference not just to the way this or that tiny stretch of discourse is interpretable, but to our understanding of *acquisition*.

No one is preventing Firth and Wagner from doing work of the kind they advocate. In fact, it would be welcomed. Their protestations at feeling like "trespassers" on SLA "private property" (Firth and Wagner, 1998, p. 91 et infra) are simply absurd. However, it seems that evidence is in fact unlikely to be forthcoming, from them at least, any time soon. Near the end of their 1997 paper, they write: "In essence, we call for work within SLA that endeavors to adopt what we have referred to as a holistic approach.... A crucially important and challenging *next step* is to develop, in much greater detail, the *theoretical bases*, a *research agenda*, and a set of *methodological approaches* that are aligned with the 'reconceptualization' here espoused" (p. 296, emphases added). It seems that these critics, at least, have not only not produced any work of the kind they nevertheless think the whole field should start doing, but have also yet to work out even what is to be done, or how. Until they or someone else antes up (for one attempt, see Tarone & Liu, 1995), the basic stance of SLA researchers will likely remain the same, and for good reason.

Whether or not eventually turning out to be influenced by social factors and social context, SLA is certainly, in large part, at least, a mental process: the acquisition of new linguistic *knowledge*. Language acquisition usually takes place in a social setting, to be sure, as do most internal processes—learning, thinking, remembering, sexual arousal, and digestion, for example—and that does not obviate the need for theories of those processes or shift the goal of inquiry to the settings themselves. Remove a learner from the social setting and the L2 grammar does not change or disappear. Change the social setting altogether (e.g., from street to classroom), or from a foreign to a second language environment and, as far as we know, the way the learner acquires does not change much either (as suggested, e.g., by comparisons of error types, developmental sequences, processing constraints, and other aspects of the acquisition process in and out of classrooms; see, e.g., R. Ellis, 1989; Johnston, 1985, 1998; Lightbown, 1983; Pica, 1984). An eight-hour flight from a foreign language to a second language environment does not alter a learner's brain after all, so why should one *expect* any basic differences? Conversely, alter the *cognitive*, or *psycholinguistic*, dimensions of a task or of task conditions—attentional focus, planning time, familiarity, difficulty, complexity, provision of negative feedback, processing constraints, and so on—and performance changes in ways that seem relevant for acquisition (see, e.g., Doughty & J. Williams, 1998a; N. Ellis, 1995; N. Ellis & Laporte, 1995; Gilabert Guerrero, 2004; J. Hulstijn, 1992; J. Hulstijn & W. Hulstijn, 1984; Mackey, 1995;

Manheimer, 1993; Newton & Kennedy, 1996; Norris & Ortega, 2000; Ortega, 1999; Pienemann, 1989; Rahimpour, 1997; Robinson, Ting, & Urwin, 1995; Schmidt, 1995).

Unfortunately, the cognitive and the psycholinguistic are not the dimensions of context that interest Firth and Wagner and their "discourse" colleagues, probably because they see language primarily as a social and cultural phenomenon and, as we have seen, are really more interested in language *use* than acquisition. Psycholinguistic results do interest SLA researchers, however, because one of our major goals is to understand how changes in the internal mental representation, or interlanguage grammar, are achieved; why they sometimes appear to cease (so-called stabilization and fossilization); and which learner, linguistic, and social factors (and if relevant, which instructional practices) affect and effect the acquisition process. Firth and Wagner may be making a valuable contribution by arguing for a broader, context-sensitive, participant-sensitive, emic approach, and for the use of more naturalistic data sampled from a wider range of acquisition settings (and, I would add, on a wider range of languages). Given the thus-far-productive focus on SLA as a mental process, however, and given the absence of any evidence to support a fundamental change in approach, cognitive factors and what Firth and Wagner refer to as "cognitively oriented theories and methodologies" will inevitably remain high on the agenda, whether or not those laying siege to SLA from the "discourse" camp approve.

Before closing this section, it is important to note that, symptomatic of the confusion among several of SLA's loudest critics, Firth and Wagner attempt to bolster their "social context" case by an unfortunate appeal to epistemological relativism, thereby conflating what are two quite separate issues. Already in the second paragraph of their article, they write: "Our critical assessment of some of SLA's core concepts is, in part, a reaction to recent discussions on theoretical issues in the field [by Beretta, Crookes, Ellis, Gregg, and Long, which reflect a desire] to introduce 'quality control' on the basis of 'established' and 'normal' scientific standards" (1997, pp. 285–286). Noting that Block (1996) had challenged assumptions underlying such discussions, Firth and Wagner side with him in disputing the desirability of "normal science," and in viewing the existence of multiple theories of SLA as unproblematic. Indeed, they go further than Block in one regard, asserting multiplicity of theories to be a *given* in their world: "The fact remains [NB: there are *facts* in Firth and Wagner's world] that the branch of the discipline dealing with discourse and communication is, and always has been, *of necessity multitheoretical* in its adopted approaches and conceptual apparatus" (1997, p. 286, emphasis added). They offer no evidence or reasoning (there could be none) to support their assertion concerning the *necessity* of such a situation. The remark is important in the present context, however, because it reveals basic misunderstandings of the differences between accepting multiple theories and multiple compet-

ing, or oppositional, theories, and the interpretations relativists and rationalists (e.g., realists) would put on either situation. Both are subjects to
which we will return. As we shall see, as part of their postmodernist critique of SLA research, Block (1996) and Lantolf (1996b) make the same
egregious error—confusing pluralism and relativism—and are then allowed by journal editors to use it as a stick with which to beat rationalists.
Whereas Firth and Wagner's subsequent reanalyses of excerpts from other
researchers' work show that, in fact, they do not really share Block's relativist views, some critics of SLA do, so let us now turn to the second group
of besiegers, the postmodernists.

MODERNISM

After some two decades of ferment in many literature, cultural studies,
philosophy, and political science departments at universities in Europe
and North America, postmodernism made an appearance in SLA and applied linguistics only fairly recently (see, e.g., Markee, 1994; Pennycook,
1996; van Lier, 1994). The pace is picking up, however. A 1996 issue of *Language Learning* included a lengthy article by Lantolf (1996) purporting to
provide a "postmodernist critical analysis" of some work on theory construction and evaluation in SLA by Beretta, Crookes, Gregg, and Long, and
an issue of *Applied Linguistics* in the same year unleashed what can only be
described as a postmodernist attack article (Block, 1996), aimed principally at the usual suspects, but once again encompassing more general expressions of its author's unhappiness with the whole field. An evaluation
of these criticisms requires some understanding of their philosophical underpinnings.

Dating from the late 18-century Enlightenment, *modernism* is associated
with beliefs in the self-motivated, rational subject, individual freedom,
self-determination, the possibility of steady progress through scientific
discovery, and a capacity for self-emancipation in the struggle for a more
just, humane society. Modernists put their faith, in particular, in rational
thinking and science. *Postmodernism* is the antithesis of all that.[3]
Postmodernists espouse a belief in decentered, socially constructed subjects. In place of science and reason, various of them value chaos, desire,
and the unconscious. As with all forms of epistemological relativism,
claims for the existence of "correct" ways of knowing (e.g., scientific
ways), or for "correct" knowledge systems (e.g., accepted research findings), are regarded as spurious. Belief systems like rationality and science
are examples of what Lyotard (1984) and other postmodernists call "grand
narratives," which they view with "incredulity." For them, *all knowledge is*

---

[3]For accessible introductions to postmodernist ideas, see Rosenau (1992) and Usher and
Edwards (1994).

socially constructed. It exists only in discourses, in texts, and not even objectively in the texts themselves, but in *each writer's or reader's interpretation of those texts.* There is no fact of the matter (although *that* is supposed to be accepted as a fact), but instead multiple interpretations and multiple realities; and, for some relativists at least (so-called judgmental relativists), anyone's construction of reality is as good as anyone else's. Thus, Lechte (1994, p. 236) reports that in a notorious series of articles in the French newspaper, *Liberation,* a leading French postmodernist, Baudrillard, appeared to claim that the Gulf Massacre of 1991 had not taken place. The personal horror stories and misery of 200,000 young Iraqi widows and orphans had no more *truth* to them than the musings of an aging French intellectual thousands of miles away. For postmodernists and relativists in general, we all "construct our own narratives," our own versions and understandings of events and of the world, and there is no objective way of distinguishing among them or any point in doing so.[4]

For postmodernists, as Usher and Edwards (1994) describe, one sort of evidence that modernist beliefs are ill-founded—or, at least, what postmodernists count as evidence—consists of the continuing existence of social ills: war, famine, disease, genocide, and environmental pollution. If science and reason can do what modernists claim for them, then why have they not been able to deal with those problems? Thus, for some postmodernists, horrific, "irrational" human acts count as evidence for their position. Bauman (1992) and Lyotard (1992), for example, see the Holocaust as the ultimate in the cold, calculated use of scientific principles for social engineering and, hence, an indictment of rationality and science.

The allegation that major human problems continue to exist due to a failure of science and reason—as opposed to the more obvious culprits, the selfish acts of corporate-sponsored elites wielding state power[5]—although silly enough, deteriorates still further into a denunciation of "the" scientific method (as if there were just one), usually equated with positivism. Predictably, therefore, as is discussed later, positivism is one of many accusations made by Lantolf (e.g., 1996, p. 714) against named individuals in SLA, despite its being a philosophy to which, to the best of my knowledge,

---

[4]This, incidentally, is one of many places where Firth and Wagner can be seen not really to be relativists at all, despite their endorsement of Block, because they attempt, whether or not successfully, to show that their analyses of other researchers' data are truer to reality than those of the original authors.

[5]Several of the leading lights in French postmodernism spent their early years as members of a variety of Stalinist and Maoist sects. It comes as no surprise, therefore, given the traditional authoritarian socialist need to discredit the libertarian ideas they rightly fear (see, also, Brumfit, 1997, pp. 25–26), that some French (or French-style) intellectuals claim that the writings of one of the most widely respected living anarchist philosophers, Noam Chomsky (an anarcho-syndicalist), employ outdated strategies that are "unable to accommodate the subtleties of political movements" (Barsky, 1997, p. 197). Chomsky's reply to this is that the French intelligentsia are unwilling to see what is clearly set out before them, and should learn "how to tell the truth, to pay attention to facts, and to reach standards of minimal rationality" (March 31, 1995, letter to Robert Barsky, quoted in Barsky, 1997, p. 197).

not a single SLA researcher subscribes. Given its allegedly poor results, "the scientific method" must also be flawed, postmodernists claim, particularly when it comes to its advocates' (alleged) claims to objectivity, neutrality, and an ability to produce value-free, true knowledge. Knowledge is not universal or independent of time, place, and the people producing it, the postmodernists claim; instead, it is incomplete, local, particular, socially and historically conditioned, fluid, not static, and serves the interests of those in power.

Ideological underpinnings and motives aside, however, the postmodernists raise some serious issues. They have a direct impact on the ways researchers proceed (or if they proceed at all), and those in turn can have major consequences for the success of their work and the benefits to interested parties. A key example is the role of theory construction. To illustrate, consider how things play out when a realist—perhaps the most common variant of rationalist among today's SLA researchers—and a relativist confront the same situation in SLA: a case of multiple theories in the same domain.

Whereas there are several different varieties of *realism*, and many nuances within those varieties, realists believe that even if it can never be fully comprehended, an objective, external world exists, independent of any individual's or group's (social) construction of it, and there are *universals* as well, of course, as individual differences and particularities of time and place. Thus, realists do not believe that, say, the laws of gravity or of thermodynamics only apply in Spain, only to short people, only on Tuesdays, or only to those who believe in them. They maintain that it is possible to demonstrate this by repeated observation (e.g., that apples always fall to the ground, never float up into the sky), whenever and wherever a study is conducted, and no matter who conducts it. That is to say, they believe *there are facts of the matter*. Realists also believe that although imperfect, our methods of inquiry permit us to discover whether at least some of our beliefs about that objective world are true, or more or less likely to be true than other beliefs, that is, to differentiate among conflicting views (e.g., rival theories), by measuring the degree to which they are or are not borne out by observations of events and experiences. In other words, it is possible at least to approximate the truth, without necessarily ever being able to be sure that a belief *is* the truth. Contrary to what is often alleged, realism entails no allegiance to any one method of inquiry, or to the idea that one method (e.g., the so-called scientific method) is better than others—simply an allegiance to *rational inquiry*. Nor, it needs to be emphasized, does it entail a belief in absolute truth. Thus, as Gregg (2000, p. 390) points out, if epistemological realists see two or more theories in some domain of SLA, especially—but not only—oppositional ones, their reaction will be that, because there is only one objective reality, (a) one of the theories *may* be correct, (b) all of them *may* be false, (c) all but one *must* be false, and (d) empirical observation, among other approaches, can potentially find out which is which. One might add, although this is not part of the realist's brief *qua* realist, that if that is then done, and if the increased understanding provided by the supported theory offers some practical benefits (e.g., a potential application in technology, medicine, or language teaching), then our collective knowledge of the world has increased and some people's lot within it may improve as a result.

As already noted, the same situation for a *relativist* is quite different. If a relativist sees the same multiplicity of theories, the tendency will be simply to accept the situation as unproblematic, an inevitable reflection of everyone having "their own narrative," their own construction of reality. Even if the texts in which theories live are "interpreted," and however "richly," there is no independent way of arbitrating between rival interpretations in the event that the participants cannot agree, and no need to do so. If the meaning of a text is rightfully, and in each case differently, in the mind of the writer and each reader, then, as Gregg (2000) notes, "there's no arguing about what a given text means" (p. 386).

And there's the rub. Contrary to what the postmodernists claim, comparing and evaluating theories is not an option, not a luxury, not an ivory tower activity, not a game, not impossible, but *essential* for progress in science. In fact, it is what progress consists in, because theories are our current approximations to truth—perhaps as close as we will ever come—our interim understandings, or explanations, of how things work. And not all explanations are as good as others. Maintaining that they are is a fundamental flaw in the relativist argument. It misses the fact, and it is a fact, that what decides whether or not a theory is good, or better than another theory, is not whether we say it is, but how well it works. How does the theory fare when tested against the way the world is (i.e., when tested empirically)? How many problems of different kinds does it solve? Holding that a plurality of theories is unproblematic,[6] even inevitable, therefore, is to obstruct progress in SLA, and shows that in science, as in the political arena, postmodernism and relativism are inherently reactionary and inhibitory of progress, because they permit any position to be defended equally well, regardless of its apparent truth or the social consequences. Far from threatening the status quo, therefore, postmodernists and relativists help perpetuate it. As with Marxist, Stalinist, Maoist, and other authoritarian socialist political goals, there is no interest in changing the system itself, just who, or in this case, which theories are in a position of power within it.[7]

Building on assertions first made in his plenary address to the 1995 British Association for Applied Linguistics (BAAL) conference (Lantolf, 1996), Lantolf's main claim in *Language Learning* (Lantolf, 1996) was that theories

---

[6]Strangely, in what is generally an excellent defense of critical realism in SLA research, Jordan (2004) endorses the relativists' "the more the merrier" position on theory proliferation. His stance, however, is qualified in important ways, as described in chapter 3.

[7]According to L. Laudan (1990), "The displacement of the idea that facts and evidence matter by the idea that everything boils down to subjective interests and perspectives is—second only to American political campaigns—the most prominent and pernicious manifestation of anti-intellectualism in our time."

of SLA, like all theories, are simply *metaphors,* whose productivity as stimuli for research, he further asserted—as Gregg notes (2000, p. 388), against all the evidence from the natural and social sciences—is in inverse proportion to their acceptance within a discipline. Theory (or metaphor) proliferation is something to be welcomed, therefore, as new theories (or metaphors) are likely to stimulate more research of diverse kinds. Beretta (1991) and Long (1993a), conversely, argued that progress in SLA was being hampered by an unwillingness to test or cull theories, especially oppositional theories, or to evaluate them comparatively using reasonably well-established standards from other sciences. Long suggested four candidate criteria from a much longer list of possibilities: simplicity, the ability to explain phenomena different from those for which the theory was invented to account, (possibly) the ability to make surprising novel predictions, and (provided it is not applied too early in the theory development process) empirical adequacy. Lantolf rejected any such proposals, arguing that the field should let all the flowers bloom.

Lantolf's view is reminiscent of the metaphor of SLA theories as "pictures in an art gallery," proposed by Schumann (1983) during his brief flirtation with relativism 15 years earlier.[8] It is a stance, in my view, that trivializes the field and ignores (for those who believe in such things) some rather salient facts, not the least of which is the fact that most SLA researchers, like researchers in other fields, do not simply trade "metaphors" (or "pictures") back and forth; they formulate increasingly precise predictions and test them against what is thought to be known about language learning, however imperfect and incomplete—*and very possibly wrong*—that knowledge may turn out to be. Whereas a new claim's initial acceptance may sometimes depend in part on the power or rhetorical persuasiveness of its advocates, in the long run it will survive if it receives empirical support (i.e., appears to be correct when compared against events in the natural world, and will be dropped if not). Something fundamental the postmodernists refuse to deal with is that the success or failure of theories depends on how they match up with the way the world is (in this case, how people learn languages), not the way the theorists say it is. This is a cardinal distinction between science, on the one hand, and *irrational* belief systems, like relativism, on the other. Relativists can continue to do business because they can find enough people willing, for a variety of reasons, to accept what they say the world is like, regardless of perceived reality, without the need for evidence or independent verification, or because while personally disagreeing with some claims, they believe that "anything goes" and are fatalistic with regard to human progress. Rationalists may not have higher standards, but they do have different ones.

When rival theories exist in a domain, Lantolf explained that there are two basic possibilities. If the observer is of the *judgmental relativist* persua-

---

[8]Schumann publicly disavowed any continuing allegiance to relativism in 1991 at the Michigan State University conference on "Theory and Research Methodology in SLA."

sion, which holds that all knowledge—being socially constructed and merely a reflection of the current distribution of power—is equally valid, then that will be the end of the matter. If an *epistemic relativist*, then the individual concerned may seek to determine which theory is more successful, not via empirical testing, but through the interpretation (sometimes the interpretation of interpretations) of texts (i.e., what Lantolf, 1996, p. 734, refers to euphemistically as "rational social discourse").

In a cogent response to Lantolf, Gregg (2000, 2003) notes that epistemic relativism, as portrayed by Lantolf, sounds like having your relativist cake and eating it too. He writes, paraphrasing Lantolf: "We can maintain that there is no objective reality out there and hence no way of preferring one theory to another on grounds of explanatory adequacy or empirical adequacy, while still making rational choices among theories.... Would that it were that simple. For one thing, on what *relativistic* grounds does one reject judgmental relativism" (Gregg, 2000, p. 394)?

Gregg dismantles Lantolf's theory-as-metaphor argument and provides some timely comments on the postmodernist "contribution" to SLA in general. He also documents a number of major misrepresentations, misunderstandings, and ill-founded accusations in Lantolf's critique of the rationalist SLA theory construction literature. For example, offering no evidence (there is none), but following the standard postmodernist script described earlier, Lantolf accuses Gregg and others of "a commitment to the rationalist epistemology and ... the *positivist* legacy that continues to pervade SLA research" (1996b, p. 714, emphasis added). In fact, not only have none of the accused ever expressed such a commitment, Gregg et al. (1997, p. 550) explicitly reject any allegiance to positivism (it is doubtful whether anyone in SLA has ever really subscribed to that position), and also stated their allegiances quite clearly: "A 'critical realist' ontology ('reality exists but can never be fully comprehended') combine[d] with a 'modified objectivist' epistemology ('objectivity remains a regulatory ideal') and a 'modified experimental/manipulative' methodology" (p. 550). This is about as explicit as one could get, and many steps removed from positivism, but it did not deter Lantolf from making his groundless accusation, or *Language Learning* from publishing it.

Elsewhere in his paper, having stated without evidence and quite untruly that "SLA theory builders share ... a common fear of the dreaded 'relativism'" (p. 715), Lantolf cites Long's statement concerning the typical coexistence of three or more theories even during a period of Kuhnian normal science, and concludes that "apparently, for Long relativism is not so bad after all, provided it is a constrained relativism" (1996b, p. 732). Echoing the earlier discussion, I can do no better than cite Gregg (2000) on this blatant misunderstanding of fundamental concepts:

> To start with, Lantolf confuses relativism with pluralism.... The situation Long describes [where there are three competing theories in a given domain] justifies no conclusion whatever as to what the epistemological commitments

of the theoreticians are. A relativist would presumably think that all three theories are OK, where a realist or a positivist would argue that, of the three, at least two are incorrect, if not all three.... In other words, the question of plurality of theories is a red herring as far as the relativism issue goes. (p. 390)

Firth and Wagner, we saw, made the same error when they stated that discourse studies in SLA must of necessity always be multitheoretical.

Another accusation that occurs with some frequency in the writings of the postmodernist critics of SLA, although it is not limited to them, is the accusation that researchers interested in theory evaluation are suffering from some form of misplaced "science envy." Lantolf writes, for example, that Long (1993a, p. 235) illustrates the "SLA theory builders' reverence for the natural science model" (Lantolf, 1996, p. 716), and later that "the theory builders are experiencing an episode of ... 'physics envy'" (p. 717). Block (1996, p. 73) dutifully repeats the allegation. Gregg et al. (1997, p. 544) point out, however, that this name-calling reflects more on those making the accusations than on those charged. Lantolf, Block, and others apparently think that SLA is not a science, and the rationalists' goal is to make it one. In fact, rationalist SLA researchers (i.e., the overwhelming majority of SLA researchers) are already doing science, however well or poorly. The writing on theory construction is no different from that by some of the same individuals and many others on L2 research methods; the goal in each case is to improve the quality of work in our field and to speed up progress. Writing on research methods addresses research quality issues at the grassroots level, so to speak; writing about theory construction and philosophy of science issues deals with broader disciplinary matters. Why the latter (alone) should come in for so much abuse remains a mystery. But it does, and none more so of late than from Block (1996, 2003).

Block's (1996) article in *Applied Linguistics* is a distressingly convoluted and ill-informed exposition of the relativist case. Among numerous charges against the usual suspects, Block chastises Long (1990a) for having suggested the existence of some "widely accepted findings" in SLA for which a theory of SLA should account. Block denies that such findings exist—without providing any evidence for his view, so presumably based on the relativist assertion that there is no "correct" knowledge, thereby confusing "correct" with what had been claimed (i.e., that the findings were "widely accepted"). He rejects even the surely uncontroversial generalization to the effect that "(I)nterlanguages, the psycholinguistic equivalent of idiolects, exhibit systematicity and variability at any time in their development (Selinker, 1969; Huebner, 1985)" (Long, 1990a, p. 658). Yet, Block approves of the existence of multiple theories of SLA. As Gregg et al. (1997, pp. 549–550) point out in their response, this is an odd position, even for a relativist. There is normally some agreement in science about many of the phenomena (i.e., putative "findings") to be explained, but disagreement about the correct explanation for them. Block, conversely, endorses a multiplicity of explanations for phenomena he claims SLA researchers have not yet agreed exist.

Block confuses "theory" and "paradigm," by which term Kuhn meant "dominant theory" (see, also, L. Laudan & R. Laudan, 1989), and also fails to grasp Kuhn's discussions of "pre-science" and "normal science." As Gregg et al. (1997, p. 546) underscore, Kuhn held that fields begin with a prescientific period, characterized by a chaos of competing theories that makes progress difficult. When a dominant theory emerges, a stage of normal science begins, during which research becomes cumulative, and applications of the theory can be harvested. This is achieved because the scientific community concerned has agreed on the basic issues and unified behind the dominant theory, or paradigm. Nonparadigmatic research typically continues, however, with histories of science showing three or more theories to be the norm, *even during such periods* (Collins, 1989), and substantive discoveries arising from research conducted outside the dominant paradigm.

Block also denies the need for, or indeed the very possibility of, either replication studies or control of extraneous variables in SLA research, which he states is "probably not even desirable" (p. 74), while admitting that this is "a major philosophical difference between my stance and that of many authors" (p. 74). Indeed, it is. He asks rhetorically (p. 74), "What good does a theory developed to explain the general do for a situation which is particular?" and thereby reveals another fundamental misunderstanding about the scope and purpose of all theories. He strongly rejects any move to reduce the number of competing theories in SLA in favor of a controlling paradigm, although that is something none of the accused had ever suggested, or could bring about even if they wished to do so.

It is not just replication studies, control of variables, and normal science to which Block objects, but rational inquiry in general. In its place, he advocates relativism as a viable basis for a research program in SLA, yet he offers absolutely no indication as to what such an alternative might look like, and (like Firth & Wagner) points to no examples of such work—probably because, to the best of my knowledge, none exists. Instead, he simply pledges allegiance to "constructivism" (see Lincoln, 1990). Constructivism involves the belief that the results of inquiries are always a function of the interaction of the inquirer and the inquired into, such that "what can be known and the individual who comes to know it are fused into a coherent whole" (Guba, 1990, p. 26). The methodology is hermeneutic and dialectic, with each inquirer required to compare and contrast their individual construction of reality with every other such individual construction "so that each respondent must confront the constructions of others and come to terms with them" (Guba, 1990, p. 26). What this would mean in SLA research, Block says nothing about. Would advocates of mutually exclusive oppositional theories have to negotiate a compromise: half the abstract syntactic principles posited for UG are innate, half learned, and so on? A hint of the "insights" in store can perhaps be found, however, in Block's criticism of Long's (1990b) according of primacy to cognitive factors (over social and affective ones) in SLA theory. Block claims (1996, p. 76) that this risks widening the gap between researchers and practitioners because, he says, it ignores the fact that "language lessons [not SLA theory, note] are essentially social events which are co-constructed by the individuals participating in them."

As if all this were not more than enough, Block throws in several sociology of science issues for good measure—"black boxing," linguistic imperialism, male chauvinism in teacher education, unequal power relationships in applied linguistics, the obligatory "science envy" charge, and so on—alleging that such problems exist, as always without providing any evidence, but nonetheless making insinuations. To give but one example, he suggests that writers languishing in the (undefined) geographical (note, not intellectual) "periphery" and/or espousing views that ran counter to prevailing opinion, might find their work rejected by journals in the (undefined) anglophone "center" if theoretical pluralism were reduced, and then uses that entirely unsupported speculation as an argument against the suggested need for theory evaluation. It is worth quoting him on this point, because I will be returning to the question of the editing of purportedly scholarly journals in our field when suggesting some ways of breaking the siege. In a stunning series of paranoid speculations and non sequiturs masquerading as an argument, Block (1996) writes:

> While *I have no reason to believe* that qualitatively different views about research exist in [other] parts of the world, *I would venture to say* that *if they did exist* they would not be *likely* to get into print.... In addition different views *might* run into resistance from the gatekeepers of the profession, the journal editors and the reviewers themselves, who *might* not consider the research reported to be in line with the expressed "line" of the journal. (p. 67, emphases added)

He offers no evidence for any of this, as usual, and again it is not something that anyone could ever prove does *not* occur. The onus is on Block to come up with, if not an example of this happening, at least some reasons for believing that it might. He fails to do that, while spicing the pot with equally unsubstantiated allegations of anglophone cultural hegemony. As documented by Gregg et al. (1997), the rest of Block (1996) contained numerous additional vague charges against individuals and organizations in SLA—charges of dishonesty, bad faith, discrimination, and so forth—all unsubstantiated, as well as gross misrepresentations of our and others' work. And again, Block's piece was accepted for publication by the editors of *Applied Linguistics* at the time (Lantolf and McCarthy), a supposedly scholarly journal. It took over 18 months for them to publish Gregg et al.'s reply, which due to the time lapse and separation from the original was never seen by many readers of the original attack article.

It is *not* true that a multiplicity of theories in a field is unproblematic—especially when some of those theories are oppositional, but not only then—because that is tantamount to a declaration of irresponsibility, or else a belief that progress is unattainable, an acceptance that "anything goes." And that is untrue if SLA is, as I have tried to show (see, e.g., Long, 1990a), a field that has made considerable empirical progress during its short existence, and unacceptable if, as I have also tried to show (see, e.g., Doughty & Long, 2003b), it is a field with considerable social consequence for millions of people all over the world.

Claims that theory proliferation is of no concern because there is no objective reality, no facts of the matter, that people are their own theorists, that all knowledge is socially constructed and nongeneralizable, are quickly forgotten in the face of a rapidly approaching Mack truck. Every time relativists cross a street, they make use of the same rapid mental calculations based on distance and the velocity of oncoming traffic as everyone else. It is hard to believe that "anything goes" is an attitude, moreover, that the postmodernists or relativists would dream of accepting for one moment in the purveyors of social services they routinely utilize (i.e., doctors, dentists, nurses, architects, engineers, mechanics, airline pilots, etc.), people whose work is successful precisely because it is based on the accumulated research findings of decades of *rational* inquiry in the basic and applied sciences, the very kind of research the critics claim to reject in SLA.[9] Are postmodernists and relativists prepared to accept something less in language teachers, in educators, or in those who work with disadvantaged populations? Why is SLA different? Why are the countless people (immigrants, refugees, school children, etc.) who stand to benefit from SLA research findings different? Can Lantolf, Block, and their supposed sympathizers, like Firth and Wagner, explain why those people and their needs are unimportant and why SLA is unimportant? And can the editors of journals who publish such shoddily argued material explain their reasons for doing so?

IRRELEVANCE FOR LANGUAGE TEACHING

The third group currently laying siege to SLA are some defenders of the status quo in language teaching, often commercial textbook writers. This may come as something of a surprise, particularly to those many SLA researchers who, like myself, entered the field after substantial and varied experience as classroom teachers and teacher educators. Many SLA researchers have witnessed firsthand the relatively few successes and the widespread failures of even the best-intentioned classroom instruction, and many were first motivated to undergo training as SLA researchers with a view to improving that state of affairs.

---

[9]Redhead (1995, p. 15) put it this way: "For quarks it may not matter so much, but in everyday life I believe it really does make a difference whether we believe in medical science as against witchcraft and spells, and I know for sure which jetliner I want to travel in—the realist's, not the relativist's!"

Language teaching has been going on for a very long time. Histories of the field (see, e.g., Howatt, 1984; Kelly, 1969; Musumeci, 1997) show that many of the same issues debated by pedagogues today have occupied their predecessors for centuries, with first one side and then the other emerging victorious—temporarily. In the absence of either a widely accepted theory of language learning or a solid empirical base for classroom practice, teachers and learners have always been, and will always be, vulnerable to drastic pendulum swings of fashion, the coming and going of various unconventional and unlamented "Wonder Methods" being an obvious recent example. The sad truth is that after at least 2,000 years, most language teaching takes place on a wing and a prayer—sometimes successfully, but often a relative failure. As Richards (1994) showed, this makes the field prey to charismatic personalities (e.g., the Methods gurus of the 1970s and 1980s) and to powerful governmental and commercial interests; these interests sometimes act in concert, as when a government's cultural attaches promote the books of publishers from the country whose commercial interests they represent, and the publishers themselves have a heavy investment in, and expect huge profits from, a textbook series implementing this or that approach to teaching.[10]

Bigger political forces are often also at work.[10] When then U.S. Vice-President Dan Quayle, not a renowned expert on language matters, publicly urged thousands of young Americans to join the Peace Corps and go to newly "liberated" eastern Europe to teach thirsty Hungarians, Romanians, and others English, was it because of a sudden interest in foreign language learning on his part, or because of a realization that English is the language of international capitalism, and that, as Pennycook (1995) pointed out, "English in the world" quickly becomes "the world in English?" And it was not just the Peace Corps whose credibility suffered from Quayle's support. Once again, teaching EFL was tacitly represented as an activity requiring no special knowledge or training, something that could be done at the drop of a trade barrier by the next God-fearing citizen with a sudden urge to share American culture with unsuspecting foreigners.

Against this backdrop of many more L2 beginners and repeatedly "false beginners" than finishers, a lack of theoretical or empirical grounding, and a consequent susceptibility to pendulum swings, one might have expected research on SLA to be welcomed with open arms, especially—but by no means only—when it has implications (and occasionally even applications) for the classroom. SLA, after all, is the process that language teaching is designed to facilitate. Welcomes, at least from self-appointed pedagogic gatekeepers, are few and far between, however. Instead, suggestions from SLA researchers (many of them experienced classroom lan-

---

[10]For an analysis of the (sometimes unwitting) role of various quasi-governmental agencies, including the Peace Corps, in projecting U.S. foreign policy abroad, see the special issue of *Covert Action Information Bulletin* 39, Winter 1991–1992. More recently, it has become official government policy that two of the typical eight years of military service required of those joining the U.S. armed forces can be fulfilled by service as Peace Corps volunteers.

guage teachers themselves, remember), especially if explicit, and it seems especially if perceived as presenting a challenge to current commercial interests and orthodoxy, have been swiftly and repeatedly subjected to attack. Explicit, relatively detailed proposals, such as those for various kinds of task-based language teaching (e.g., Long, 1985b; Long & Crookes, 1992; Long & Norris, 2000; Nunan, 1991; Skehan, 1998), seem especially threatening to some, who miss the point that explicitness (as distinct from dogmatism) is, of course, valued in rational inquiry because the more explicit a claim is, the more easily testable and, hence, quickly falsifiable. Explicitness is a plus for people who are seriously interested in progress, because it helps if bad ideas are easily identifiable as such. Opaque distinctions and vaguely worded claims, conversely, are less easily recognized as empty when that is the case, and so tend to have unwarrantedly long shelf-lives, thereby inhibiting progress. As in the political arena, so in language teaching, people will be less likely to search for alternatives as long as they think existing options may one day turn out to be adequate.

Advocates for the status quo, or in some cases for times past,[11] offer a variety of arguments against SLA-influenced language teaching proposals. Sheen, for example, has repeatedly asserted that proposed innovations that lack massive, repeated, longitudinal field testing in real classrooms should not be allowed into real classrooms (Sheen, 1994, and elsewhere). The fact that any pedagogic innovation from SLA research or anywhere else must, by definition, be allowed into classrooms before it can be tested there, much less validated, seems to escape him. So does the absence, which is simply ignored, of any such testing, much less empirical vindication of his own preferred practices (e.g., grammar translation and "principled eclecticism"; Sheen, 1998), whatever that might be. Different proposals apparently warrant different standards. Sheen and his ilk arrogantly claim perceived classroom successes as victories for their "methods," and dismiss failures, if they acknowledge them at all, sometimes even blaming the students. During an attack on an EFL teacher in Japan who had questioned the widespread use of grammar translation in that country, for example, Sheen (1992) wrote:

> The eclectic approach which Bailey espouses does not preclude the use of elements of the GTM [Grammar Translation Method]. As both a learner and teacher, I would regard them as essential.… I have taught both French and English … and have often found the students equally baffled by the simplest of questions after more than five years of study using methods ranging from the GTM to the most functional. If we have not learned much else in the last decades of intensive research, surely we have learned to resist the temptation to lay such store by the method used and lay at its feet the failings of the students. (p. 45)

---

[11]See, for example, "In defense of grammar translation" (Sheen, 1992).

When things go wrong, it is not the teacher or the Method that is to blame, but the students. The Sheens of this world ignore the very real possibility that some learners succeed despite their methods, and it is the failures for which they should claim credit.

Some of the language teaching establishment's loudest critics of SLA research-influenced proposals ignore the fact that there is often a complete lack of anything more than impressionistic evidence for the teaching strategies they advocate. Those include the imposition of a pre-set, external, synthetic grammatical syllabus, regardless of learners' current readiness to learn the items on Monday morning's menu or to do so in the order presented; the use of explicit grammar rules; and "error correction" to prevent or undo "fossilization," something literally impossible (given that *permanence* is part of the definition) if fossilization is real, which arguably has yet to be demonstrated (see Long, 2003). The strategies are frequently incompatible with SLA theory and research findings in both naturalistic and instructed settings, but that is apparently of no concern to them. At the same time, some (like Sheen) complain bitterly about what they assert (usually wrongly) is a lack of evidence for proposals emanating from SLA researchers. It is as if a physician continued to advocate blood-letting as a cure for cancer, claimed success in the cases of the few patients who recovered for other reasons, dismissed the numerous failures as having been caused by aggravating factors beyond their control (e.g., patients not trying to stay alive hard enough), and vociferously attacked any researchers and practitioners with other ideas and research findings to back them up, especially if they proposed trying them out in hospitals.

Another line of assault on SLA, and a handy way of dismissing whatever ideas are under discussion without having to deal with them, is to deny that SLA research alone constitutes an adequate basis on which to make proposals for the classroom. But who has ever suggested that SLA alone is an adequate base? Most SLA researchers with an interest in classroom teaching have espoused some variant of the far more inclusive approaches described by Crookes (1997a, 1997b); Doughty and Long (2003a); R. Ellis (1997a, 1997b); Long (2005a, 2005c); and Long and Crookes (1992), among others, in which information from *multiple* sources is utilized in program design—needs and means analyses, SLA, micro- and macrosociolinguistics, language analysis, psychology, education, educational psychology, and more—and in which, moreover, the information flow between those sources and classroom teaching experience is anything but unidirectional. A variant of the critics' gambit is to assert that language teaching is "an art," and that it is therefore wrong and ultimately hopeless to try to bring "scientific" findings to bear on the potentially endless, sometimes centuries-long, arguments among self-appointed experts on pedagogy. Would the same people claim that medicine is an art, or engineering, or law, or architecture? Why is education different in kind?

When all else fails, as it does, the assailant may always resort to a charge of political correctness. Thus, Sheen pronounced Task-Based Language Teaching, as proposed by Long & Crookes (1992), to be a product of "the liberal ethos that has permeated the (sic) approach to teaching in recent decades, particularly in the field of ESL" (Sheen, 1994, p. 144). Despite having been exposed as confused, confusing, and riddled with misrepresentations (see, e.g., Long, 1994; Nunan, 1994), Sheen's endlessly repetitious diatribes against a mystifyingly select subgroup of SLA researchers (mostly Krashen, Long, R. Ellis, Nunan, and Lightbown) have been published for over 10 years now in *TESOL Quarterly, RELC Journal, Applied Linguistics*, and *Canadian Modern Language Review*, among other places. Why?

Fortunately, not all discussions of SLA-influenced proposals for language teaching within pedagogy and applied linguistics circles are pitched at such a low level. Several prominent applied linguists, including some who have made important contributions to syllabus design, have begun to reevaluate their own earlier proposals in light of SLA findings and, probably more important in the long run, increasing numbers of experienced practicing teachers with formal training in SLA are doing so. However, even here, the discussion is sometimes less substantive or rigorous than might have been expected. Thus, to cite but one example, due to space limitations, in a plenary address to the Korean Association of Language Teachers conference, Wilkins (1994) reviewed some basic options in syllabus design in the light of SLA research findings, particularly proposals for Task-Based Language Teaching (Long, 1985b, in press), as summarized in Long and Crookes (1992).

Unlike Block or Sheen, Wilkins starts by acknowledging several facts about interlanguage development uncovered by SLA research (e.g., that learning often exhibits U-shaped and zigzag learning curves); that students do not learn isolated L2 items one at a time, in additive, linear fashion; that learners rarely, if ever, move from zero to target-like mastery of new items in one step; that both naturalistic and classroom learners pass through fixed developmental sequences, stages that often entail quite lengthy periods of non-TLU of forms; and that these sequences (*not* SLA in toto, note) seem impervious to instruction. He also recognizes the major problems such findings pose for advocates of approaches to language teaching that involve synthetic (e.g., structural) syllabuses and accompanying methodology, as well as for the use of linguistically simplified texts, as found in commercially published "graded readers" series, and the research findings' greater compatibility with analytic (e.g., task-based) approaches. So far, so good.

Wilkins next claims that the notional syllabus, with which his name is rightly associated, is not really synthetic, as Long and Crookes had stated, simply because it itemized linguistic content. Referring to his crucial distinction (Wilkins, 1976) between synthetic and analytic syllabuses (in my view, one of the single most important ever made in writing on language teaching), he continues:

> It was my view that all syllabuses that provide linguistic diversity should be considered to be analytic and this would include the notional and functional syllabuses.... Generally speaking, any individual social function or semantic category is associated with diverse linguistic forms. It may be that the difference of view arises from different perceptions of how those syllabuses might actually be implemented. (Wilkins, 1994, p. 47)

First, quite apart from the fact that "linguistic diversity" is undefined (would a grammatical syllabus that included a wide range of target structures qualify as linguistically diverse, and so as analytic?), this is a rather different understanding of what constitutes an analytic syllabus from that which Wilkins proposed 30 years ago. The synthetic/analytic distinction then had to do with the learner's role, respectively, either as synthesizer of linguistic forms presented discretely, or as analyzer of gestalt target language samples presented holistically. Second, Wilkins may be right in suggesting that the way both types of syllabus might be implemented could affect perceptions of them. However, there have been one or two (admittedly small-scale) studies of how variants of notional-functional syllabuses and communicative language teaching, at least, are implemented (see, e.g., Long, Adams, McLean, & Castanos, 1976; Nunan, 1987; Phillips & Shettlesworth, 1975), which all found that they tended to look uncannily like structural language teaching in the classroom. Wilkins does not refer to any of those studies, or to any in support of his speculation that notional syllabuses really can be implemented differently.

There then follows, in light of his earlier acknowledgment of various relevant SLA research findings, a rather puzzling attempt to defend synthetic syllabuses, which is even more troubling. For example, he asserts that structurally graded, inauthentic materials are not inevitably bad, and notes that: "(N)o evidence is cited [by Long & Crookes, 1992] that learners cannot learn language from what the authors would regard as non-authentic material" (1994, p. 51). Once again, one is being asked to offer evidence that something cannot occur. Along with the impossibility of meeting such a demand, shouldn't some evidence more legitimately be expected of, and more easily produced by, those advocating an approach that has long been implemented in classrooms all over the world? Lack of authenticity, Wilkins continues, is virtually a given and, in any case unproblematic:

> The fact is that in any ordinary sense of the word authentic there are virtually no authentic uses of language in the classroom other than those which relate to the functioning of the classroom itself.... This is not a problem.... It is doubtful whether authenticity is an issue with which learners themselves are greatly concerned.... The urge to (so-called) authenticity should be seen as the shibboleth that it is. (1994, pp. 51–52)

Here, Wilkins, like every discussant of the "authenticity" issue from a peda-gogic perspective that I am aware of, misses its crucial psycholinguistic di-mension (see Long, 1997a). In any case, Long and Crookes had not argued for the use of "found" texts (texts originally produced for communication among NSs, not written for language teaching), which is the traditional meaning of "authentic." He also misses the distinction between authentic *texts* and authentic *tasks* as the relevant starting point both in classroom lan-guage learning and for the discussion itself (see, again, Long, 1997a, and chap. 5 in this volume). Next, apart from the fact that it is pure speculation, the suggestion that (some? all?) learners may not be "greatly concerned" about authenticity is surely irrelevant. Learners may or may not even be aware of, much less concerned about, a great many issues and options in language teaching, but then that is not their responsibility but ours as teach-ers and applied linguists. Far from being "a shibboleth," successful manipu-lation of the psycholinguistic dimension of authenticity (e.g., where *elaboration*, rather than simplification, is utilized to increase comprehensibil-ity without removing learnable grammatical or lexical L2 forms from the in-put) is probably a critical factor in determining the success or failure of language teaching. As yet, no one knows for sure, but Wilkins dismisses the issue out of hand, apparently unaware of the numerous studies of the rela-tive effectiveness of (what he considers) "authentic" texts, and simplified and elaborated versions thereof (for data and reviews, see, e.g., Long, 1997a, 2003; Oh, 2001; Yano et al., 1994; and chap. 5, this volume).

Elsewhere in his discussion, Wilkins suggests that structural syllabuses do not necessarily preempt the operation of developmental processes: "It can be said, though, in defense of the structural approach to language teaching, that *however damaging this may be to the principles on which such an approach is based,* the practice inevitably involved a degree of holistic learn-ing" (1994, p. 48, emphasis added). But even if that were true (and Wilkins provides no evidence that it is), how is the *possibility that X might not always fail* a legitimate argument against the *probability of Y succeeding*? Then co-mes a demand for *more* empirical studies and for answers to questions (most already available in the SLA literature) before a suggestion should be seriously entertained, while again, like Sheen, glossing over the absence of any such evidence for the position he is defending: "What is the sequen-tial relationship, if any, between the different syntactic categories [in the developmental sequences]?… What were the methods by which the acqui-sition data were collected?… How much variation is there between indi-viduals?… Just how impervious to instruction are these sequences" (1994, pp. 49–52)? There is sometimes a tinge of straw-man argumentation here, too: "The step from seeing second language learning as a holistic process to concluding that it consists of 'fixed developmental sequences' 'impervi-ous to instruction' is a very large one. In my view the evidence needs to be far more comprehensive and convincing than it is at the moment before we would wish to establish this as the sole basis for language teaching practice" (1994, p. 49). Lightbown, Long and Crookes, Pienemann, and others nowhere claim, as is implied here, either that SLA is "impervious to instruction" (on the contrary, for reviews of research showing multiple *effects* of instruction, see, e.g., Doughty, 2003; Long, 1983a, 1988; Long & Robinson, 1998; Norris & Ortega, 2000) or that this idea and "fixed developmental sequences" should form the "sole basis" for language teaching practice or indeed for anything at all. And, once again, there is a demand for "far more comprehensive and convincing" evidence. How much more? Convincing to whom? What is inadequate about the dozens of studies of these issues to date? Why is the lack of empirical evidence supporting the position Wilkins is defending not of equal concern?

In sum, although not typical of all discussion of SLA findings for language teaching, many of which are positive, these papers by Sheen and Wilkins are representative (at very different levels of scholarship) of much of it. In addition to the problems pointed out, there is a disappointing unwillingness to recognize the insights that language teaching has quietly absorbed from SLA theory and research over the past three decades (see chap. 5 in this volume), with their source now seemingly forgotten. Since the hey-day of the Contrastive Analysis Hypothesis and Audiolingualism 40 years ago, for example, when linguists ruled the language teaching roost, SLA has furnished far from complete, but very much improved, *data-based* understandings of many aspects of language learning in and out of classrooms, including the role of positive and negative evidence; L1 transfer; learner error; a range of implicit and explicit forms of negative feedback; a number of options in modifying target language samples so as to improve their comprehensibility without sacrificing learning targets; practice, automatization, and restructuring; variation; accuracy, complexity and fluency; attention and metalinguistic awareness; individual differences; incidental, implicit, and explicit learning; and the relative utility of a focus on the target language as object or medium of communication. For accessible sources on the implications for language teaching of research findings on many of these and other topics, see H. D. Brown (1994), Doughty and Williams (1998a, 1998b), Lightbown and Spada (1993), Doughty and Long (2003a), and Robinson (1997, 1998), as well as chapter 5 in this volume. There have no doubt been some ill-founded proposals, but with this fairly solid record overall, why should current ideas be dismissed out of hand?

BREAKING THE SIEGE

The Danger of a Siege Mentality

Paying too much attention to those laying siege to SLA risks legitimizing some of the woollier critics, who might be better simply ignored, as well as some of their more absurd criticisms. Worse, it could gradually create a siege mentality and isolate the field from its constituents and from neighboring disciplines. On the other hand, completely ignoring all the current assaults (and insults) also seems ill advised. First, whereas most of the charges are unsupported now, as far as one can tell, perhaps in the case of the "social context" criticisms at least, some may eventually turn out to have merit. Second, however convoluted the prose, the attention postmodernist critiques draw to the often hidden dimensions of expertise, patriarchy, and power relationships in science, among other matters usually treated by the sociology of science, while unrecognized as coming decades after anarchist exposés of many of the same issues (see, e.g., Hales, 1986; Igor, 1985; Kropotkin, 1899/1975, 1899/1985; Martin, 1991; Purchase, 1996) is also valuable, even if the postmodernists' *solutions* are not. Third, equally clearly, it would be foolish to ignore critiques of language teaching proposals by experienced and reputable applied linguists, like Wilkins. Fourth, discouraging or reducing diversity (as opposed to chaos) is almost always a bad idea in any walk of life, and theoretical and methodological diversity in SLA research is likely to be no exception.

By the same token, it does seem important to respond swiftly and forcefully to some critics and charges before they damage SLA as a field and its potential beneficiaries more than they already have, especially when the criticisms are published in what in a few cases are currently (but how much longer?) considered major journals. Some of these people, especially the postmodernists, a few journal editors (postmodernists themselves, in one or two cases), and publishers are having the effect of portraying SLA, unjustifiedly, as fundamentally misguided, as a dangerous threat, or both. This is harmful for research funding prospects, obstructs progress, diverts attention from the real issues, wastes a lot of people's time and energy, and hinders improvement in language teaching and other domains that stand to benefit from SLA findings.

Postmodernism, in particular, has had a pernicious effect in many areas, from literature, art, and architecture to political science and cultural studies, as well as on social activism (see, e.g., Albert, 1996, and discussions in subsequent issues of Z Magazine). The hollowness of the postmodernist critique of science has been revealed on numerous occasions, not least by publication of Sokal's (1996) famous hoax article in the North American postmodernist journal, Social Text, along with the substantial commentaries that followed elsewhere. The postmodernist critique of SLA should be exposed for what it is right away, before this field also becomes mired in the same unproductive "debates" that have sidetracked other disciplines. Even in the short term, strident voices repeatedly asserting that research is futile and academic debates within SLA are just a game are likely to damage SLA's credibility with such groups as university administrators, language teachers, funding agencies, and individuals from other disciplines sitting on university promotion and tenure committees. The standard of scholarship and argumentation found in some of the published critiques, moreover—*whatever* one thinks of their contents—is sometimes so low (replete with ad hominem attacks, distortions, straw men, unsupported assertions, and mis-citations) that the credibility of one or two of the journals concerned has already been adversely affected, thereby potentially risking *all* publications in them being tainted in the eyes of some observers. One can easily envisage the day when work in those journals will no longer be considered relevant by university administrators and faculty making decisions about such matters as the future of units and degree programs concerned with SLA, just as has already happened in some instances when applied linguists have attempted to establish new programs or have sought promotion and tenure from committees made up primarily of members from other disciplines, such as linguistics.

The hostility toward language teaching proposals based partly on SLA research findings from some (although, thankfully, by no means all) applied linguists and language teachers is a different matter. A healthy skepticism toward premature proposals is obviously to be welcomed and is not a problem at all. Reasoned debate of the *issues*, moreover, suggests a growing maturity in the field (e.g., the existence of a recognized knowledge base, i.e., widely accepted findings, to which proposals can be held accountable). Trashing suggestions for no good reason, conversely, apart from being insulting to the people doing the hard work, is likely (perhaps intended?) to frighten off teachers and prospective graduate students who could benefit from a grounding in SLA research, but who understandably do not yet know enough about the original studies to judge for themselves, and so have to rely on the self-appointed intermediaries, some of whom obviously know precious little about SLA research, either. It is also damaging to the ultimate consumers (i.e., classroom language learners), whose instruction will remain subject to the vicissitudes of fashion and to the undue influence of government agencies and commercial publishers until the situation changes. As should be obvious from the previous discussion, this is *not* to say SLA research has all the answers, of course, or that it ever will; and, it certainly does not mean that current proposals, including those for Task-Based Language Teaching or focus on form, for instance, are correct. It is simply to protect the integrity of a field, many of whose participants have already contributed much to language teaching, and who will assuredly contribute much more if given a hearing.

Gate-Keeping, Structural Fault Lines, and Potential Remedies

A number of experienced SLA researchers (from a variety of "schools") who have commented informally on the spate of attack articles have wondered openly how individuals who were in some cases quite unknown and untrained as SLA researchers themselves could publish so easily in supposedly scholarly journals, especially when their allegations lacked substance and, in one or two cases, were so poorly articulated. SLA, like several areas of applied linguistics, has its own knowledge base, but one would never know it from reading some of the literature discussed earlier. How likely is it that people with little or no formal training or publication record in, say, linguistics, psychology, biology, or chemistry, and with minimal familiarity with their literature, would be given access to major journals in those fields in order to indict all previous work in them, unless the indictments were well reasoned and supported? Would the individuals and field attacked lose credibility, or would it be the editors and journals concerned?

Some of the publications already discussed raise many questions about the current state of SLA and its potential as a discipline. They suggest the existence of structural fault lines, including a number usually dealt with elsewhere under the rubric of the sociology of science, most of which are outside the (already broad enough) scope of this chapter. An obvious one in the present context, however, is the state of journals and journal editing in the field. There are one or two fine journals, and there have been—and are—some fine editors, but this often appears fortuitous because there is usually an obvious lack of procedures in place to ensure that quality is maintained or, in some cases, ever achieved. Many aspects of how some journals are run give serious cause for concern, especially when it is remembered that peer review is one of the important ways in which bias is minimized and quality maximized in a field. The refereed literature in any area has a status different from that of commercial publications, and this should be the case in SLA too. In fact, a survey of senior scholars in the field (VanPatten & J. Williams, 2002) showed agreement among them that this is indeed already the case (e.g., with regard to the criteria considered most relevant when evaluating an application for promotion and tenure).

Who comes to publish in the supposedly refereed SLA literature? Who are the gatekeepers? Why are almost all SLA and applied linguistics journals controlled or owned by commercial publishers and/or a particular university department? Does it matter that their editors are often selected behind closed doors, on the say-so of proprietary company representatives or of one or two powerful individuals inside or outside the field, or the editors thus chosen are then in some cases free to restock editorial advisory boards with like-minded individuals, some of whom have a minimal track record or none at all in the journal concerned, or even in the field, over which they are now to exercise considerable power? How it is that in some notorious cases the individuals attacked have subsequently been denied an opportunity to respond by the same editors, including one or two well known to share the views of the authors they *have* published and then seemed anxious to protect from rebuttal? Is it important that few journals have any written policies or procedures at all covering such matters as "right of reply" or even refereeing, or that some editors appear to flout such policies as do exist when so inclined? Is it important that *all* articles in a purportedly refereed journal are in fact refereed? Can any journal in the field be edited satisfactorily by only one or two people any longer, given the diversity and technicality of so much work in SLA today, or is a team of specialist coeditors, each with their own panel of expert reviewers, now needed? Is it a justified concern that no remedies exist when arbitrary and capricious decisions are made?

Solutions to these problems, if it is agreed that they are problems, may vary, and obviously require careful discussion. In the short term, to set the ball rolling, on a par with (say) the Linguistic Society of America and its prestigious journal, *Language*, the time has come to establish one or more international SLA associations, whose principal function would be to publish one or more SLA journals of the highest caliber, a journal or journals whose editors, editorial board members, and outside reviewers were selected openly, democratically, and on merit by members of the associations, and whose policies and procedures were written, open to public inspection, applied rigorously, and above all, applied consistently. The association(s) would be inclusive, open to anyone, and charge minimal dues. These would be chiefly to pay the subscription costs of the journal(s). Procedures would be in place from the outset to ensure that all schools of thought could be represented, and that no one viewpoint could dominate simply through bias in the way editors were selected, or in the composition of editorial boards or reviewer panels.

Again following worthy examples in linguistics, psychology, and other more mature disciplines, there is a parallel need for high quality e-mail discussion lists in SLA. These would be open to all, but some (not all) of them would be moderated so as to exclude personal attacks, and perhaps the number of posts any one person can make per day would be limited in some rational way in order to prevent subscribers' in-boxes from being deluged with incessant diatribes from the same individuals. Some leading scholars have commented that tightening up scholarly journal practices (and in other areas of gate-keeping not discussed here) may be necessary to keep SLA viable long enough institutionally for the field to show what it can contribute in cognitive science and to society as a whole.

Some of these matters are simply teething problems common to any emerging discipline and are fairly easy to remedy. In the longer term, I believe the solution is to emphasize and encourage rational inquiry and empirical research. SLA has more than enough intellectually stimulating and socially important problems to be solved, and more than enough hard work to go around. If given the opportunity, it will ultimately succeed or fail as a discipline on its achievements, and there is every reason for optimism here.

One area where the training given future researchers in the field could be improved, however, is in the philosophy of science. Few even of the top graduate programs in SLA and applied linguistics provide coursework in this area as yet (two that do are the PhD in SLA programs at the University of Hawai'i and the University of Maryland), but I think it should become routine, just as training in research methods now is. What sense is there in turning out SLA researchers with a thorough grounding in qualitative and quantitative research methods, in numerous procedures for gathering and analyzing language data, and expertise in measurement and statistics, but who know little or nothing about theory construction and change, or about how sciences work? Are SLA researchers fully competent if well versed in day-to-day, grassroots research procedures, but lacking an idea of how what they are doing fits in with other work in the field (i.e., of how to assess the big picture)? Excellent written sources exist for those with an initial interest in such matters (see, e.g., Corvalis, 1997; Diesing, 1991; Kitcher, 1993; L. Laudan, 1990, 1996a; Riggs, 1992b), and some of the best known and respected authors in the area, like Laudan, also happen to be first-rate classroom teachers of the material. I would suggest that one or more of them should be invited to provide intensive courses designed especially for our field, perhaps at summer institutes, so that not only graduate students, but also the many people currently training future SLA researchers could attend. Experts in SLA and applied linguistics with advanced formal training in philosophy of science are sorely needed, and it is pleasing to note a major contribution in this area in the form of a recent doctoral dissertation by an ex-student of Popper, among other notable philosophers of science (Jordan, 2002b, 2004).

Whether or not these ideas alone would solve any of the problems discussed, I look forward to the day when SLA is more widely recognized as the serious and socially responsive discipline I believe it can be. Chapters like this one (unpleasant for writer and assuredly some readers alike) would no longer be needed. One could instead concentrate on the genuine controversies and excitement in SLA and L3A: the roles of nature and nurture; special and general nativism; child–adult differences and the possibility of maturational constraints; cross-linguistic influence; acquisition and socialization; cognitive and social factors; resilience; stabilization, fossilization, and other putative mechanisms and processes in interlanguage change; the feasibility of pedagogical intervention; and, most of all, the development of viable theories.

References

Albert, M. (1996). Science, post-modernism, and the left. *Z Magazine,* July/August, 64–69.

Allwright, R. (1975). Problems in the study of the language teacher's treatment of learner error. In M. Burt & H. Dulay (Eds.), *On TESOL '75: New directions in language learning, teaching and bilingual education* (pp. 96–109). Washington, DC: TESOL.

Allwright, R., & Bailey, K. M. (1991). *Focus on the language classroom.* Cambridge, England: Cambridge University Press.

Andersen, R. W. (1989). The theoretical status of variation in interlanguage development. In S. M. Gass, C. Madden, D. Preston, & L. Selinker (Eds.), *Variation in second language acquisition: Vol. II. Psycholinguistic issues* (pp. 46–64). Philadelphia: Multilingual Matters.

Avrich, P. (1980). *The modern school movement. Anarchism and education in the United States.* Princeton, NJ: Princeton University Press.

Ayoun, D. (1998, March). *The effect of implicit negative feedback in L2 French.* Paper presented at the third PacSLRF, Aoyama Gakuin University, Tokyo.

Ayoun, D. (2001). The role of negative and positive feedback in the second language acquisition of passé composé and imparfait. *Modern Language Journal, 85*(2), 226–243.

Bachman, L. F. (2002). Some reflections on task-based language performance assessment. *Language Testing, 19*(4), 453–476.

Bachman, L. F., & Cohen, A. D. (Eds.). (1998). *Interfaces between second language acquisition and language testing research.* Cambridge, England: Cambridge University Press.

Baker, C. L. (1979). Syntactic theory and the projection problem. *Linguistic Inquiry, 10,* 533–581.

Baker, N. D., & Nelson, K. E. (1984). Recasting and related conversational techniques for triggering syntactic advances by young children. *First Language, 5,* 3–22.

Bardovi-Harlig, K. (1987). Markedness and salience in second language acquisition. *Language Learning, 37*(2), 385–407.

Barsky, R. (1997). *Noam Chomsky: A life of dissent.* Cambridge, MA: MIT Press.

Bartlett, N. J. D. (2005). A double shot 2% mocha latté, please, with whip: Service encounters in two coffee shops and at a coffee cart. In M. H. Long (Ed.), *Second language needs analysis* (pp. 305–343). Cambridge, England: Cambridge University Press.

Bates, E., & MacWhinney, B. (1989). Functionalism and the competition model. In B. MacWhinney & E. Bates (Eds.), *The cross-linguistic study of sentence processing* (pp. 3–73). Cambridge, England: Cambridge University Press.

Bauman, Z. (1992). *Intimations of postmodernity.* London: Routledge.

Beck, M., & Eubank, L. (1991). Acquisition theory and experimental design: A critique of Tomasello and Herron. *Studies in Second Language Acquisition, 13*(1), 73–76.

Beebe, L., & Giles, H. (1984). Speech-accommodation theories: A discussion in terms of second language acquisition. *International Journal of the Sociology of Language, 46*(1), 1–32.

Beretta, A. (1991). Theory construction in SLA: Complementarity and opposition. *Studies in Second Language Acquisition, 13*(4), 493–511.

Bialystok, E. (1997). The structure of age: In search of barriers to second language acquisition. *Second Language Research, 13*(2), 116–137.

Bialystok, E. (2002). On the reliability of robustness. A reply to DeKeyser. *Studies in Second Language Acquisition, 24*(3), 481–488.

Bialystok, E., & Hakuta, K. (1999). Confounded age: Linguistic and cognitive factors in age differences for second language acquisition. In D. Birdsong (Ed.), *Second language acquisition and the critical period hypothesis* (pp. 161–81). Mahwah, NJ: Lawrence Erlbaum Associates.

Bialystok, E., & Miller, B. (1999). The problem of age in second-language acquisition: Influences from language, structure, and task. *Bilingualism: Language and Cognition, 2*(2), 127–145.

Bickerton, D. (1984). The language bioprogram hypothesis. *Behavioral and Brain Science, 7,* 173–187.

Birdsong, D. (1992). Ultimate attainment in second language acquisition. *Language, 68*(4), 706–755.

Birdsong, D. (1999). Introduction: Whys and why nots of the critical period hypothesis for second language acquisition. In D. Birdsong (Ed.), *Second language acquisition and the critical period hypothesis* (pp. 1–22). Mahwah, NJ: Lawrence Erlbaum Associates.

Birdsong, D., & Molis, M. (2001). On the evidence for maturational constraints in second-language acquisition. *Journal of Memory and Language, 44,* 235–249.

Blau, E. K. (1982). The effect of syntax on readability for ESL students in Puerto Rico. *TESOL Quarterly, 16*(4), 517–528.

Blau, E. K. (1990). The effect of syntax, speed, and pauses on listening comprehension. *TESOL Quarterly, 24*(4), 746–753.

Blau, E. K. (1991). *More on comprehensible input: The effect of pauses and hesitation markers on listening comprehension.* (ERIC Document Reproduction Service No. ED340 234)

Bley-Vroman, R. (1989). What is the logical problem of foreign language learning? In S. M. Gass & J. Schachter (Eds.), *Linguistic perspectives on second language acquisition* (pp. 41–68). Cambridge, England: Cambridge University Press.

Bley-Vroman, R. (1990). The logical problem of foreign language learning. *Linguistic Analysis, 20*(1–2), 3–49.

Bley-Vroman, R. (1997, October). *Features and patterns in foreign language learning.* Plenary address to the Second Language Research Forum, Michigan State University, East Lansing, MI. Retrieved from http://www.lll.hawaii.edu/bley-vroman/

Block, D. (1996). Not so fast: Some thoughts on theory culling, relativism, accepted findings and the heart and soul of SLA. *Applied Linguistics, 17*(1), 63–83.

Block, D. (2003). *The social turn in second language acquisition.* Washington, DC: Georgetown University Press.

Bohannon, J. N. M., MacWhinney, B., & Snow, C. (1990). No negative evidence revisited: Beyond learnability or who has to prove what to whom. *Developmental Psychology, 26,* 221–226.

Bohannon, J. N., Padgett, R. J., Nelson, K. E., & Mark, M. (1996). Useful evidence on negative evidence. *Development Psychology, 24*, 684–689.

Bongaerts, T. (1999). Ultimate attainment in L2 pronunciation: The case of very advanced late L2 learners. In D. Birdsong (Ed.), *Second language acquisition and the critical period hypothesis* (pp. 133–159). Mahwah, NJ: Lawrence Erlbaum Associates.

Bongaerts, T., Mennen, S., & van der Slik, F. (2000). Authenticity of pronunciation in naturalistic second language acquisition. The case of very advanced learners of Dutch as a second language. *Studia Linguistica, 54*, 298–308.

Bongaerts, T., Planken, B., & Schils, E. (1995). Can late starters attain a native accent in a foreign language? A test of the critical period hypothesis. In D. Singleton & Z. Lengyel (Eds.), *The age factor in second language acquisition* (pp. 30–50). Clevedon, England: Multilingual Matters.

Bongaerts, T., van Summeren, C., Planken, B., & Schils, E. (1997). Age and ultimate attainment in the pronunciation of a foreign language. *Studies in Second Language Acquisition, 19*(4), 447–465.

Boom, R. (1998). *A longitudinal study of the use of recasts in adult second language acquisition.* Unpublished manuscript, University of Hawai'i at Manoa.

Borden, G., Gerber, A., & Milsark, G. (1983). Production and perception of the /r/-/l/ contrast in Korean adults learning English. *Language Learning, 33*(4), 499–526.

Bornstein, M. H. (Ed.). (1987). *Sensitive periods in development: Interdisciplinary perspectives.* Hillsdale, NJ: Lawrence Erlbaum Associates.

Braidi, S. M. (1999). Functional approaches. In *The acquisition of second language syntax* (pp. 139–167). London: Arnold.

Braidi, S. M. (2002). Reexamining the role of recasts in native-speaker/nonnative-speaker interactions. *Language Learning, 52*(1), 1–42.

Brock, C., Crookes, G., Day, R. R., & Long, M. H. (1986). Differential effects of corrective feedback in native speaker–nonnative speaker conversation. In R. R. Day (Ed.), *"Talking to learn": Conversation in second language acquisition* (pp. 229–236). Rowley, MA: Newbury House.

Brown, H. D. (1994). *Teaching by principles: An interactive approach to language pedagogy.* NJ: Prentice-Hall Regents.

Brown, R. (1987). A comparison of the comprehensibility of modified and unmodified reading materials for ESL. *University of Hawai'i Working Papers in ESL, 6,*(1), 49–79.

Brumfit, C. (1997). Theoretical practice: applied linguistics as pure and practical science. In A. Mauranen & K. Sajavaara (Eds.), *Applied linguistics across disciplines. AILA Review, 12,* 18–30.

Calvé, P. (1992). Corriger ou ne pas corriger, la n'est pas la question [To correct or not to correct, that is not the question]. *Canadian Modern Language Review, 48,* 458–471.

Carroll, S. (1997). On the irrelevance of verbal feedback to language learning. In L. Eubank, L. Selinker, & M. Sharwood-Smith (Eds.), *The current state of interlanguage* (pp. 73–88). Amsterdam: Benjamins.

Carroll, S., & Swain, M. (1993). Explicit and implicit negative feedback: An empirical study of the learning of linguistic generalizations. *Studies in Second Language Acquisition, 15,* 357–386.

Carroll, S., Swain, M., & Roberge, Y. (1992). The role of feedback in adult second language acquisition: Error correction and morphological generalizations. *Applied Psycholinguistics, 13,* 173–198.

Chambers, J. K. (1992). Dialect acquisition. *Language, 68,*(4), 673–705.

Chaudron, C. (1977). A descriptive model of discourse in the corrective treatment of learners' errors. *Language Learning, 27*(1), 29–46.

Chaudron, C. (1982). Vocabulary elaboration in teachers' speech to L2 learners. *Studies in Second Language Acquisition, 4*(2), 170–180.

Chaudron, C. (1985). Intake: On models and methods for discovering learners' processing of input. *Studies in Second Language Acquisition, 7*(1), 1–14.

Chaudron, C. (1987). The role of error correction in second language teaching. In B. Das (Ed.), *Patterns of classroom interaction in southeast Asia* (pp. 17–50). Singapore: SEAMEO Regional Language Centre.

Chaudron, C., Doughty, C., Kim, Y., Kong, D., Lee, J., Lee, Y., Long, M. H., Rivers, R., & Urano, K. (2005). A task-based needs analysis of a tertiary Korean as a foreign language program. In M. H. Long (ed.), *Second language needs analysis* (pp. 225–261). Cambridge, England: Cambridge University Press.

Chaudron, C., & Richards, J. C. (1986). The effects of discourse markers on the comprehension of lectures. *Applied Linguistics, 7*(2), 113–127.

Chiang, C. S., & Dunkel, P. (1992). The effect of speech modification, prior knowledge, and listening proficiency on EFL lecture learning. *TESOL Quarterly, 26*(2), 345–374.

Choi, M.-Y. (2000). *Effects of recasts on irregular past tense verb morphology in web-chat.* Unpublished master's thesis, University of Hawai'i, Honolulu, HI.

Chung, H. (1995). *Effects of elaborative modification on second language reading comprehension and incidental vocabulary learning.* Unpublished master's thesis, University of Hawai'i, Honolulu, HI.

Clahsen, H., & Muysken, P. (1986). The availability of universal grammar to adult and child learners—a study of the acquisition of German word order. *Second Language Research, 2,* 93–119.

Clyne, M. (1977). Multilingualism and pidginization in Australian industry. *Ethnic Studies, 1,* 40–55.

Cochran, B. P., McDonald, J. L., & Parault, S. J. (1999). Too smart for their own good: The disadvantage of a superior processing capacity for adult language learners. *Journal of Memory and Language, 41,* 30–58.

Collins, R. (1989). Towards a theory of intellectual change: The social causes of philosophies. *Science, Technology, and Human Values, 14*(2), 107–140.

Coppieters, R. (1987). Competence differences between native and near-native speakers. *Language, 63,* 544–573.

Corvalis, G. (1997). *The philosophy of science: Science and objectivity.* Thousand Oaks, CA: Sage.

Crookes, G. (1992).Theory format and SLA theory. *Studies in Second Language Acquisition, 14*(4), 425–449.

Crookes, G. (1997a). SLA and teachers; a socio-educational perspective. *Studies in Second Language Acquisition, 19*(1), 93–116.

Crookes, G. (1997b). What influences how and what second language teachers teach. *Modern Language Journal, 81,*(1), 67–79.

Culp, R. E., Watkins, R. V., Lawrence, H., Letts, D., Kelly, D. J., & Rice, M. L. (1991). Maltreated children's language and speech development: Abused, neglected, and abused and neglected. *First Language, 11,* 377–389.

Cummins, J. (1991). Interdependence of first and second language proficiency in bilingual children. In E. Bilaystok (Ed.), *Language processing in bilingual children* (pp. 70–89). Cambridge, England: Cambridge University Press.

Curtiss, S. (1977). *Genie: A linguistic study of a modern day "wild child."* New York: Academic Press.

Cushing, J. T. (1989).The justification and selection of scientific theories. *Synthese, 78,* 1–24.

Darden, L. (1991). *Theory change in science: Strategies from Mendelian genetics.* New York: Oxford University Press.

Davies, A. (1991). *The native speaker in applied linguistics.* Edinburgh, Scotland: Edinburgh University Press.

DeKeyser, R. (1993). The effect of error correction on L2 grammar knowledge and oral proficiency. *Modern Language Journal, 77*(4), 501–514.

DeKeyser, R. (2000). The robustness of critical period effects in second language acquisition. *Studies in Second Language Acquisition, 22*(4), 499–533.

DeKeyser, R. (2003). Implicit and explicit learning. In C. J. Doughty & M. H. Long (Eds.), *Handbook of SLA* (pp. 313–348). Oxford, England: Blackwell.

DeKeyser, R., & Larson-Hall, J. (2005). What does the critical period really mean? In J. Kroll & A. M. B. de Groot (Eds.), *Handbook of bilingualism: Psycholinguistic approaches* (pp. 88–108). Oxford, England: Oxford University Press.

DeKeyser, R., Ravid, D., & Alfi-Shabtay, I. (2004, May). *Age effects in Russian immigrants acquiring English or Hebrew.* Paper presented at the annual meeting of the American Association for Applied Linguistics, Portland, OR.

Diesing, P. (1991). *How does social science work? Reflections on practice.* Pittsburgh, PA: University of Pittsburgh Press.

Derwing, T. (1996). Elaborative detail: Help or hindrance to the NNS listener? *Studies in Second Language Acquisition, 18,* 283–297.

Doughty, C. J. (1994). Fine-tuning of feedback by competent speakers to language learners. In J. Alatis (Ed.), *GURT: Strategic interaction and language acquisition: Theory, practice, and research* (pp. 96–108). Washington, DC: Georgetown University Press.

Doughty, C. J. (1999, March). *Psycholinguistic evidence for recasting as focus on form.* Paper presented at the American Association for Applied Linguistics conference, Stamford, CT.

Doughty, C. J. (2001). Cognitive underpinnings of focus on form. In P. Robinson (Ed.), *Cognition and SLA* (pp. 206–257). Cambridge, England: Cambridge University Press.

Doughty, C. J. (2003). Instructed SLA; constraints, compensation, and enhancement. In C. J. Doughty & M. H. Long (Eds.), *Handbook of SLA* (pp. 256–310). Oxford, England: Blackwell.

Doughty, C. J., Izumi, S., Maciukaite, S., & Zapata, G. (1999, September). *Recasts, focused recasts, and models: Effects of L2 Spanish word order.* Paper presented at the Second Language Research Forum, University of Minnesota, Minneapolis, MN.

Doughty, C. J., & Long, M. H. (2003a). Optimal psycholinguistic environments for distance foreign language learning. *Language Learning and Technology, 7*(3), 50–80. Retrieved from http://llt.msu.edu

Doughty, C. J., & Long, M. H. (2003b). The scope of inquiry and goals of SLA. In C. J. Doughty & M. H. Long (Eds.), *Handbook of second language acquisition* (pp. 3–15). Oxford, England: Blackwell.

Doughty, C. J., & Varela, E. (1998). Communicative focus on form. In C. J. Doughty & J. Williams (Eds.), *Focus on form in classroom second language acquisition* (pp. 114–138). Cambridge, England: Cambridge University Press.

Doughty, C. J., & Williams, J. (Eds.). (1998a). *Focus on form in classroom second language acquisition.* Cambridge, England: Cambridge University Press.

Doughty, C. J., & Williams, J. (1998b). Pedagogical choices in focus on form. In C. J. Doughty & J. Williams (Eds.), *Focus on form in classroom second language acquisition* (pp. 197–261). Cambridge, England: Cambridge University Press.

Dunkel, P., & Davis, J. N., (1994). The effects of rhetorical signaling cues on recall. In J. Flowerdew (Ed.), *Academic listening: Research perspectives* (pp. 55–74). Cambridge, England: Cambridge University Press.

Dyson, B. (2000). *Focus on learnable form in a communicative context: A framework for second language acquisition in the classroom.* Unpublished manuscript, University of Western Sydney, Macarthur.

Eckman, F. R. (1994). The competence–performance issue in second language acquisition theory: A debate. In E. E. Tarone, S. M. Gass, & A. D. Cohen (Eds.), *Research methodology in second language acquisition* (pp. 3–15). Hillsdale, NJ: Lawrence Erlbaum Associates.

Eckman, F. R. (1996). A functional-typological approach to second language acquisition theory. In W. C. Ritchie & T. K. Bhatia (Eds.), *Handbook of second language acquisition* (pp. 195–211). San Diego: Academic Press.

Eckman, F. R. (2004). From phonemic differences to constraint rankings. Research on second language phonology. *Studies in Second Language Acquisition, 26*(4), 513–549.

Ellis, N. C. (1995). Consciousness in second language acquisition: A review of field studies and laboratory experiments. *Language Awareness, 4*(3), 123–146.

Ellis, N. C., & Laporte, L. (1995). Contexts of acquisition: Effects of formal instruction and naturalistic exposure on second language acquisition. In A. M. B. de Groot & J. F. Kroll (Eds.), Tutorials in Bilingualism: *Psycholinguistic perspectives* (pp. 53–83). Mahwah, NJ: Lawrence Erlbaum Associates.

Ellis, R. (1989). Are classroom and naturalistic acquisition the same? A study of the classroom acquisition of German word order rules. *Studies in Second Language Acquisition, 11*(3), 305–328.

Ellis, R. (1990). An integrated theory of instructed second language learning. In *Instructed second language acquisition: Learning in the classroom* (pp. 174–198). Oxford, England: Blackwell.

Ellis, R. (1995). Modified oral input and the acquisition of word meanings. *Applied Linguistics, 16*(4), 409–441.

Ellis, R. (1997a). SLA and language pedagogy: An educational perspective. *Studies in Second Language Acquisition, 19*(1), 69–92.

Ellis, R. (1997b). *SLA research and language teaching.* Oxford, England: Oxford University Press.

Ellis, R., Basturkmen, H., & Loewen, S. (2001). Learner uptake in communicative classrooms. *Language Learning, 51*(2), 281–318.

Ellis, R., Tanaka, Y., & Yamazaki, A. (1994). Classroom interaction, comprehension, and L2 vocabulary acquisition. *Language Learning, 44*(4), 449–491.

Elman, J. L., Bates, E. A., Johnson, M. H., Karmiloff-Smith, A., Parisi, D., & Plunkett, K. (Eds.). (1996). *Rethinking innateness: A connectionist perspective on development.* Cambridge, MA: MIT Press.

Eubank, L. (1996). Negation in early German-English interlanguage: More valueless features in the L2 initial state. *Second Language Research, 12*(1), 73–106.

Eubank, L., & Gregg, K. R. (1999). Critical periods and (second) language acquisition: Divide et impera. In D. Birdsong (Ed.), *Second language acquisition and the critical period hypothesis* (pp. 65–99). Mahwah, NJ: Lawrence Erlbaum Associates.

Fanselow, J. (1977). The treatment of error in oral work. *Foreign Language Annals, 10*, 583–593.

Farrar, M. J. (1990). Discourse and the acquisition of grammatical morphemes. *Journal of Child Language, 17*, 607–624.

Farrar, M. J. (1992). Negative evidence and grammatical morpheme acquisition. *Developmental Psychology, 28*(1), 90–98.

Feyerabend, P. (1981). More clothes from the Emperor's bargain basement. *British Journal of Philosophy of Science, 32*, 57–94.

Firth, A. (1996). The discursive accomplishment of "normality": On lingua franca English and conversational analysis. *Journal of Pragmatics, 26*, 237–259.

Firth, A., & Wagner, J. (1997). On discourse, communication, and (some) fundamental concepts in SLA research. *Modern Language Journal, 81*(3), 285–300.

Firth, A., & Wagner, J. (1998). SLA property: No trespassing! *Modern Language Journal, 82*(1), 91–94.

Flege, J. E. (1981). The phonological basis of a foreign accent: A hypothesis. *TESOL Quarterly, 15*(4), 443–455.

Flege, J. E. (1995). Second language speech learning: Findings and problems. In W. Strange (Ed.), *Speech perception and linguistic experience: Theoretical and methodological issues* (pp. 233–273). Timonium, MD: York Press.

Flege, J. E. (1999). Age of learning and second language speech. In D. Birdsong (Ed.), *Second language acquisition and the critical period hypothesis* (pp.101–131). Mahwah, NJ: Lawrence Erlbaum Associates.

Flege, J. E., & Fletcher, K. L. (1992). Talker and listener effects on degree of perceived foreign accent. *Journal of the Acoustical Society of America, 91*(1), 370–389.

Flege, J. E., Munro, M., & Mackay, I. (1995). Factors affecting degree of perceived foreign accent in a second language. *Journal of the Acoustical Society of America, 97*, 3125–3134.

Flege, J. E., Yeni-Komshian, G. H., & Liu, S. (1999). Age constraints on second language acquisition. *Journal of Memory and Language, 41*, 78–104.

Flynn, S. (1996). A parameter-resetting approach to second language acquisition. In W. Ritchie & T. J. Bhatia (Eds.), *Handbook of second language acquisition* (pp. 121–158). San Diego: Academic Press.

Flynn, S., & Manuel, S. (1991). Age-dependent effects in language acquisition: An evaluation of "critical period" hypotheses. In L. Eubank (Ed.), *Point-counterpoint: Universal grammar in the second language* (pp. 117–146). Amsterdam: Benjamins.

Fraser Gupta, A. (1994). *The step tongue. Children's English in Singapore*. Philadelphia: Multilingual Matters.

Fuller, J. K. (1978). *An investigation of natural and monitored morpheme difficulty orders by non-native adult students of English*. Unpublished doctoral dissertation, Florida State University, Tallahassee, FL.

Gardner, R. C. (1985). *Social psychology and second language learning: The role of attitude and motivation*. London: Edward Arnold.

Gardner, R. (1988).The socio-educational model of second language learning: Assumptions, findings, and issues. *Language Learning, 38*(1), 101–126.

Gass, S. M. (1997). *Input, interaction, and the second language learner*. Mahwah, NJ: Lawrence Erlbaum Associates.

Gass, S. M. (1998). Apples and oranges; or, why apples are not orange and don't need to be. A response to Firth and Wagner. *Modern Language Journal, 82*(1), 82–90.

Gass, S. M. (2003). Input and interaction. In C. J. Doughty & M. H. Long (Eds.), *Handbook of Second Language Acquisition* (pp. 224–255). Oxford, England: Blackwell.

Gass, S. M., & Mackey, A. (2000). *Stimulated recall methodology in second language research*. Mahwah, NJ: Lawrence Erlbaum Associates.

Gass, S. M., & Varonis, E. M. (1994). Input, interaction, and second language production. *Studies in Second Language Acquisition, 16*, 283–302.

Gasser, M. (1990). Connectionist models. *Studies in Second Language Acquisitions, 12*(2), 179–199.

Gholson, B., & Barker, P. (1985). Kuhn, Lakatos, and Laudan. Applications to the history of physics and psychology. *American Psychologist, 40*(7), 755–769.

Gilabert Guerrero, R. (2004). *Task complexity and L2 narrative oral production*. Unpublished doctoral dissertation, Universitat de Barcelona, Barcelona, ES.

Givon, T. (1979). *On understanding grammar*. New York: Academic Press.

Goldschneider, J., & DeKeyser, R. (2001). Explaining the "natural order of L2 morpheme acquisition" in English: A meta-analysis of multiple determinants. *Language Learning, 51*(1), 1–50.

González-Lloret, M. (2003). Designing task-based CALL to promote interaction: En Busca de Esmeraldas. *Language Learning & Technology, 7*(1), 86–104. Retrieved February 3, 2003, from http://llt.msu.edu/vol7num1/gonzalez/default.html

Gregg, K. R. (1984). Krashen's monitor and Occam's razor. *Applied Linguistics, 5*(2), 79–100.

Gregg, K. R. (1990). The variable competence model of second language acquisition and why it isn't. *Applied Linguistics, 11*, 364–383.

Gregg, K. R. (1993). Taking explanation seriously; or, let a couple of flowers bloom. *Applied Linguistics, 14*(3), 276–294.

Gregg, K. R. (1996). The logical and developmental problems of second language acquisition. In W. C. Ritchie & T. K. Bhatia (Eds.), *Handbook of second language acquisition* (pp. 49–81). San Diego: Academic Press.

Gregg, K. R. (2000). A theory for every occasion: Postmodernism and SLA. *Second Language Research, 16*(4), 343–359.

Gregg, K. R. (2001). Learnability and SLA theory. In P. Robinson (Ed.), *Cognition and second language instruction* (pp. 152–180). Cambridge, England: Cambridge University Press.

Gregg, K. R. (2002). A garden ripe for weeding: A reply to Lantolf. *Second Language Research, 18*(1), 79–81.

Gregg, K. R. (2003). SLA theory: Construction and assessment. In C. J. Doughty & M. H. Long (Eds.), *Handbook of second language acquisition* (pp. 831–865). Oxford, England: Blackwell.

Gregg, K. R., Long, M. H., Jordan, G., & Beretta, A. (1997). Rationality and its discontents in SLA. *Applied Linguistics, 18*(4), 539–559.

Grimshaw, J., & Pinker, S. (1989). Positive and negative evidence in language acquisition. *Behavioral and Brain Sciences, 12*, 341–342.

Griffiths, R. (1992). Speech rate and listening comprehension: Further evidence of the relationship. *TESOL Quarterly, 26*(2), 385–390.

Grobler, A. (1990). Between rationalism and relativism. On Larry Laudan's model of scientific rationality. *British Journal for the Philosophy of Science, 41*, 493–507.

Guba, E. (1990). The alternative paradigm dialog. In E. Guba (Ed.), *The paradigm dialog* (pp. 17–29). Newbury Park, CA: Sage.

Haig, Y. (1995). *The provision and use of recasts: The effect of task types and prosodic cues.* Unpublished master's thesis, University of Western Australia, Nedlands, WA.

Hakuta, K., Bialystok, E., & Wiley, E. (2003). Critical evidence: A test of the critical-period hypothesis for second language acquisition. *Psychological Science, 14*, 31–38.

Hales, M. (1986). *Science or society: The politics of the work of scientists.* London: Free Association Books.

Hamilton, R. L. (1994). Is implicational generalization unidirectional and maximal? Evidence from relativization instruction in a second language. *Language Learning, 44*(1), 123–157.

Harley, B. (1986). *Age in second language acquisition.* Clevedon, England: Multilingual Matters.

Harley, B., & Hart, D. (1987). Language aptitude and second language proficiency in classroom learners of different starting ages. *Studies in Second Language Acquisition, 19*, 379–400.

Harley, B., & Wang, W. (1997). The critical period hypothesis: Where are we now? In A. M. de Groot & J. F. Kroll (Eds.), *Tutorials in bilingualism: Psycholinguistic perspectives* (pp. 19–51). Mahwah, NJ: Lawrence Erlbaum Associates.

Hatch, E., Flashner, V., & Hunt, L. (1986). The experience model and language teaching. In R. R. Day (Ed.), *Talking to learn: Conversation in second language acquisition* (pp. 5–22). Rowley, MA: Newbury House.

Hatch, E. M. (1978). Discourse analysis and second language acquisition. In E. M. Hatch (Ed.), *Second language acquisition: A book of readings* (pp. 402–435). Rowley, MA: Newbury House.

Hatch, E. M. (1979). Apply with caution. *Studies in Second Language Acquisition, 2*(1), 123–143.

Havranek, G. (1999). The effectiveness of corrective feedback: Preliminary results of an empirical study. *Acquisition et Interaction en Langue Etrangere, 2*, 189–206.

Hendrickson, J. (1978). Error correction in foreign language teaching: Recent research and practice. *Modern Language Journal, 62*, 387–398.

Hilles, S. (1991). Access to universal grammar in second language acquisition. In L. Eubank (Ed.), *Point counterpoint: Universal grammar in the second language* (pp. 305–338). Amsterdam: Benjamins.

Hoetker, J., & Ahlbrand, W. P. (1969). The persistence of the recitation. *American Educational Research Journal, 6*(1), 145–167.

Howatt, A. P. R. (1984). *A history of English language teaching.* Oxford, England: Oxford University Press.

Huebner, T. (1983). *A longitudinal analysis of the acquisition of English.* Ann Arbor, MI: Karoma.

Huebner, T. (1985). System and variability in interlanguage syntax. *Language Learning, 35*(2), 141–163.

Hulstijn, J. (1992). Retention of inferred and given word meanings: Experiments in incidental vocabulary learning. In P. Arnaud H. & Bejoint (Eds.), *Vocabulary and applied linguistics* (pp. 113–125). London: Macmillan.

Hulstijn, J., & Hulstijn, W. (1984). Grammatical errors as a function of processing constraints and explicit knowledge. *Language Learning, 34*(1), 23–43.

Hyltenstam, K. (1984). The use of typological markedness conditions as predictors in second language acquisition: The case of pronominal copies in relative clauses. In R. W. Andersen (Ed.), *Second languages: A cross-linguistic perspective* (pp. 39–58). Rowley, MA: Newbury House.

Hyltenstam, K. (1988). Lexical characteristics of near-native L2 learners of Swedish. *Journal of Multilingual and Multicultural Development, 9*, 67–84.

Hyltenstam, K. (1992). Non-native features of near-native speakers: On the ultimate attainment of childhood L2 learners. In R. J. Harris (Ed.), *Cognitive processing in bilinguals* (pp. 351–368). Amsterdam: Elsevier.

Hyltenstam, K., & Abrahamsson, N. (2001). Age and L2 learning: The hazards of matching practical "implications" with theoretical "facts." (Comments on Stefka H. Marinova-Todd, D. Bradford Marshall, and Catherine E. Snow's "Three misconceptions about age and L2 learning"). *TESOL Quarterly, 35*, 151–170.

Hyltenstam, K., & Abrahamsson, N. (2003). Maturational constraints in second language acquisition. In C. J. Doughty & M. H. Long (Eds.), *Handbook of second language acquisition* (pp. 539–588). Oxford, England: Blackwell.

Igor, B. (1985). *And yet it moves: The realization and suppression of science and technology.* New York: Zamisdat Press.

Inagaki, S., & Long, M. H. (1999). The effects of implicit negative feedback on the acquisition of Japanese as a second language. In K. Kanno (Ed.), *The acquisition of Japanese as a second language* (pp. 9–30). Amsterdam: Benjamins.

Ioup, G., Boustagui, E., El Tigi, M., & Moselle, M. (1994). Reexamining the critical period hypothesis. A case study of successful adult SLA in a naturalistic environment. *Studies in Second Language Acquisition, 16*(1), 73–98.

Ishida, S. (2002). *The effect of recasts on the acquisition of aspect in JFL.* Unpublished manuscript, University of Hawai'i, Honolulu, HI.

Ishida, S. (2004, May). *Taking pronunciation to task: Exploring methodological issues in maturational constraints research.* Paper presented at the annual meeting of the American Association of Applied Linguistics, Portland, OR.

Iwashita, N. (1999). *The role of task-based conversation in the acquisition of Japanese grammar and vocabulary.* Unpublished doctoral dissertation, University of Melbourne, Melbourne, AU.

Iwashita, N. (2003). Negative feedback and positive evidence in task-based interaction: Differential effects of L2 development. *Studies in Second Language Acquisition, 25*(1), 1–36.

Izumi, S. (2000). Implicit negative feedback in adult NS–NNS conversations: Its availability, utility, and the discourse structure of the information gap task. *Applied Language Learning, 11*, 289–321.

Jacobs, B. 1988. Neurobiological differentiation of primary and secondary language acquisition. *Studies in Second Language Acquisition, 10*(3), 303–337.

Jacobson, W. H. (1986). An assessment of the communication needs of non-native speakers of English in an undergraduate physics lab. *English for Specific Purposes, 5*(2), 189–195.

Jansen, B., Lalleman, J., & Muysken, P. (1981). The alternation hypothesis: Acquisition of Dutch word order by Turkish and Moroccan foreign workers. *Language Learning, 31*, 315–336.

Jia, G., & Aaronson, D. (2003). A longitudinal study of Chinese children and adolescents learning English in the United States. *Applied Psycholinguistics, 24*(1), 131–161.

Jia, G., Aaronson, D., & Wu, Y. (2002). Long-term language attainment of bilingual immigrants: Predictive variables and language group differences. *Applied Psycholinguistics, 23*(4), 599–621.

Johnson, J., & Newport, E. (1989). Critical period effects in second language learning: The influence of maturational state on the acquisition of English as a second language. *Cognitive Psychology, 21*, 60–99.

Johnson, J. S., & Newport, E. L. (1991). Critical period effects on universal properties of language: The status of subjacency in the acquisition of a second language. *Cognition, 39*, 215–258.

Johnson, K. (1996). *Language teaching and skill learning.* Oxford, England: Blackwell.

Johnston, M. (1985). *Syntactic and morphological progression in learner English.* Research Report. Canberra: Department of Immigration and Ethnic Affairs, Commonwealth of Australia.

Johnston, M. (1998). *Development and variation in learner language.* Unpublished doctoral dissertation, Australian National University, Canberra.

Jordan, G. (2002a). *Property is cleft: Gregg and theory construction in SLA.* Unpublished manuscript.

Jordan, G. (2002b). *Theory construction in second language acquisition.* Unpublished doctoral dissertation. University of London. London.

Jordan, G. (2004). *Theory construction in second language acquisition.* Amsterdam: Benjamins.

Kanno, K. (1997). The acquisition of null and overt pronominals in Japanese by English speakers. *Second Language Research, 13*, 265–287.

Kasper, G. (1997). "A" stands for acquisition: A response to Firth and Wagner. *Modern Language Journal, 81*(3), 307–312.

Keenan, E., & Comrie, B. (1976). Noun phrase accessibility and universal grammar. *Linguistic Inquiry, 8*, 63–99.

Kelch, K. (1985). Modified input as an aid to comprehension. *Studies in Second Language Acquisition, 7*(1), 81–90.

Kelly, L. G. (1969). *Twenty-five centuries of language teaching.* Rowley, MA: Newbury House.

Kersten, A. W., & Earles, J. L. (2001). Less really is more for adults learning a miniature artificial language. *Journal of Memory and Language, 44*, 250–273.

Kilborn, K., & Ito, T. (1989). Sentence-processing in Japanese-English and Dutch-English bilinguals. In B. MacWhinney & E. Bates (Eds.), *The crosslinguistic study of sentence processing* (pp. 257–291). Cambridge, England: Cambridge University Press.

Kim, Y. (1996). *Effects of text elaboration on intentional and incidental foreign language vocabulary learning.* Unpublished master's thesis, University of Hawai'i, Honolulu, HI.

Kim, Y. (2003). *Effects of input elaboration and enhancement on vocabulary acquisition through reading by Korean EFL learners.* Unpublished doctoral dissertation, University of Hawai'i, Honolulu, HI.

Kitcher, P. (1993). *The advancement of science: Science without legend, objectivity without illusions.* New York: Oxford University Press.

Kong, D.-K. (2002). *Effects of task complexity on second-language production.* Unpublished master's thesis, University of Hawai'i at Manoa, Honolulu, HI.

Krashen, S. D. (1979). A response to McLaughlin, "The monitor model: Some methodological considerations." *Language Learning, 29*(1), 151–167.

Krashen, S. D. (1984). Response to Ioup. *TESOL Quarterly, 18*(2), 350–352.

Krashen, S. D. (1985). *The input hypothesis: Issues and implications.* New York: Longman.

Krashen, S. D. (1993). The effect of formal grammar teaching: Still peripheral. *TESOL Quarterly, 27*(4), 722–725.

Krashen, S. D., Butler, J., Birnbaum, R., & Robertson, J. (1978). Two studies in language acquisition and language learning. *ITL: Review of Applied Linguistics, 39–40*, 73–92.

Krashen, S. D., Long, M. H., & Scarcella, R. C. (1979). Age, rate, and eventual attainment in second language acquisition. *TESOL Quarterly, 13*(4), 573–582.

Krashen, S. D., & Scarcella, R. (1978). On routines and patterns in second language acquisition and performance. *Language Learning, 28*(2), 283–300.

Krashen, S. D., Sferlazza, V., Feldman, L., & Fathman, A. (1976). Adult performance on the SLOPE test: More evidence for a natural order in adult second language acquisition. *Language Learning, 26*, 145–151.

Krashen, S. D., & Terrell, T. (1983). *The natural approach: Language acquisition in the classroom.* Oxford, England: Pergamon.

Kropotkin, P. (1975). *An appeal to the young.* In E. Capouya & K. Tomkins (Eds.), *The essential Kropotkin* (pp. 10–27). New York: Liveright. (Original work published 1899)

Kropotkin, P. (1985). *Fields, factories and workshops tomorrow* (C. Ward, Ed.). London: Freedom Press. (Original work published 1899)

Lantolf, J. (1996). SLA theory building: "Letting all the flowers bloom!" *Language Learning, 46*(4), 713–749.

Lantolf, J. P. (2002). Commentary from the flower garden: Responding to Gregg, 2000. *Second Language Research, 18*, 72–78.

Lardiere, D. (1998a). Case and tense in the "fossilized" steady-state. *Second Language Research, 14*, 1–26.

Lardiere, D. (1998b). Dissociating syntax from morphology in a divergent L2 end-state grammar. *Second Language Research, 14*, 359–375.

Larsen-Freeman, D., & Long, M. H. (1991). *An introduction to second language acquisition research.* London: Longman.

Laudan, L. (1977). *Progress and its problems: Towards a theory of scientific growth.* Berkeley: University of California Press.

Laudan, L. (1989). If it ain't broke, don't fix it. *British Journal for the Philosophy of Science, 40*, 369–375.

Laudan, L. (1990). *Science and relativism: Some key controversies in the philosophy of science.* Chicago: University of Chicago Press.

Laudan, L. (1996a). *Beyond positivism and relativism: Theory, method, and evidence.* Boulder, CO: Westview.

Laudan L. (1996b). A problem-solving approach to scientific progress. In *Beyond positivism and relativism: Theory, method, and evidence* (pp. 77–87). Boulder, CO: Westview.

Laudan, L. (1997). Una teoría de la evaluación comparativa de teorías científicas [A theory of the comparative evaluation of scientific theories]. In W. Gonzalez (Ed.), *Jornadas en torno al pensamiento de L. Laudan.* Ferrol, Spain: Universidad de la Coruna.

Laudan, L., & Laudan, R. (1989). Dominance and disunity of method: Solving the problems of innovation and consensus. *Philosophy of Science, 56*, 221–237.

Lechte, J. (1994). *Fifty key contemporary thinkers: From structuralism to postmodernity.* London: Routledge.

Lee, D. (1992). Universal grammar, learnability, and the acquisition of English reflexive binding by L1 Korean speakers. Doctoral dissertation, University of Souther California, Los Angeles.

Lee, J. (1998). *Is there a sensitive period for second language collocational knowledge?* Unpublished master's thesis, University of Hawai'i, Honolulu, HI.

Lee, Y.-G. (2002). *Effects of task complexity on the complexity and accuracy of oral production in L2 Korean.* Unpublished doctoral dissertation. University of Hawai'i, Honolulu, HI.

Leeman, J. (2000). *Towards a new classification of input: An empirical study of the effect of recasts, negative evidence, and enhanced salience on L2 development.* Unpublished doctoral dissertation, Georgetown University, Washington, DC.

Leeman, J. (2003). Recasts and L2 development: Beyond negative evidence. *Studies in Second Language Acquisition, 25*(1), 37–63.

Lightbown, P. M. (1983). Exploring relationships between developmental and instructional sequences. In H. W. Seliger & M. H. Long (Eds.), *Classroom-oriented research on second language acquisition* (pp. 217–243). Rowley, MA: Newbury House.

Lightbown, P. M. (1998). The importance of timing in focus on form. In C. J. Doughty & J. Williams (Eds.), *Focus on form in classroom second language acquisition* (pp. 177–196). Cambridge, England: Cambridge University Press.

Lightbown, P. M., & Spada, N. (1993). *How languages are learned.* Oxford, England: Oxford University Press.

Lincoln, Y. (1990). The making of a constructivist: A remembrance of transformations past. In E. Guba (Ed.), *The paradigm dialog* (pp. 67–87). Newbury Park, CA: Sage.

Lipton, P. (1991). *Inference to the best explanation.* London: Routledge.

Lochtman, K. (2000, August 24–26). *The role of negative feedback in experiential vs. analytic foreign language teaching.* Paper presented at the Conference on Instructed Second Language Learning, Brussels, Belgium.

Loewen, S., & Philp, J. (2005). Recasts in the adult L2 classroom: Characteristics, explicitness and effectiveness. *Modern Language Journal, 26.*

Long, M. H. (1977). Teacher feedback on learner error: Mapping cognitions. In H. D. Brown, C. A. Yorio, & R. H. Crymes (Eds.), *On TESOL '77* (pp. 278–293). Washington, DC: TESOL.

Long, M. H. (1983a). Does second language instruction make a difference? A review of research. *TESOL Quarterly, 17*(3), 359–382.

Long, M. H. (1983b). Linguistic and conversational adjustments to non-native speakers. *Studies in Second Language Acquisition, 5* (2), 177–193.

Long, M. H. (1983c). Native speaker/non-native speaker conversation and the negotiation of comprehensible input. *Applied Linguistics, 4*(2), 126–141.

Long, M. H. (1985a). Input and second language acquisition theory. In S. M. Gass & C. G. Madden (Eds.), *Input in second language acquisition* (pp. 377–393). Rowley, MA: Newbury House.

Long, M. H. (1985b). A role for instruction in second language acquisition: Task-based language teaching. In K. Hyltenstam & M. Pienemann (Eds.), *Modeling and assessing second language development* (pp. 77–99). Clevedon, England: Multilingual Matters.

Long, M. H. (1988). Instructed interlanguage development. In L. M. Beebe (Ed.), *Issues in second language acquisition: Multiple perspectives* (pp. 115–141). Cambridge, MA: Newbury House/Harper and Row.

Long, M. H. (1989). Task, group, and task-group interactions. *University of Hawai'i Working Papers in ESL, 8*(2), 1–26.

Long, M. H. (1990a). The least a second language acquisition theory needs to explain. *TESOL Quarterly, 24*(4), 649–666.

Long, M. H. (1990b). Maturational constraints on language development. *Studies in Second Language Acquisition, 12,* 251–285.

Long, M. H. (1991). Focus on form: A design feature in language teaching methodology. In K. de Bot, R. B. Ginsberg, & C. Kramsch (Eds.), *Foreign language research in cross-cultural perspective* (pp. 39–52). Amsterdam: Benjamins.

Long, M. H. (1993a). Assessment strategies for second language acquisition theories. *Applied Linguistics, 14,* 225–249.

Long, M. H. (1993b). Second language acquisition as a function of age: Research findings and methodological issues. In K. Hyltenstam & A. Viberg (Eds.), *Progression and regression in language* (pp. 196–221). Cambridge, England: Cambridge University Press.

Long, M. H. (1994). On the advocacy of the task-based syllabus. *TESOL Quarterly, 28*(4), 782–790.

Long, M. H. (1996). The role of the linguistic environment in second language acquisition. In W. C. Ritchie & T. J. Bhatia (Eds.), *Handbook of second language acquisition* (pp. 413–468). New York: Academic Press.

Long, M. H. (1997a). Authenticity and learning potential in L2 classroom discourse. In G. M. Jacobs (Ed.), *Language classrooms of tomorrow: Issues and responses* (pp. 148–169). Singapore: SEAMEO Regional Language Centre.

Long, M. H. (1997b). Construct validity in SLA research: A response to Firth and Wagner. *Modern Language Journal, 81*(3), 318–323.

Long, M. H. (1998). Focus on form in task-based language teaching. *University of Hawai'i Working Papers in ESL, 16*(2), 35–49.

Long, M. H. (2003). Stabilization and fossilization in interlanguage development. In C. J. Doughty & M. H. Long (Eds.), *Handbook of second language acquisition* (pp. 487–535). Oxford, England: Blackwell.

Long, M. H. (2005a). Methodological issues in learner needs analysis. In M. H. Long (Ed.), *Second language needs analysis* (pp. 19–76). Cambridge, England: Cambridge University Press.

Long, M. H. (2005b). Problems with supposed counter-evidence to the critical period hypothesis. *International Review of Applied Linguistics, 43*(4), 287–317.

Long, M. H. (2005c). *Second language needs analysis.* Cambridge, England: Cambridge University Press.

Long, M. H. (2006). *Task-based language teaching.* Unpublished manuscript.

Long, M. H., Adams, L., McLean, M., & Castanos, F. (1976). Doing things with words: Verbal interaction in lockstep and small group classroom situations. In J. Fanselow & R. Crymes (Eds.), *On TESOL '76* (pp. 137–153). Washington, DC: TESOL.

Long, M. H., Brock, C., Crookes, G., Deicke, C., Potter, L., & Zhang, S. (1984). *The effect of teachers' questioning patterns and wait-time on pupil participation in public high school classes in Hawaii for students of limited English proficiency (Tech. Rep. No. 1).* Honolulu: Center for Second Language Classroom Research, Social Science Research Institute, University of Hawai'i at Manoa.

Long, M. H., & Crookes, G. (1987). Intervention points in second language classrooms. In B. Das (Ed.), *Patterns of interaction in classrooms in Southeast Asia* (pp. 177–203). Singapore: Regional English Language Centre.

Long, M. H., & Crookes, G. (1992). Three approaches to task-based language teaching. *TESOL Quarterly, 26*(1), 27–56.

Long, M. H., & Crookes, G. (1993a). The authors respond … *TESOL Quarterly, 27*(4), 729–733.

Long, M. H., & Crookes, G. (1993b). Units of analysis in syllabus design: The case for task. In G. Crookes & S. M. Gass (Eds.), *Tasks in pedagogical context: Integrating theory and practice* (pp. 9–54). Clevedon, England: Multilingual Matters.

Long, M. H., Doughty, C. J., Kim, Y., Lee, J.-H., & Lee, Y.-G. (2003). *Task-based language teaching: A demonstration module.* Honolulu, HI: National Foreign Language Research Center.

Long, M. H., Inagaki, S., & Ortega, L. (1998). The role of implicit negative feedback in SLA: Models and recasts in Japanese and Spanish. *Modern Language Journal, 82*(3), 357–371.

Long, M. H., Kim, Y., Lee, Y.-G., & Doughty, C. J. (2003). *Task-based language teaching: A demonstration* (NFLRC RN No.37v). Honolulu: University of Hawai'i, Second Language Teaching and Curriculum Center.

Long, M. H., & Norris, J. M. (2000). Task-based teaching and assessment. In M. Byram (Ed.), *Encyclopedia of language teaching* (pp. 597–603). London: Routledge.

Long, M. H., & Robinson, P. (1998). Focus on form: Theory, research, and practice. In C. J. Doughty & J. Williams (Eds.), *Focus on form in classroom second language acquisition* (pp. 15–41). Cambridge, England: Cambridge University Press.

Long, M. H., & Ross, S. (1993). Modifications that preserve language and content. In M. Tickoo (Ed.), *Simplification: Theory and application* (pp. 29–52). Singapore: SEAMEO Regional Language Centre.

Lugg, A. (1986). An alternative to the traditional model? Laudan on disagreement and consensus in science. *Philosophy of Science, 53,* 419–424.

Lyotard, J. F. (1984). *The postmodern condition: A report on knowledge.* Manchester, England: Manchester University Press.

Lyotard, J. F. (1992). *The postmodern explained to children: Correspondence 1982–1984.* London: Turnaround.

Lyster, R. (1998a). Negotiation of form, recasts, and explicit correction in relation to error types and learner repair in immersion classrooms. *Language Learning, 48*(2), 183–218.

Lyster, R. (1998b). Recasts, repetition and ambiguity in L2 classroom discourse. *Studies in Second Language Acquisition, 20*(1), 51–81.

Lyster, R. (1999). La négotiation de la forme: la suite … mais pas la fin [Negotiation of form: The sequel … but not the end]. *Canadian Modern Language Review, 55*(3), 355–384.

Lyster, R., & Ranta, L. (1997). Corrective feedback and learner uptake: Negotiation of form in communicative classrooms. *Studies in Second Language Acquisition, 19*(1), 37–66.

Mackey, A. (1995). *Stepping up the pace: Input, interaction and interlanguage development. An empirical study of questions in ESL.* Unpublished doctoral dissertation, University of Sydney.

Mackey, A. (1999). Input, interaction and second language development. *Studies in Second Language Acquisition, 21*(4), 557–587.

Mackey, A., Gass, S. M., & McDonough, K. (2000). How do learners perceive interactional feedback? *Studies in Second Language Acquisition, 22,* 471–497.

Mackey, A., & Oliver, R. (2002). Interactional feedback and children's L2 development. *System, 30,* 459–477.

Mackey, A., & Philp, J. (1998). Conversational interaction and second language development: Recasts, responses, and red herrings? *Modern Language Journal, 82*(3), 338–356.

MacWhinney, B. (1997). Second language acquisition and the competition model. In A. M. B. de Groot & J. F. Kroll (Eds.), *Tutorial in bilingualism: Psycholinguistic perspectives* (pp. 113–142). Mahwah, NJ: Lawrence Erlbaum Associates.

Manheimer, R. (1993). Close the task, improve the discourse. *Estudios de Linguistica Aplicada, 17,* 18–40.

Marcus, G. (1993). Negative evidence in language acquisition. *Cognition, 46,* 53–85.

Marinova-Todd, S. H., Marshall, D. B., & Snow, C. E. (2000). Three misconceptions about age and L2 learning. *TESOL Quarterly, 34*(1), 9–34.

Markee, N. (1994). Towards an ethnomethodological respecification of second language acquisition studies. In E. Tarone, S. M. Gass, & A. D. Cohen (Eds.), *Research methodology in second language acquisition* (pp. 89–116). Mahwah, NJ: Lawrence Erlbaum Associates.

Martin, B. (1991). *Strip the experts.* London: Freedom Press.

Martohardjono, G., & Flynn, S. (1995). Language transfer: What do we really mean? In L. Eubank, L. Selinker, & M. Sharwood-Smith (Eds.). *The current state of interlanguage* (pp. 205–217). Philadelphia: Benjamins.

Mayberry, R. (1993). First-language acquisition after childhood differs from second-language acquisition: The case of American Sign Language. *Journal of Speech and Hearing Research, 36,* 1258–1270.

Mayberry, R. I., & Lock, E. (2003). Age constraints on first versus second language acquisition: Evidence for linguistic plasticity and epigenesis. *Brain and Language, 87,* 369–384.

McLaughlin, B. (1978). The monitor model: Some methodological considerations. *Language Learning, 28,* 309–332.

Meisel, J. M. (1991). Principles of universal grammar and strategies of language learning: Some similarities and differences between first and second language acquisition. In L. Eubank (Ed.), *Point counterpoint: Universal grammar in the second language* (pp. 231–276). Amsterdam: Benjamins.

Meisel, J. M. (1997). The acquisition of the syntax of negation in French and German: Contrasting first and second language acquisition. *Second Language Research, 13,* 227–263.

Meisel, J. M., Clahsen, H., & Pienemann, M. (1981). On determining developmental stages in natural second language acquisition. *Studies in Second Language Acquisition, 3*(1), 109–135.

Mellow, D., Reeder, K., & Kennedy, E. (1996). Using time series research designs to investigate the effects of instruction on SLA. *Studies in Second Language Acquisition, 18*(3), 325–350.

Mislevy, R. J., Steinberg, L. S., & Almond, R. G. (2002). Design and analysis in task-based language assessment. *Language Testing, 19*(4), 477–496.

Mitchell, R., & Myles, F. (1998). *Second language learning theories.* London: Arnold.

Moyer, A. (1999). Ultimate attainment in L2 phonology: The critical factors of age, motivation and instruction. *Studies in Second Language Acquisition, 21*(1), 81–108.

Mito, K. (1993). *The effects of modeling and recasting on the acquisition of L2 grammar rules.* Unpublished manuscript, University of Hawai'i, Honolulu, HI.

Mohan, B., & Beckett, G. H. (2001). A functional approach to research on content-based language learning: Recasts in causal explanations. *Canadian Modern Language Review, 58*(1), 133–155.

Mori, H. (1998, March). *Corrective feedback and learner uptake in Japanese immersion classrooms at different grade levels.* Paper presented at the third PacSLRF, Aoyama Gakuin University, Tokyo.

Moroishi, M. (2001). Recasts and learner uptake in Japanese classroom discourse. In X. Bonch-Bruevich, W. Crawford, J. Hellermann, C. Higgins, & N. Nguyen (Eds.), *The past, present, and future of second language research: Selected proceedings of the 2000 Second Language Research Forum* (pp. 197–208). Sommerville, MA: Cascadilla.

Morris, F. A. (2002). Negotiation moves and recasts in relation to error types and learner repair in the foreign language classroom. *Foreign Language Annals, 35*(4), 395–404.

Muranoi, H. (1998, March). *Corrective recasts and JSL learners' modification of interlanguage systems.* Paper presented at the third PacSLRF, Aoyama Gakuin University, Tokyo.

Musumechi, D. (1997). *An exploration of the historical relationship between theory and practice in second language teaching.* New York: McGraw-Hill.

Nation, P. (Ed.). (1986). *Vocabulary lists: Words, affixes and stems* (rev. ed.). Occasional Publication No. 12. Wellington: English Language Institute, Victoria University of Wellington.

Nelson, K. E. (1987). Some observations from the perspective of the rare event cognitive comparison theory of language acquisition. In K. Nelson & D. van Kleeck (Eds.), *Childrens' language* (Vol. 6, pp. 289–331). Mahwah, NJ: Lawrence Erlbaum Associates.

Netten, J. (1991). Toward a more language oriented second language classroom. In L. Malav & G. Duquette (Eds.), *Language, culture, and cognition* (pp. 284–304). Clevedon, England: Multilingual Matters.

Neufeld, G. (1977). Language learning ability in adults: A study on the acquisition of prosodic and articulatory features. *Working Papers on Bilingualism, 12,* 46–60.

Neufeld, G. 1978. On the acquisition of prosodic and articulatory features in adult language learning. *Canadian Modern Language Review, 34,* 163–174.

Neufeld, G. (1988). Phonological asymmetry in second-language learning and performance. *Language Learning, 38,* 531–559.

Neufeld, G. (2001). Non-foreign-accented speech in adult second language learners: Does it exist and what does it signify? *ITL Review of Applied Linguistics, 133–134,* 185–206.

Newport, E. (1990). Maturational constraints on language learning. *Cognitive Science, 14*(1), 11–28.

Newton, J., & Kennedy, G. (1996). Effects of communication tasks on the grammatical relations marked by second language learners. *System, 24*(3), 309–322.

Nicholas, H., Lightbown, P. M., & Spada, N. (2001). Recasts as feedback to language learners. *Language Learning, 51*(4), 719–758.

Norris, J. M. (2002). Interpretations, intended uses and designs in task-based language assessment. *Language Testing, 19*(4), 337–346.

Norris, J. M., Brown, J. D., Hudson, T., & Yoshioka, J. (1998). Task-based assessment. In J. M. Norris, J. D. Brown, T. Hudson, & J. Yoshioka, *Designing second language performance assessments* (pp. 53–62). (Tech. Rep. No.18). Honolulu, HI: Second Language Teaching and Curriculum Center, University of Hawai'i at Manoa.

Norris, J. M., & Ortega, L. (2003). Defining and measuring SLA. In C. J. Doughty & M. H. Long (Eds.), *Handbook of second language acquisition* (pp. 717–761). Oxford, England: Blackwell.

Norris, J., & Ortega, L. (2000). Effectiveness of L2 instruction: A research synthesis and quantitative meta-analysis. *Language Learning, 50*(3), 417–528.

Nunan, D. (1987). Communicative language teaching: Making it work. *English Language Teaching Journal, 41*(2), 136–145.

Nunan, D. (1991). Communicative tasks and the language curriculum. *TESOL Quarterly, 25*(2), 279–295.

Nunan, D. (1994). A reader reacts. *TESOL Quarterly, 28*(4), 781–782.

Nystrom, N. (1983). Teacher–student interaction in bilingual classrooms: Four approaches to error feedback. In H. W. Seliger & M. H. Long (Eds.), *Classroom-oriented research in second language acquisition* (pp. 169–188). Rowley, MA: Newbury House.

Odlin, T. (1989). *Language transfer: Cross-linguistic influence in language learning.* Cambridge, England: Cambridge University Press.

O'Grady, W. (1996). Language acquisition without universal grammar: A general nativist proposal for L2 learning. *Second Language Research, 12*(4), 374–397.

O'Grady, W. (2003). The radical middle: Nativism without universal grammar. In C. J. Doughty & M. H. Long (Eds.), *Handbook of second language acquisition* (pp. 43–62). Oxford, England: Blackwell.

Oh, S.-Y. (2001). Two types of input modification and EFL reading comprehension: Simplification versus elaboration. *TESOL Quarterly, 35*(1), 69–96.

Ohta, A. S. (2000). Rethinking recasts: A learner-centered examination of corrective feedback in the Japanese language classroom. In J. K. Hall & L. S. Verplaeste (Eds.), *The construction of second and foreign language learning through classroom instruction* (pp. 47–71). Mahwah, NJ: Lawrence Erlbaum Associates.

Oliver, R. (1995). Negative feedback in child NS–NNS conversation. *Studies in Second Language Acquisition, 18*(4), 459–481.

Oliver, R. (1998). Negotiation of meaning in child interactions: The relationship between conversational interaction and second language acquisition. *Modern Language Journal, 82*(3), 372–386.

Oliver, R. (2000). Age differences in negotiation and feedback in classroom and pairwork. *Language Learning, 50*(1), 119–151.

Ono, L., & Witzel, J. (2002). Recasts, salience, and morpheme acquisition. Unpublished manuscript, University of Hawai'i, Honolulu, HI.

Ortega, L. (1999). Planning and focus on form in L2 oral performance. *Studies in Second Language Acquisition, 21*(1), 109–148.

Ortega, L., & Long, M. H. (1997). The effects of models and recasts on the acquisition of object topicalization and adverb placement in L2 Spanish. *Spanish Applied Linguistics, 1*(1), 65–86.

Oyama, S. (1976). A sensitive period for the acquisition of a nonnative phonological system. *Journal of Psycholinguistic Research, 5*(3), 261–283.

Oyama, S. (1978). The sensitive period and comprehension of speech. *Working Papers on Bilingualism, 16*, 1–17.

Oyama, S. (1979). The concept of the sensitive period in developmental studies. *Merrill-Palmer Quarterly, 25*, 83–103.

Palmen, M.-J., Bongaerts, T, & Schils, E. (1997). L'autheticite de la pronunciation dans l'acquisition d'une language etrangere au-dela de la periode critique: Des apprenants neerlandais parvenus a un niveau tres avance en francais. *Adquisicion et Interaction en*

Langue Etrangere [Authenticity of pronunciation in post-critical period foreign language acquisition: Dutch learners who have reached very advanced levels in French. *Foreign Language Acquisition and Interaction*] 9, 173–191.

Panova. I. (1999). *Patterns of corrective feedback and uptake in an adult ESL classroom*. Unpublished master's thesis, McGill University, Montreal.

Parker, K., & Chaudron, C. (1987). The effects of linguistic simplification and elaborative modification on L2 comprehension. *University of Hawai'i Working Papers in ESL, 6*(2), 107–133.

Patkowski, M. (1980). The sensitive period for the acquisition of syntax in a second language. *Language Learning, 30*(2), 449–472.

Patkowski, M. (1982). The sensitive period for the acquisition of syntax in a second language. In S. D. Krashen, R. C. Scarcella, & M. H. Long (Eds.), *Child–adult differences in second language acquisition* (pp. 52–63). Rowley, MA: Newbury House.

Pavesi, M. (1986). Markedness, discoursal modes, and relative clause formation in a formal and an informal context. *Studies in Second Language Acquisition, 8*(1), 38–55.

Payne, A. (1980). Factors controlling the acquisition of the Philadelphia dialect by out-of-state children. In W. Labov (Ed.), *Locating language in time and space* (pp. 143–178). New York: Academic Press.

Pennycook, A. (1995). English in the world/the world in English. In J. W. Tollefson (Ed.), *Power and inequality in language education* (pp. 34–58), Cambridge, England. Cambridge University Press.

Pennycook, A. (1996). Borrowing others' words: Text, ownership, memory, and plagiarism. *TESOL Quarterly, 30*(2), 201–230.

Perez-Leroux, A. T., & Glass, W. R. (1997). OPC effects on the L2 acquisition of Spanish. In A. T. Perez-Leroux & W. R. Glass (Eds.), *Contemporary perspectives on the acquisition of Spanish* (pp. 149–165). Somerville, MA: Cascadilla.

Phillips, M., & Shettlesworth, C. (1975, August). *Questions in the design and use of courses in English for specialized purposes*. Paper presented at the fourth International Congress of Applied Linguistics, Stuttgart.

Philp, J. (1997). *Do learners notice recasts in task-based interaction?* Paper presented at the Second Language Research Forum, Michigan State University, East Lansing.

Philp, J. (1999). *Interaction, noticing and second language acquisition: An examination of learners' noticing of recasts in task-based interaction*. Unpublished doctoral dissertation, University of Tasmania, Hobart.

Philp, J. (2003). Constraints on "noticing the gap": Non-native speakers' noticing of recasts in NS–NNS interaction. *Studies in Second Language Acquisition, 25*.

Pica, T. (1983). Adult acquisition of English as a second language under different conditions of exposure. *Language Learning, 33*(4), 465–497.

Pica, T. (1994). Research on negotiation: What does it reveal about second-language learning conditions, processes, and outcomes? *Language Learning, 44*(3), 493–527.

Pica, T. (1988). Interlanguage adjustments as an outcome of NS–NNS negotiated interaction. *Language Learning, 38*, 45–73.

Pica, T., Doughty, C. J., & Young, R. (1986). Making input comprehensible: Do interactional modifications help? *ITL Review of Applied Linguistics, 72*, 1–25.

Pica, T., Lincoln-Porter, F., Paninos, D., & Linnel, J. (1996). Language learners' interaction: How does it address the input, output and feedback needs of L2 learners? *TESOL Quarterly, 30*(1), 59–83.

Pienemann, M. (1984). Psychological constraints on the teachability of languages. *Studies in Second Language Acquisition, 6*(2), 186–214.

Pienemann, M. (1985). Learnability and syllabus construction. In K. Hyltenstam & M. Pienemann (Eds.), *Modeling and assessing second language acquisition* (pp. 23–75). Clevedon, England: Multilingual Matters.

Pienemann, M. (1989). Is language teachable? Psycholinguistic experiments and hypotheses. *Applied Linguistics, 10*(1), 52–79.

Pienemann, M. (1998). *Language processing and second language development: Processability theory.* Amsterdam: Benjamins.

Pinker, S. (1989). Resolving a learnability paradox in the acquisition of the verb lexicon. In M. L. Rice & R. L. Schiefelbusch (Eds.), *The teachability of language* (pp. 13–61). Baltimore: Brookes.

Piske, T., MacKay, I., & Flege, J. E. (2001). Factors affecting degree of foreign accent in an L2: A review. *Journal of Phonetics, 29*, 191–215.

Plunkett, K. (1995). Connectionist approaches to language acquisition. In P. Fletcher & B. MacWhinney (Eds.), *The handbook of child language* (pp. 36–72). Oxford, England: Blackwell.

Poulisse, N. (1997). Some words in defense of the psycholinguistic approach. *Modern Language Journal, 81*(3), 324–328.

Purchase, G. (1996). *Evolution and revolution: An introduction to the life and thought of Peter Kropotkin.* Sydney: Jura Books.

Rabie, S. R. (1996). *Negative feedback, modeling, and vocabulary acquisition in task-based interaction.* Unpublished master's thesis, University of Hawai'i at Manoa, Honolulu, HI.

Rahimpour, M. 1997. *Task condition, task complexity and variation in oral L2 narrative discourse.* Unpublished doctoral dissertation, CLTR, University of Queensland, Brisbane.

Rampton, B. (1987). Stylistic variability and not speaking "normal" English: Some post-Labovian approaches and their implications for the study of interlanguage. In R. Ellis (Ed.), *Second language acquisition in context* (pp. 47–58). Englewood-Cliffs, NJ: Prentice-Hall.

Rampton, B. (1995). *Crossing: Language and ethnicity among adolescents.* London: Longman.

Rampton, B. (1997a). Retuning in applied linguistics. *International Journal of Applied Linguistics, 7*(1), 3–25.

Rampton, B. (1997b). Second language research in late modernity. *Modern Language Journal, 81*(3), 329–333.

Rampton, B. (1997c). A sociolinguistic perspective on L2 communication strategies. In G. Kasper & E. Kellerman (Eds.), *Communication strategies: Psycholinguistic and sociolinguistic perspectives* (pp. 279–303). London: Longman.

Reber, A. S., & Allen, R. (2000). Individual differences in implicit learning: Implications for the evolution of consciousness. In R. G. Kunzendorf & B. Wallace (Eds.), *Individual differences in conscious experience* (pp. 227–247). Amsterdam: Benjamins.

Redhead, M. (1995). *From physics to metaphysics.* Cambridge, England: Cambridge University Press.

Richards, B. (1994). Child-directed speech and influences on language acquisition: Methodology and interpretation. In C. Galloway & B. Richards (Eds.), *Input and interaction in language acquisition* (pp. 74–106). Cambridge, England: Cambridge University Press.

Richardson, M.A. (1995). *The use of negative evidence in the second language acquisition of grammatical morphemes.* Unpublished master's thesis, University of Western Australia, Perth.

Riggs, P. J. (1992a). Laudan's theory of evolving research traditions. In *Whys and ways of science: Introducing philosophical and sociological theories of science* (pp. 95–123). Carlton, Victoria: Melbourne University Press.

Riggs, P. J. (1992b). *Whys and ways of science. Introducing philosophical and sociological theories of science.* Carlton, Victoria: Melbourne University Press.

Roberts, M. A. (1995). Awareness and the efficacy of error correction. In R. W. Schmidt (Ed.), *Attention and awareness in foreign language learning* (Tech. Rep. No.9) (pp. 163–182). Honolulu, HI: Second Language Teaching and Curriculum Center.

Robinson, P. (1995a). Aptitude, awareness, and the fundamental similarity of implicit and explicit second language learning. In R. W. Schmidt (Ed.), *Attention and awareness in foreign language learning* (pp. 303–358). Honolulu, HI: Second Language Teaching and Curriculum Center.

Robinson, P. (1995b). Task complexity and second language narrative discourse. *Language Learning, 45*, 99–140.

Robinson, P. (1997). State of the art: SLA research and second language teaching. *The Language Teacher* (Japan), *21*(7), 7–16.

Robinson, P. (1998). State of the art: SLA theory and second language syllabus design. *The Language Teacher, 22*(4), 7–14.

Robinson, P. (2001a). Task complexity, cognitive resources, and syllabus design. In P. Robinson (Ed.), *Cognition and second language instruction* (pp. 287–318). Cambridge, England: Cambridge University Press.

Robinson, P. (2001b). Task complexity, task difficulty and task production: Exploring interactions in a componential framework. *Applied Linguistics, 22*(1), 27–57.

Robinson, P. (2003). Attention and memory during SLA. In C. J. Doughty & M. H. Long (Eds.), *Handbook of second language acquisition* (pp. 631–678). New York: Blackwell.

Robinson, P., Ting, S. C.-C., & Urwin, J. J. (1995). Investigating second language task complexity. *RELC Journal, 26*(2), 62–79.

Rosenau, P. M. (1992). *Post-modernism and the social sciences: Insights, inroads, and intrusions.* Princeton, NJ: Princeton University Press.

Sato, C.J. (1986). Conversation and interlanguage development: Rethinking the connection. In R. R. Day (Ed.), *Talking to learn: Conversation and second language acquisition* (pp. 23–45). Rowley, MA: Newbury House.

Sato, C. J. (1988). Origins of complex syntax in interlanguage development. *Studies in Second Language Acquisition, 10*(3), 371–395.

Sato, C. J. (1989). A nonstandard approach to Standard English. *TESOL Quarterly, 23*(2), 259–282.

Sato, C.J. (1990). *The syntax of conversation in interlanguage development.* Tubingen: Gunter Narr.

Saxton, M. (1997). The contrast theory of negative input. *Journal of Child Language, 24*, 139–161.

Saxton, M., Kulscar, B., Greer, M., & Rupra, M. (1998). Longer-term effects of corrective input: An experimental approach. *Journal of Child Language, 25*, 701–721.

Scarcella, R. C., & Higa, C. (1981). Input, negotiation, and age differences in second language acquisition. *Language Learning, 31*(2), 409–437.

Schachter, J. (1981). The hand signal system. *TESOL Quarterly, 15*(1), 125–138.

Schachter, J. (1988). Second language acquisition and its relationship to universal grammar. *Applied Linguistics, 9*,219–235.

Schachter, J. (1990). On the issue of completeness in second language acquisition. *Second Language Research, 6*(2), 93–124.

Schachter, J. (1991). Corrective feedback in historical perspective. *Second Language Research, 7*(2), 89–102.

Schmidt, R. W. (1983). Interaction, acculturation, and the acquisition of communicative competence; A case study of an adult. In N. Wolfson & E. Judd (Eds.), *Sociolinguistics and second language acquisition* (pp. 137–174). Rowley, MA: Newbury House.

Schmidt, R. W. (1990). The role of consciousness in second language learning. *Applied Linguistics, 11*, 129–158.

Schmidt, R. W. (1995). Consciousness and foreign language learning: A tutorial on the role of attention and awareness in learning. In R. W. Schmidt (Ed.), *Attention and awareness in foreign language learning* (pp. 1–63) *(Tech. Rep. No. 9)*. Honolulu, HI: Second Language Teaching and Curriculum Center.

Schmidt, R. (2001). Attention. In P. Robinson (Ed.), *Cognition and second language instruction* (pp. 3–32). Cambridge, England: Cambridge University Press.

Schumann, J. H. (1978). The acculturation model for second language acquisition. In R. Gingras (Ed.), *Second language acquisition and foreign language teaching* (pp. 27–50). Arlington, VA: Center for Applied Linguistics.

Schumann, J. H. (1983). Art and science in second language acquisition research. In M. Clarke & J. Handscombe (Eds.), *On TESOL '82* (pp. 107–124). Washington, DC: TESOL.

Schumann, J. H. (1986). Research on the acculturation model for second language acquisition. *Journal of Multilingual and Multiculutural Development, 7*, 379–392.

Schwartz, B. (1992). Testing between UG-based and problem-solving models of L2A: Developmental sequence data. *Language Acquisition, 2*(1), 1–19.

Schwartz, B. D. (1993). On explicit and negative evidence effecting and affecting competence and "linguistic behavior." *Studies in Second Language Acquisition, 15*(2), 147–163.

Schwartz, B. D. (1998). The second language instinct. *Lingua, 106*, 133–160.

Schwartz, B. D., & Sprouse, R. A. (1996). L2 cognitive states and the full transfer/full access hypothesis. *Second Language Research, 12*(1), 40–72.

Schwartz, B., & Gubla-Ryzak, M. (1992). Learnability and grammar reorganization in L2A: Against negative evidence causing the unlearning of verb movement. *Second Language Research, 8*(1), 1–38.

Scovel, T. (1988). *A time to speak: A psycholinguistic inquiry into the critical period for human speech.* Rowley, MA: Newbury House.

Scovel, T. (2000). A critical review of the critical period hypothesis. *Annual Review of Applied Linguistics, 20*, 213–223.

Seedhouse, P. (1997). The case of the missing "no": The relationship between pedagogy and interaction. *Language Learning, 47*(4), 547–583.

Seliger, H. W. (1978). Implications of a multiple critical periods hypothesis for second language learning. In W. C. Ritchie (Ed.), *Second language acquisition research: Issues and implications* (pp. 11–19). New York: Academic Press.

Seliger, H. W., Krashen, S. D., & Ladefoged, P. (1975). Maturational constraints in the acquisition of second language accent. *Language Sciences, 36*, 20–22.

Selinker, L. (1969). Language transfer. *General Linguistics, 9*, 67–92.

Selinker, L. (1979). On the use of informants in discourse analysis and "language for specialized purposes." *International Review of Applied Linguistics, 17*(3), 189–215.

Shavelson, R. L., & Stern, P. (1981). Research on teachers' pedagogical thoughts, judgments and behavior. *Review of Educational Research, 51*(4), 455–498.

Sheen, R. (1992). In defense of grammar translation. *The Language Teacher* (Japan) *16*, 43–45.

Sheen, R. (1994). A critical analysis of the advocacy of the task-based syllabus. *TESOL Quarterly, 28*(1), 127–151.

Sheen, R. (1998, March). *The case for an eclectic approach.* Paper presented at the annual meeting of the American Association for Applied Linguistics, Seattle.

Shotton, J. (1993). *No master high or low: Libertarian education and schooling in Britain, 1890–1990.* Bristol, England: Libertarian Education.

Sibata, T. (1990). *Conditions controlling standardization.* Excerpt from *Nihon no hogen* [The dialects of Japan] (M. Sawaki, Trans.). Tokyo: Iwanami Shoten. (Original work published 1958)

Siegel, J. (2003). Social context. In C. J. Doughty & M. H. Long (Eds.), *Handbook of second language acquisition* (pp. 178–223). Oxford, England: Blackwell.

Silva, A. D. (2000). Text elaboration and vocabulary learning. Unpublished master's thesis, University of Hawai'i, Honolulu, HI.

Sinclair, J. M., & Coulthard, M. (1975). *Towards an analysis of discourse: The English used by teachers and pupils.* Oxford, England: Oxford University Press.

Singleton, D. (1989). *Language acquisition: The age factor.* Clevedon, England: Multilingual Matters.

Skehan, P. (1998). *A cognitive approach to language learning.* Oxford, England: Oxford University Press.

Slimani, E. (1992). The role of topicalization in classroom language learning. *System*, *17*,223–234.

Smith, M. P. (1983). *The libertarians and education*. London: Allen & Unwin.

Snow, C., & Hoefnagel-Hohle, M. (1978). The critical period for language acquisition: Evidence from second language learning. *Child Development, 49*, 1114–1128.

Sokal, A. (1996). Transgressing the boundaries: Towards a transformative hermeneutics of quantum gravity. *Social Text 46/47, 14*(1–2), 217–252.

Sorace, A. (2003). Near-nativeness. In C. J. Doughty & M. H. Long (Eds.), *Handbook of second language acquisition* (pp. 130–151). New York: Blackwell.

Spada, N. (1997). Form-focused instruction and second language acquisition: A review of classroom and laboratory research. *Language Teaching Abstracts, 30*, 73–87.

Spadaro, K. (1996). *Maturational constraints on lexical acquisition in a second language*. Unpublished doctoral dissertation, University of Western Australia, Perth.

Speidel, G., & Nelson, K. E. (Eds.). (1989). *The many faces of imitation in language learning*. New York: Springer-Verlag.

Spolsky, B. (1989). *Conditions for second language learning*. Oxford, England: Oxford University Press.

Stevens, G. (1999). Age at immigration and second language proficiency among foreign-born adults. *Language in Society, 28*(4), 555–578.

Stevens, G. (2004, May). *The age-length-onset problem in research on second language acquisition among immigrants*. Paper presented at the annual meetings of the American Association of Applied Linguistics, Portland, OR.

Swaffer, J. K., Arens, K., & Morgan, M. (1982). Teacher classroom practices: Redefining method as task hierarchy. *Modern Language Journal, 66*(1), 24–33.

Swain, M. (1985). Communicative competence: Some roles of comprehensible input and comprehensible output in its development. In S. M. Gass & C. Madden (Eds.), *Input in second language acquisition* (pp. 235–253). Rowley, MA: Newbury House.

Swain, M. (1991). French immersion and its off-shoots: Getting two for one. In B. F. Freed (Ed.), *Foreign language acquisition research and the classroom* (pp. 91–103). Lexington, MA: Heath.

Swain, M., & Lapkin, S. (1998). Interaction and second language learning: Two adolescent French immersion students working together. *Modern Language Journal, 82*, 320–337.

Tarone, E. E. (1983). On the variability of interlanguage systems. *Applied Linguistics, 4*, 142–163.

Tarone, E. (1997, October). *A sociolinguistic perspective on an SLA theory of mind*. Paper presented at the 17th annual Second Language Research Forum, Michigan State University, East Lansing, MI.

Tarone, E., & Liu, G.-Q. (1995). Situational context, variation, and second language acquisition theory. In G. Cook & B. Seidelhofer (Eds.), *Principle & practice in applied linguistics* (pp. 107–124). Oxford, England: Oxford University Press.

Terrell, T. (1990). Natural vs. classroom input: Advantages and disadvantages for beginning language students. In J. E. Alatis (Ed.), *GURT 1990* (pp. 193–206). Washington, DC: Georgetown University Press.

Thompson, I. (1991). Foreign accents revisited: The English pronunciation of Russian immigrants. *Language Learning, 41*(2), 177–204.

Toya, M. (1992). *Form of explanation in modification of listening input in L2 vocabulary learning*. Unpublished master's thesis, University of Hawai'i, Honolulu, HI.

Truscott, J. (1996). The case against grammar correction in L2 writing classes. *Language Learning, 46*(2), 327–369.

Truscott, J. (1999). What's wrong with oral grammar correction. *Canadian Modern Language Review, 55*(4), 437–456.

Tsang, W. K. (1987). *Text modification in ESL reading comprehension*. Unpublished manuscript, University of Hawai'i, Honolulu, HI.

Urano, K. (2000). *Lexical simplification and elaboration: Sentence comprehension and incidental vocabulary acquisition.* Unpublished master's thesis, University of Hawai'i, Honolulu, HI.

U.S. Army (1994). *The soldier's manual of common tasks.* Washington, DC.

U.S. Department of Labor (1991). *Dictionary of occupational titles.* Washington, DC.

Usher, R., & Edwards, R. (1994). *Postmodernism and education.* London: Routledge.

Vainikka, A., & Young-Scholten, M. (1996). Gradual development of L2 phrase structure. *Second Language Research, 12*(1), 7–39.

van Boxtel, S. (2005). *Can the late bird catch the worm? Ultimate attainment in L2 syntax.* Utrecht, The Netherlands: LOT (Landelijke Onderzoekschool Taalwetenschap).

van Boxtel, S., Bongaerts, T., & Coppen, P.-A. (2005). Native-like attainment of dummy subjects in Dutch and the role of the L1. *International Review of Applied Linguistics, 43*(4), 355–380.

Van Lier, L. (1994). Forks and hope: Pursuing understanding in different ways. *Applied Linguistics, 15,* 3283–346.

VanPatten, B., & Williams, J. (2002). *Research criteria for tenure in second language acquisition: Results from a survey of the field.* Unpublished manuscript, University of Illinois at Chicago, Chicago, IL.

VanPatten, B., Williams, J., Rott, S., & Overstreet, M. (Eds.). (2004). *Form–meaning connections in second language acquisition.* Mahwah, NJ: Lawrence Erlbaum Associates.

Varonis, E., & Gass, S. (1985). Non-native/non-native conversations: A model for negotiation of meaning. *Applied Linguistics, 6,* 71–90.

Wagner, J. (1996). Foreign language acquisition through interaction: A critical review of research on conversational adjustments. *Journal of Pragmatics, 23*(8), 215–235.

Warner, S. L. (1996). *I ole ka 'olelo i na keiki: Ka 'apo ia ana o ka 'olelo Hawai'i e na keiki ma ke kula kaiapuna.* [A language survives through its children: The acquisition of Hawaiian by children in an immersion school.] Unpublished doctoral dissertation, University of Hawai'i at Manoa, Honolulu, HI.

Watson-Gegeo, K. A. (1992). Thick explanation in the ethnographic study of child socialization: A longitudinal study of the problem of schooling for Kwara`ae (Solomon Islands) children. In W. Corsaro & P. J. Miller (Eds.), *Interpretative approaches to children's socialization* (pp. 51–66). San Francisco: Jossey-Bass.

Wesche, M. B. (1994). Input, interaction, and acquisition: The linguistic environment of the language learner. In B. Richards & C. Galloway (Eds.), *Input and interaction in language acquisition* (pp. 219–249). Cambridge, England: Cambridge University Press.

White, L. (1987). Against comprehensible input: The input hypothesis and the development of L2 competence. *Applied Linguistics, 8,* 95–110.

White, L. (1991a). Adverb-placement in second language acquisition: Some effects of positive and negative evidence in the classroom. *Second Language Research, 7,* 133–161.

White, L. (1991b). The verb-movement parameter in second language acquisition. *Language Acquisition, 1,* 337–360.

White, L. (1996). Universal grammar and second language acquisition: Current trends and new directions. In W. C. Ritchie & T. K. Bhatia (Eds.), *Handbook of second language acquisition* (pp. 85–120). San Diego: Academic Press.

White, L. (2003a). On the nature of interlanguage representation: Universal grammar in the second language. In C. J. Doughty & M. H. Long (Eds.), *Handbook of second language acquisition* (pp. 19–42). Oxford, England: Blackwell.

White, L. (2003b). *Second language acquisition and universal grammar.* Cambridge, England: Cambridge University Press.

White, L., & Genesee, F. (1996). How native is near-native? The issue of age and ultimate attainment in the acquisition of a second language. *Second Language Research, 12*(2), 238–265.

Widdowson, H. G. (1972). The teaching of English as communication. *English Language Teaching, 27*(1), 15–19.

Wilkins, D. (1976). *Notional syllabuses*. London: Oxford University Press.

Wilkins, D. (1994). Language, language acquisition and syllabus design: Some recent issues. *English Teaching* (Korea) *49*, 41–56.

Williams, J. (1988). Zero anaphora in second language acquisition: A comparison among three varieties of English. *Studies in Second Language Acquisition, 10*(3), 339–370.

Williams, M. (1988). Language taught for meetings and language used in meetings: Is there anything in common? *Applied Linguistics, 9*(1), 45–58.

Wode, H. (1994). Nature, nurture, and age in language acquisition. *Studies in Second Language Acquisition, 16*(3), 325–345.

Wolfe-Quintero, K. (1992). Learnability and the extraction in relative clauses and wh-questions. *Studies in Second Language Acquisition, 14*(1), 39–70.

Wolfe-Quintero, K. (1996). Nativism does not equal universal grammar. *Second Language Research, 12*(4), 335–373.

Worrall, J. (1988). The value of a fixed methodology. *British Journal for the Philosophy of Science, 39*, 263–275.

Worrall, J. (1989). Fix it and be damned: A reply to Laudan. *British Journal for the Philosophy of Science, 40*, 376–388.

Yamaguchi, Y. (1994). *Negative evidence and Japanese as a foreign language acquisition*. Unpublished manuscript, University of Western Australia, Perth.

Yamaguchi, Y., Iwasaki, J., & Oliver, R. (1999, March). *Negative feedback in JFL task-based interaction*. Paper presented at the AILA conference, Waseda University, Tokyo.

Yano, Y., Long, M. H., & Ross, S. (1994). The effects of simplified and elaborated texts on foreign language reading comprehension. *Language Learning, 44*(2), 189–219.

Yeni-Komshian, G., Flege, J. E., & Liu, S. (2000). Pronunciation proficiency in the first and second languages of Korean-English bilinguals. *Bilingualism: Language and Cognition, 3*(2), 131–149.

Yeni-Komshian, G., Robbins, M., & Flege, J. E. (2001). Effects of word class differences on L2 pronunciation accuracy. *Applied Psycholinguistics, 22*, 283–299.

Zobl, H. (1982). A direction for contrastive analysis: the comparative study of developmental sequences. *TESOL Quarterly, 16*, 169–183.

Author Index

Subject Index